AMERICA'S COVERT WAR IN EAST AFRICA

T0322523

CLARA USISKIN

America's Covert War in East Africa

Surveillance, Rendition, Assassination

HURST & COMPANY, LONDON

First published in the United Kingdom in 2019 by
C. Hurst & Co. (Publishers) Ltd.,
41 Great Russell Street, London, WC1B 3PL
© Clara Usiskin, 2019
All rights reserved.
Printed in India

Distributed in the United States, Canada and Latin America by
Oxford University Press, 198 Madison Avenue, New York, NY 10016,
United States of America.

A Cataloguing-in-Publication data record for this book
is available from the British Library.

ISBN: 9781849044134 *paperback*
        9781849044547 *hardback*

This book is printed using paper from registered sustainable
and managed sources.

www.hurstpublishers.com

CONTENTS

v

CONTENTS

ACKNOWLEDGEMENTS

Many people and organisations have contributed directly or indirectly to the content of this book. I hope I have clearly acknowledged many of them within the text. Others whom I would like to acknowledge for their courage, collaboration, support and inspirational work include Suleiman Abdallah and all the other former detainees I have interviewed; Bridget Prince, Sarah El-Grew, Al-Amin Kimathi; Hussein Khalid, Francis Auma and everyone else at HAKI Africa; Sam Mohochi, Mbugua Mureithi; Binaifer Nowrojee and everyone at Open Society East Africa; George Kegoro; Clive Stafford Smith and all my former colleagues at Reprieve in particular, Tim Cooke-Hurle and Crofton Black, Cori Crider, and Chloe Davies and Polly Rossdale.

I'd also like to thank Steven Watt, Gareth Peirce and Irene Nembhard; Gus Hosein, Eric King, Claire Lauterbach and others at Privacy International; and Ron Deibert, John Scott Railton, Masashi Nishihata and Irene Poetranto of Citizen Lab.

I am grateful to Brock Chisholm, Sarah el-Grew, Rupert Stone, Amrit Singh, Joanna Buckley, Mark Scott, Tessa Gregory, Ian Cobain, Asim Qureshi, Moazzam Begg, Lorna McGregor, John Goetz, Flora Berkeley, Richard King, Graham Ennis, Jeremy Scahill, Abdalle Mumin and Alex Strick van Linschoten.

I would also like to thank Sarah Lewis and Jo Gatford of Writers' HQ, and Michael Dwyer, Daisy Leitch, Alasdair Craig, and Jon de Peyer of Hurst Publishers.

LIST OF ABBREVIATIONS

There are a number of organisations and bodies referred to within this text with long names and commonly-used acronyms. For ease of reference I have listed as many as possible here.

Human rights organisations and bodies

ACHPR	African Commission on Human and Peoples' Rights
ACLU	American Civil Liberties Union
CPJ	Committee to Protect Journalists
EFF	Electronic Frontier Foundation
HRW	Human Rights Watch
ICC	International Criminal Court
ICJ-KENYA	International Commission of Jurists—Kenya
IMLU	Independent Medico-Legal Unit (Kenya)
MHRF	Muslim Human Rights Forum (Kenya)
NGO	Non-Governmental Organisation
UNCAT	United Nations Committee against Torture, and other Cruel, Inhuman or Degrading Treatment or Punishment
UNESCO	United Nations Educational, Scientific and Cultural Organisation
UNHCR	United Nations High Commission for Refugees

LIST OF ABBREVIATIONS

Media organisations

ABC	American Broadcasting Company
NPR	National Public Radio (United States)

Governmental bodies

AFRICOM	United States Africa Command
ATPU	Anti-Terrorism Police Unit (Kenya)
BIOT	British Indian Ocean Territory
CCK	Communications Commission of Kenya
CIA	Central Intelligence Agency (United States)
CJTF-HOA	Combined Joint Task Force—Horn of Africa (United States)
CTF-150	Combined Task Force 150 (United States)
CTF-151	Combined Task Force 151 (United States)
DOD	Department of Defense (United States)
EU	European Union
FAO	Food and Agriculture Organization of the United Nations
FBI	Federal Bureau of Investigation (United States)
FCO	Foreign & Commonwealth Office (United Kingdom)
GCHQ	United Kingdom Government Communications Headquarters
GODJ	Government of Djibouti
HMG	Her Majesty's Government (United Kingdom)
ICRC	International Committee of the Red Cross
JSOC	Joint Special Operations Command (United States)
JTF—GTMO	Joint Task Force Guantánamo Bay (United States)
NATO	North Atlantic Treaty Organization

LIST OF ABBREVIATIONS

NISA (SOMALIA)	National Intelligence and Security Agency (Somalia)
NSA	National Security Agency (United States)
UKMTO	United Kingdom Maritime Trade Operations
UN	United Nations
UNEP	United Nations Environment Programme
USG	United States Government

Documents, reports and treaties

CAT	United Nations Convention Against Torture and Other Cruel, Inhuman, or Degrading Treatment or Punishment
FOIA	Freedom of Information Act
ICCPR	International Covenant on Civil and Political Rights
PDD	Presidential Decision Directive
SSCI Study	Senate Select Committee on Intelligence, *Committee Study of the Central Intelligence Agency's Detention and Interrogation Program.*[1]
UNCLOS	United Nations Convention on the Law of the Sea

Other

EEZ	Exclusive Economic Zone
ESAT	Ethiopian Satellite Television
HGV	High-value detainee
IUU	Illegal, unreported and unregulated
SLDF	Sabaot Land Defence Force (Kenya)

INTRODUCTION

I was twenty-three years old when 9/11 occurred: white, British, with little understanding then of how that event would come to define my working life. A few years later, in 2005, I began working as a volunteer at the London-based legal charity Reprieve on the cases of prisoners detained at Guantánamo Bay, and soon became interested in the network of other, more secret prisons that most detainees had been held at before arriving at Guantánamo. My job evolved into working as an investigator of the US 'rendition system', by which the CIA and military were ferrying prisoners around the world for detention under suspicion of terrorism in extraterritorial US military prisons and CIA-run facilities, and into the hands of third-party states with a reputation for mistreatment of prisoners. While my scope was global, I developed a particular interest in rendition cases involving East Africa, on the basis that very little was known about such operations in this region, and little research was being done on them, despite the fact that it was clearly an important location in the developing War on Terror. In the years since leaving Reprieve, I've continued to work on both the War on Terror in general, and the East of Africa specifically.

I am neither African nor Muslim. My aim is not to provide an introduction to a region that many other people know far better than me, or an explanation of contemporary 'Islamism'. Nor would I describe myself as a terrorism 'expert'. Understanding the War on Terror and its impact requires a multi-disciplinary, trans-national and historical approach. My perspective and experience comprise one part of this tapestry and I hope readers will go on to engage with other points of view. I've tried, in the writing of this book, to avoid the pitfalls of orientalism and I very much hope I have managed to portray my own experience and research without placing myself at the centre of the story. One consequence of my identity as an outsider at the counterterrorism ball is that I've mostly felt like a kind of ghost at the feast—neither a member of the potential victim group, that is a terrorist, nor an employee of any government, security services, or private company carrying out the War on Terror. My locus for 'being there' has always been a strong belief in the rule of law, and a concern that the human rights abuses inherent to the global War on Terror have sometimes been both perpetrated and tacitly supported by representatives of my own government, the United Kingdom. I only felt entitled to write about my work after personal experience of the sharp end of East African government security responses, when I was working on the defence investigation of Kenyan human rights defender Al-Amin Kimathi, who was facing capital charges in Uganda at the time. I care deeply about both human rights and the rule of law, which I think are worth protecting, and the realm of national security is where those sets of traditions and principles are most often compromised, both by those who seek to commit 'acts of terror', and often by those who purport to be fighting them. What I have learned in the process of the work recounted in this book is that in the 'national security' zone, dominated by the divisions of the War on Terror, there is essentially no third category beyond friend or foe, no protected space for justice and human rights.

INTRODUCTION

My work on this topic around the world, in regions other than East Africa, has made it clear to me that certain common themes emerge across regions, albeit manifesting in different ways. As I zeroed further in on the War on Terror in the region covered in this book, I began to see it as a kind of microcosm of the whole, while at the same time being completely unique. In some respects, East Africa's War on Terror has pre-empted strategies and themes that later occurred elsewhere. If US national security culture is hegemonic and viral, it collides with the various local environments to produce unintended, complex, varied and out-of-control consequences. In reality, there are many complex factors, causes and consequences contained within the War on Terror, and the simplistic mainstream discourse around the issue serves to obscure that complexity. I believe that by examining some of the indirect and officially unacknowledged aspects and ramifications of the War on Terror—the evolving, granular, local ways of describing the world and manifestations of the conflict—we can overcome the prevalent reductive narratives and begin to truly understand what is happening around us.

Within its set limits, this book is thematic rather than geographic. It is representative of my own research odyssey and the characters and problems I have stumbled upon. This book is most certainly not a seamless narrative, or even a complete series of tales. The book is not a history, official or otherwise, or a holistic explanation. For example, little is said about the important history of Sudan in the global War on Terror. Neither does the text speak of heroics, battles, or secret cells; these subjects are all covered elsewhere. As I have always worked on documenting violations carried out by governments, and am not part of the security establishment, I have necessarily taken an alternative perspective to the mainstream narratives dominating the national security field. I have tried, however, to take a position that is not oppositional, or one that disrespects victims of acts of terrorism.

What I have aimed to do is to pick out and examine some of the major themes of the War on Terror as it is waged in East Africa and the Indian Ocean, by focusing primarily on the margins and the marginal: the apparently insignificant, or at least overlooked, phenomena; the scores of unknown and insignificant rendition, extrajudicial killing and disappearance victims; the hapless Zanzibari sold for a bounty to the CIA by Somali warlords; the tiny British island in the Indian Ocean used for rendition operations; the detainee who was punished for his own fantasies; the refugee and coastal Muslim recipients of Kenyan police brutality reminiscent of colonial-era punishments, and the later adoption of some of those tactics by the United States; the human rights defender accused of the same crimes as those for whom he advocated; and the Somali journalist caught between Kenyan xenophobia and the wrath of Al-Shabaab. The book shows, I hope, a few of the ways in which the War on Terror—in all its intricacy and complexity—is unfolding in this region.

This book's nature as a fractured series of descriptions—the gaps in its explanatory narrative—are also, unavoidably, a product of the complex system of official secrecy surrounding national security matters, particularly in the United States and the United Kingdom. I've never had US, UK, or any other kind of government security clearance, nor have I ever knowingly received or repeated classified information not previously released into the public domain by the likes of Wikileaks. All research sources cited in this book are therefore either unclassified by nature of their source, or from the public domain. The peculiarities of and challenges to knowing truth and delivering justice when secrecy has become the norm are explored later in this book.

I'd like also to make it abundantly clear that I am not presenting the simple argument that American policy is the direct cause of everything covered in this book. Rather, I'm trying to make plain what might be described in Washington DC as the 'collateral damage' in this realm of US foreign policy, and to argue that in some way this collateral damage is part and parcel of, possibly intrinsic to, the global War on Terror. Contrary to the dominant, overly narrow discourse around the War on Terror, real-life consequences are often messy, and distinct from intended consequences. This is especially true in regions with an already weak rule of law, and when whole groups of vulnerable people likely not even included in the original factoring—refugees, human rights defenders, those from marginalised ethnic groups—are caught in the slipstream of operations.

I hope that by way of this unconventional approach I can communicate some of the diversity and unanswered questions of my own work on this topic and in this region, as well as point out some important work that is being done by others. Where readers identify gaps or disagree with my analysis, I hope this will stimulate rich debate and further research.

1

A ZANZIBAR GHOST

When Suleiman Abdallah arrived at the Darkness, so overpowering was the stench of rotting seaweed that he thought he had been brought home to the Indian Ocean island of Zanzibar. In fact, he was thousands of miles from the sea, in a secret CIA prison now sometimes referred to as COBALT.[1] Later, a trauma specialist would explain to Suleiman that olfactory hallucinations such as this can be the brain's way of dealing with extreme trauma—creating the illusion, when we are overwhelmed with terror and uncertainty, of something familiar to hold onto. Suleiman has since spent many years working to recover from the horrors of what happened to him after he arrived in the Darkness.

It is March 2003, and Suleiman is living in Mogadishu. He grew up on the island of Zanzibar, beside the sea, and became an itinerant trader, sailing between Somalia, Kenya and Tanzania. His father was an alcoholic whose nickname was Morris because, it was said, he drank like a Morris Minor guzzled fuel. Suleiman was called 'Little Morris', and later 'Travolta', because of his love of dancing. His childhood friend and next-door neighbour was Ahmed Ghailani, later convicted in New York for involvement in the 1998 US

Embassy bombings in Kenya and Tanzania. In Mombasa, Suleiman often stopped over at a shop owned by the mother of one of Ahmed's acquaintances. Like many Zanzibar youth, he struggled with drug addiction. After the bombing, which he maintains he wasn't involved in and had no prior knowledge of (and for which, despite lengthy US detention, he was never charged or put on trial), he stayed on in Somalia, worried that he would be caught up in the security crackdown because of the people he knew. In Somalia, he has got married and found work with a woman who, unbeknownst to him, has connections to the warlord in charge of Mogadishu, Mohammed Dheere.

Suleiman's abduction comes out of the blue: he is driving down the road with a friend when they stop to help a group of men whose car appears to have broken down by the side of the road. It is a trick. After stopping, Suleiman is attacked and bundled into the car. During the abduction, a finger, nose and tooth are broken, and Suleiman is taken to a hospital for treatment. Pain from those injuries will haunt him for years. His broken finger is never reset by any of the many medics he encounters in his journey through the US secret prison system.

From his hospital bed, Suleiman is handed over to a group of Americans and Kenyans.

He has no idea what is happening to him.[2]

Figure 1.1[3]

```
    A.  Initial Conditions.  Capture,
            contribute to the physical and psychological condition
of the HVD prior to the start of interrogation.  Of these,
"capture shock" and detainee reactions              are
factors that may vary significantly between detainees
```

Suleiman is flown first to Nairobi, Kenya, on a plane he believes is manned by Kenyans. He is detained for just over a week in a facility near the airport, dressed in a light Somali kanga, with no other clothing. He is held incommunicado, with little food, undergoing daily interrogations, before being formally handed, around 23 March 2003, to US personnel in a quiet corner of Moi International Airport.

Figure 1.2

```
DEC.30.2004  10:11PM     TOP SECRET/          /NOFORN,ORCON//MR1


            Regardless of their previous environment and
     experiences, once an HVD is turned over to CIA a predictable set
     of events occur:
```

From Nairobi, Suleiman is taken briefly back to Somalia, and from there put on a plane bound for Djibouti, the regional hub for American counterterrorism operations. This is the beginning of the rendition process. In a manner eerily similar to that described in the unclassified accounts of many other CIA rendition victims, Suleiman describes being handed to a group of people dressed head to foot in black. His clothing is cut off him. Goggles are put over his eyes, and plugs shoved into his ears. He is cuffed and shackled, dressed in a diaper, tracksuit and ear defenders.

Figure 1.3

```
1)   Rendition.

     a.   The HVD is flown to a Black Site          \
             A medical examination is conducted prior to
     the flight.  During the flight, the detainee is
     securely shackled and is deprived of sight and sound
     through the use of blindfolds, earmuffs, and hoods.
```

Figure 1.4

```
............ ... ... .. ............, ...  ....             There is
no interaction with the HVD during this rendition
movement except for periodic, discreet assessments by
the on-board medical officer.
```

Contrary to the policy (Fig. 1.4), Suleiman is beaten repeatedly during the course of his rendition. On the plane he is chained to the floor with agents sitting on either side of him. They thump his ear defenders whenever they want his attention. What the United States may seek to describe as a medical procedure in Djibouti (Fig. 1.3) is so traumatic for Suleiman that he finds himself unable to speak of it. At some point, he senses the flash of a camera.

The memories haunt him in flashbacks and nightmares. It is the most terrifying experience of his life.

After a fairly long flight, Suleiman is forced off the plane and into the back of a truck. Someone's knee in the small of his back pins him down as he is driven along a bumpy track.

Figure 1.5

```
,     ⁻        ⋅        the HVD finds himself in the complete
control of Americans;
```

He arrives at his destination: The Darkness.

The Darkness was a prison notorious amongst US detainees, so called because prisoners were held in constant, pitch black. In April 2003 the CIA's chief of interrogations explained that COBALT is 'good for interrogations because it is the closest thing [...] to a dungeon, facilitating the displacement of detainee expectations.' A US Senate Select Committee tasked with oversight of intelligence matters reported in 2008 that '[D]etainees were kept in total darkness. The guards monitored detainees using headlamps and loud music was played constantly in the facility. While in their cells, detainees were shackled to the wall and given buckets for human waste.'[4]

After Suleiman arrives in the Darkness, one song is played repeatedly. It's a love ballad, which Suleiman later identifies as 'My Love' by the Irish boy band Westlife. The interrogators tell him it's being played specially for him, since he recently married. But after his abduction, Suleiman will never see his wife Magida again.

Darkness and noise were constants in the Darkness. It later emerged that these conditions were intended both as methods of 'operational security' for the CIA, and as background elements in the wider programme of 'enhanced interrogation techniques', described so clinically by the CIA and US government lawyers.

Figure 1.6

```
we begin with a summary of the detention conditions that are
used in all CIA HVD facilities and that may be a factor in
interrogations.

        1)   Existing detention conditions.  Detention
conditions are not interrogation techniques, but they have
an impact on the detainee undergoing interrogation.
Specifically, the HVD will be exposed to white noise/loud
sounds (not to exceed 79 decibels) and constant light
during portions of the interrogation process.  These
conditions provide additional operational security:  white
noise/loud sounds mask conversations of staff members and
deny the HVD any auditory clues about his surroundings and
deter and disrupt the HVD's potential efforts to
communicate with other detainees.  Constant light provides
an improved environment for Black Site security, medical,
psychological, and interrogator staff to monitor the HVD.
```

Seventy-nine decibel noise is barely louder than a washing machine. The sounds of the Darkness, according to Suleiman and other former prisoners, are far louder than this: an ear-splitting babel of pop music, cacophonous laughing, phrases in English, Arabic and Kiswahili. Between the pop songs, Suleiman hears an echoing refrain in Arabic: 'There is no God, there is no God…' Other prisoners remember their own earworms—the Barney the Dinosaur theme tune—and angry thrash metal, on repeat. The only lights that Suleiman sees during his time in the Darkness are guards' torches, and the dim spotlights of the interrogation chamber.

Far later, music will play a key role in Suleiman's recovery. He will work with a psychologist who'll take him on a journey to relive his life and, ultimately, his torture. They will work on the beach in Zanzibar. A piece of string is Suleiman's life. Stones are events, and flowers are the good things that happen. The string is long, with lots of stones, and some flowers. A flower for his marriage, and the birth of his first child. A stone for his release from US detention. Sometimes it feels as though it would be easier to still be in prison than to be out here, physically free yet confined in a mental prison of rollicking fear and anxiety, flashbacks and nightmares.

'Reliving the torture' involves finding some agency and self-confidence through revisiting traumatic memories in a therapeutic context. Earphones are placed on Suleiman's head, and his eyes are covered. He has a controlled flashback, and is back in the Darkness. Music is played—tracks he remembers from the Darkness and finds later with the psychologist on Spotify. He takes control of the situation, turns the cacophonous noise off, and replaces it with Bob Marley's 'Sun is Shining'. He feels a sense of peace, and a warm internal glow emerges that stays with him for more than three days.

Back in the Darkness, the torture is only just beginning

Figure 1.7

Transitioning to Interrogation - The Initial Interview.
Interrogators use the Initial Interview to assess the initial resistance posture of the HVD and to determine—in a relatively benign environment—if the HVD intends to willingly participate with CIA interrogators. The standard on participation is set very high during the Initial Interview. The HVD would have to willingly provide information on actionable threats and location information on High-Value Targets at large—not lower level information—for interrogators to continue with the neutral approach.

Suleiman has no Initial Interview (Fig. 1.7). He is not interrogated until he has been in the Darkness for at least five days.

'At least six detainees [including Suleiman Abdallah] were stripped and shackled nude, placed in the standing position for sleep depriva-

tion, or subjected to other CIA enhanced interrogation techniques prior to being questioned by an interrogator in 2003.' [5]

Upon his arrival, he is stripped naked and taken to a freezing cold, pitch black cell with nothing in it except a rug and a rusty hoop fixed to the wall. He is short-shackled—hands and feet—and chained to the wall hoop in an excruciating position. He can neither sit, nor stand up. He cannot sleep and he is kept here for about a week, chained to the wall in a squatting position, in the pitch black, with deafening, constant noise. The first time he is fed is around two days after his arrival, when he is given a large bottle of water and some thin soup. Thereafter he is given the same food, every other day.

Figure 1.8

2) Conditioning Techniques. The HVD is typically reduced to a baseline, dependent state using the three interrogation techniques discussed below in combination. Establishing this baseline state is important to demonstrate to the HVD that he has no control over basic human needs. The baseline state also creates in the detainee a mindset in which he learns to perceive and value his personal welfare, comfort, and immediate needs more than the information he is protecting. The use of these conditioning techniques do not generally bring immediate results; rather, it is the cumulative effect of these techniques, used over time and in combination with other interrogation techniques and intelligence exploitation methods, which achieve interrogation objectives. These conditioning techniques require little to no physical interaction between the detainee and the interrogator. The specific conditioning interrogation techniques are:

a. Nudity. The HVD's clothes are taken and he remains nude until the interrogators provide clothes to him.

b. Sleep Deprivation. The HVD is placed in the vertical shackling position to begin sleep deprivation. Other shackling procedures may be used during interrogations. The detainee is diapered for sanitary purposes, although the diaper is not used at all times.

c. Dietary manipulation. The HVD is fed Ensure Plus or other food at regular intervals. The HVD receives a target of 1500 calories per day per OMS guidelines.

Some years after his release, it slowly became clear that Suleiman was an involuntary participant in an experiment based on the theories of two CIA contractor psychologists, James Elmer Mitchell and John 'Bruce' Jessen. Mitchell and Jessen's method for the psychic unravelling of a person was based on experiments from the 1960s by a psychologist named Martin Seligman, who subjected dogs to unbearable pain with the purpose of inducing a psychological state of absolute compliance. The experiments—an exercise in animal cruelty—demonstrated that dogs subjected to high levels of arbitrary brutalisation eventually stop making an effort to escape or avoid further pain. They become withdrawn and utterly compliant, a state Seligman described as 'learned helplessness'.[6]

Mitchell and Jessen—with no robust science to support their position—hypothesised that the same thing could be achieved with humans. In a white paper commissioned by the CIA in November 2001, 'Recognising and Developing Countermeasures to Al-Qaida Resistance to Interrogation Techniques: A Resistance Training Perspective', Mitchell and Jessen proposed that they could neutralise any 'resistance' from prisoners by inducing the same state of 'learned helplessness' in humans that Seligman had induced in dogs. They devised a series of techniques based on some of the methods they had used as instructors in a classified military training programme called SERE—an acronym for 'survival, evasion, resistance, escape'—which trained (volunteer) US military personnel to survive capture by enemies who do not observe the Geneva Conventions. In essence, they took these simulated torture methods, removed the raft of psychological safeguards that had been set up in order to ensure no permanent damage to the volunteer participants, and proposed that they be used against real prisoners of the CIA.[7]

Mitchell and Jessen's theory was that after the 'psychic demolition' job of exposure to their techniques, the victim would become a *tabula rasa*, a blank slate devoid of resistance and ready to comply with the will of the interrogators.[8] The central premise of their programme was that inducing a state of cringing terror in a dog is analogous to encouraging the disclosure of truthful statements from a human. Since this theory had no basis in any known scientific fact, the programme was, amongst other things, an experiment. It was also, ultimately, a failure on its own terms. Since the CIA had tasked Mitchell and Jessen themselves with assessing its efficacy, there is no independent analysis available of whether the techniques they proposed did indeed induce the desired state of 'learned helplessness' in victims. In its exhaustive inquiry into CIA detention, the US Senate Select Committee on Intelligence, a cross-party independent committee tasked with oversight on US intelligence matters, eventually concluded that there was no evidence to support any claim that the CIA torture programme had ever produced reliable or helpful intelligence.[9]

Back in the Darkness, a CIA interrogator describes how the prisoners 'literally looked like a dog that has been kennelled.' When the doors to their cells are opened, 'they [cower].'[10] The only time Suleiman leaves his cell in that first week is around two days after his arrival when he is taken, blindfolded, by two guards to meet a man he assumes is a doctor, although he does not introduce himself. A medical examination is conducted. The doctor pays particular attention to the broken finger, and puts Suleiman's hand and arm in a cast. Later, Suleiman recounts, the cast is removed when moisture gets under it during water torture.

Figure 1.9

```
     c.  A Medical Officer interviews the HVD and a
medical evaluation is conducted to assess the physical
condition of the HVD.  The medical officer also
determines if there are any contraindications to the
use of interrogation techniques.
```

Painkillers are prescribed, and thereafter delivered to him regularly. Suleiman stockpiles the pills, hiding them in his cell.

After approximately a week, two guards dressed head to foot in black come to Suleiman's cell. In the pitch black they work with torches, unchaining Suleiman from the wall, cuffing and shackling him, and walking him to a dimly lit room. In this room there are around seven or eight men; all except one is masked. Suleiman is made to sit on a chair. The unmasked man—referred to by his colleagues as Viram—approaches Suleiman with a razor, and starts to shave his hair off. The razor is passed around the group of men and they take turns, leaving Suleiman feeling utterly humiliated.

Figure 1.10

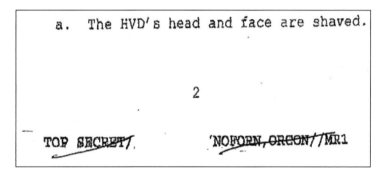

a. The HVD's head and face are shaved.

2

TOP SECRET/ 'NOFORN,ORCON//MR1

Now for the water torture (Fig. 1.11). He is made to lie, naked and shackled, in the centre of a large tarpaulin that has been placed over the floor. He is doused in ice-cold water, so cold that it leaves him breathless.

Figure 1.11

```
    4) Coercive Techniques. Certain interrogation
techniques place the detainee in more physical and
psychological stress and, therefore, are considered more
effective tools in persuading a resistant HVD to
participate with CIA interrogators.. These techniques--
walling, water dousing, stress positions, wall standing,
and cramped confinement--are typically not used in
combination, although some combined use is possible.  For
example, an HVD in stress positions or wall standing can be
water doused at the same time.  Other combinations of these
techniques may be used while the detainee is being
subjected to the conditioning techniques discussed above
(nudity, sleep deprivation, and dietary manipulation).
Examples of coercive techniques include:
```

He is kicked, slapped, and rolled up in the plastic sheet, shivering violently.

Figure 1.12

```
    3)  Corrective Techniques. Techniques that require
physical interaction between the interrogator and detainee
are used principally to correct, startle, or to achieve
another enabling objective with the detainee.  These
techniques-the insult slap, abdominal slap, facial hold,
and attention grasp-are not used simultaneously but are
often used interchangeably during an individual
interrogation session.  These techniques generally are used
while the detainee is subjected to the conditioning
techniques outlined above (nudity, sleep deprivation, and
dietary manipulation).  Examples of application include:
```

Naked and freezing, he is taken to another room, where he is restrained, with a spotlight shining in his face. Questions are fired at him in English, which at that point he does not understand. For the first and only time during his many interrogations, there is a translator. However, the translator speaks Somali—not Suleiman's first language. After half an hour of questioning, Suleiman is taken back to the first room. His head is covered with a bag and he is placed on the plastic tarpaulin. Ice-cold water is thrown on him and the cloth bag sticks to his face. He is colder than he has ever been, and he feels as though he is drowning. He is wrapped up in the wet tarpaulin again, kicked and beaten, before returning to the interrogation room.

After the water torture, Suleiman is stuffed, naked and chained, inside a small wooden box. It is pitch black and he vomits in pain.

Figure 1.13

> e. <u>Cramped Confinement.</u> Current OMS guidance on the duration of cramped confinement limits confinement in the large box to no more than 8 hours at a time for no more than 18 hours a day, and confinement in the small box to 2 hours.
>
> Because of the unique aspects of cramped confinement, it cannot be used in combination with other corrective or coercive techniques.

At the end of the day, Suleiman is taken back to his cell and chained, naked, to the metal ring on the wall. The din of the music is constant. He is naked and cold. No sleep. The next day, the treatment is repeated.

On the third day, he is taken to a room with a specially constructed wooden wall. A foam collar, attached to a leash, is placed around his neck. The interrogator uses the leash to slam Suleiman into the wall. As he rebounds, the interrogator punches him in the stomach.

Figure 1.14

> a. <u>Walling.</u> Walling is one of the most effective interrogation techniques because it wears down the HVD physically, heightens uncertainty in the detainee about what the interrogator may do to him, and creates a sense of dread when the HVD knows he is about to be walled again.
>
> interrogator
>
> An HVD may be walled one time (one impact with the wall) to make a point or twenty to thirty times consecutively when the interrogator requires a more significant response to a question. During an interrogation session that is designed to be intense, an HVD will be walled multiple times in the session. Because of the physical dynamics of walling, it is impractical to use it simultaneously with other corrective or coercive techniques.

After walling, there is more interrogation. Then Suleiman is shut in a coffin-shaped box, pitch black with music blaring. More questions, and then back to the cell. Chained to the iron ring, naked, freezing cold. No sleep. A chain attached to a large iron ball is placed on Suleiman's waist. Naked, with a bag on his head, he is made to drag it around the perimeter of the room. He collapses from exhaustion. He is strapped onto a wooden board on pivots and spun 360 degrees. This is a waterboard. It is sometimes used without the water.

At the beginning of the third week, he is subjected to a new CIA torture technique: prolonged, standing sleep deprivation.

Figure 1.15

b. Sleep Deprivation. The HVD is placed in the vertical shackling position to begin sleep deprivation. Other shackling procedures may be used during interrogations. The detainee is diapered for sanitary purposes, although the diaper is not used at all times.

Two guards take him into a tiny, pitch-black room. By torchlight, they chain his arms above his head to a metal rod that runs the width of the room. They position him so that the balls of his feet just touch the floor, then leave him hanging naked in the darkness with the deafening music. This is a twist on the 'strappado' torture method used during the Spanish Inquisition: to sleep is to invite searing physical pain as the body starts to drop. He is left hanging there for four to five days, taken down only for interrogations. He cannot sleep because as soon as he drifts off, excruciating pain shoots through his arms, shoulders and back as his body weight is no longer supported. When he is finally cut down, his legs are swollen and his arm smells rotten under the plaster cast.

Figure 1.16

> g. The interrogators' objective is to transition
> the HVD to a point where he is participating in a
> predictable, reliable, and sustainable manner.
> Interrogation techniques may still be applied as
> required, but become less frequent.

Around the fourth or fifth week, Suleiman no longer wants to continue living. He gathers all of the painkillers he has stockpiled. But as he starts to take the pills, guards storm into his cell and stop him.

Shortly after the suicide attempt he is forced into shorts and a t-shirt, with his feet and arms shackled and his ears plugged. A hood is placed over his head, with goggles and headphones over the hood. He is pushed into the back of a truck and driven to a new location.

THE SPIDER'S WEB[1]

The place Suleiman called the Darkness was one of a network of secret overseas prisons set up by the CIA in the years following 9/11.[2] The location of the Darkness has never been conclusively established, a task further complicated by the fact that there have been successive prisons in Afghanistan with similar names. An investigator working with me to confirm the location of the Darkness was first led by villagers to a derelict prison near a village on the Kabul Road, dating from the time of the Soviet occupation. Later Afghan 'Dark Prisons' include at least one on the US Military Airforce Base at Bagram, called 'Tor Jail' by former Afghan prisoners.[3]

The Darkness, it is thought, was the same prison referred to as COBALT by the Senate Select Intelligence Committee (the CIA's own code name remains classified).[4] According to the Committee's report, COBALT was the CIA's first prison in Afghanistan. It had twenty cells, and operated between September 2002 and April 2004, during which time sixty-four prisoners, including Suleiman Abdallah, were reportedly held there by the CIA.[5]

Other CIA prisons confirmed by the Senate Committee included three more in Afghanistan, and facilities in Thailand, Lithuania, Romania and Poland.[6] According to his testimony, Suleiman's next stop in the CIA spider's web was a location he now calls the 'Salt Pit'. It is still not known if the Salt Pit and the Darkness were in fact two parts of one facility. For Suleiman, there were no 'enhanced interrogation techniques' in the Salt Pit. Indeed, there were hardly any interrogations there at all. In the Salt Pit, rather than perpetual darkness, there was fluorescent lighting. Suleiman was held in the Salt Pit for approximately fourteen months, and remembers being visited by Americans who told him they were from the FBI, and from the International Committee of the Red Cross (ICRC), asking him for full contact details for his family. The ICRC later denied ever visiting prisoners in the CIA prisons, thus suggesting that these people were not from the ICRC at all.

One fellow prisoner in the Salt Pit was the German citizen Khaled el-Masri, whose case was later described by the CIA's inspector general as an 'erroneous rendition'.[7] In efforts to preserve their spirits and imagine a future freedom, Khaled and Suleiman discussed working together when they were both released. Khaled, a used-car salesman, suggested that he might be able to send cars to Suleiman, to sell for a profit in Zanzibar. Khaled was released after just under a year in US detention, dumped by a CIA plane on an Albanian hillside with his passport and belongings, and told to walk down a deserted road and not look back.[8]

Khaled was the first CIA prisoner to attempt to sue the CIA in the US courts for what was done to him in their custody. Tragically for him, his case was dismissed at the earliest possible opportunity, after the US government raised the 'state secrets' doctrine, claiming that any judicial examination, even of the publicly available evidence in the case, would create an untenable risk for US national security.[9] At the time of writing, this remains the legal position for any former prisoners seeking to sue the CIA directly in the US courts for alleged wrongs committed in the course of their rendition and detention operations. Following his ordeal, and the failure of any state since to fully admit responsibility for it, Khaled suffered a catastrophic mental breakdown.[10]

I first came across Suleiman's case in 2006. At that time, my work at the British legal charity Reprieve involved searching for information about prisoners who had been 'disappeared' by the United States as part of the War on Terror. Finding these people was like assembling a jigsaw puzzle after hunting down each of the pieces. Evidence of Suleiman's existence was fragmentary: a 2003 CNN report that one Suleiman Abdallah had been captured by Somali and Kenyan security personnel,[11] and other media reports suggesting that there had been help from plain-clothes American officers and a notorious Somali warlord named 'Mr Tall'.[12] A subsequent report placed Suleiman in Kenya, whose security minister announced that he was to be flown to the United States for trial, for offences related to the 1998 US Embassy bombings in Nairobi and Dar es Salaam.[13]

In fact, Suleiman never arrived in the United States, and none of the authorities involved in his abduction ever disclosed his whereabouts. He joined the growing list of disappeared Muslim prisoners held at undisclosed US interrogation sites around the world, with no access to lawyers or the outside world.[14] As in other countries caught in US crosshairs following the 9/11 attacks of 2001, a bounty system emerged in Somalia, whereby US forces paid handsomely for people they were told by locals were members of al-Qaeda. In pursuit of the War on Terror, the CIA compensated for their ignorance of local cultures and languages with bags of cash and blank cheques. In the years after 9/11, the CIA conducted detainee operations in Somalia, including in collaboration with the euphemistically-named 'Alliance for the Restoration of Peace and Counterterrorism'. During these operations, people were captured by local warlords and sold to the CIA as 'terror suspects' in return for cash. In lawless Somalia, anyone without local protection is highly vulnerable. The main terror suspects believed by the US to be East African al-Qaeda kingpins remained at large during this time, having managed to develop networks among Somali clans, including familial relations. The main operating factor in Suleiman's initial abduction—like that of many others—appears to have been that he was a foreigner with few local connections.[15]

As East Africa's quiet War on Terror became an increasing focus of my work, Suleiman's file grew steadily more intriguing. Shuttled through the global system of secret US prisons, he remained mostly invisible. His existence was suggested only by clues, his presence echoing faintly and from an unknown place. His name appeared in the margins of a confession rejected by a Kenyan court in 2005 for having been obtained through torture.[16] Its author confirmed, in a snatched conversation with a colleague of mine, that Kenyan police were particularly insistent during his interrogations that he should falsely point the finger at Suleiman. This was before Suleiman's release, and several years after he had been rendered via Kenya to Afghanistan. The detention in Kenya, and the interest of Kenyan interrogators in implicating him, suggested ongoing Kenyan involvement in his case. This proposition is further supported by Suleiman's recollection that he was rendered from Somalia into Kenya by Kiswahili-speaking Kenyan personnel. Indeed, one General Kimanzi of the Kenyan military was deployed to assist the US Combined Joint Task Force–Horn of Africa (CJTF-HOA) between March and November 2003—precisely the period during which Suleiman was captured. CJTF-HOA's activities at this time expressly 'involved detecting and disrupting terrorism through a direct approach':

> In the earliest inception of Combined Joint Task Force–Horn of Africa, at a time when *countering terrorism had a more direct approach*, East African coalitions were fewer and Djibouti was almost unheard of, the country of

Kenya sent a colonel and two other officers to team-up with the task force's U.S. Marines. They were about to embark on a historical occasion, transferring the task force from a ship to land-based Camp Lemonnier.

It was 2003. [...] Now the brigade commander for Kenya's Ministry of Defense, Kimanzi was the colonel who came with two junior Kenyan officers and 17 other coalition officers to assist in establishing CJTF-HOA.

'I was the Senior Liaison Officer—at that time I was an O-6 [colonel] and two left colonels with me,' Kimanzi said. 'The mission at that time was kinetic. We use [sic] to have a lot of activity, especially missions into Somalia.'[17]

Some commentators misrepresented Suleiman as a Yemeni.[18] Elsewhere, media reports confirmed that, as a young man, Suleiman's nicknames were 'Chuck Norris' and 'Travolta' because of his love of dancing.[19] Despite this intriguing and sometimes contradictory information, I still had no confirmation of where Suleiman was being held. My questions probing his whereabouts elicited only blank faces from the former US prisoners I interviewed. In 2007, I learned off-record that Suleiman was being held at Bagram Air Base in the Parwan Province of Afghanistan by the American military. Efforts at locating a family member who could give authorisation for his legal representation hit a brick wall.

Finally, about a year later, I discovered that Suleiman had been released, and arranged to visit him at home on the Indian Ocean island of Zanzibar.

At our first meetings in Stone Town, the crumbling capital of Zanzibar, Suleiman turned up wild-eyed and exhausted after mostly sleepless nights. He had been refusing food because eating upset his stomach.

In the time since his capture, Suleiman had learnt English, and the two of us soon forged a routine of driving alone into the bush, where he said he could find a temporary sense of peace. On our first trip, Suleiman drove me to a derelict underground prison that had once been used by Arab slave traders, a dungeon that he said resembled the first place he was held in Afghanistan, the secret prison he called 'the Darkness'.

In mid-2003, Suleiman arrived at the military-run prison at Bagram Air Base,[20] then Guantánamo Bay's lesser-known twin, where prisoners were never allowed direct access to legal counsel. At Bagram, Suleiman was ordered to stand within the outline of a square drawn on the floor. 'From today onward, your name is 1075,' the American guards told him. 'You are in our box, and we have five basic rules. One: no talking. Two: don't look round. Keep your face down. Three: don't touch anything around the cage. Four: don't speak. Five: don't run.' Later, one of the guards looked at tall, skinny Suleiman—one of only two African-looking prisoners in Bagram at that time—and said, 'You must be related to Snoop Dogg. Maybe he's your father.' After this, Suleiman's name at Bagram was Snoop.

At Bagram, Suleiman never saw the sun, only the constant, blinding lights hanging just above his wire mesh cage. He told me he watched the birds flying among the rafters, swooping down to peck around his cage. Bird droppings fell from the high ceiling through the mesh. Watching them, Suleiman would think, *Look at me today! I am on the side the birds ought to be on. I am in the cage, and they are free!*

Suleiman was not the only person abducted from East Africa for rendition into the CIA's wider prison network. Djibouti, the tiny state at the tip of the Horn of Africa to which Suleiman was taken before his rendition to Afghanistan, appears to have functioned as a rendition hub, or staging post, for prisoners taken from locations across the region. *Military Times* has suggested that, according to a source within the US administration, during 2001–5 'seven or eight' terror suspects were rendered by the CIA from Somalia via Djibouti to the Salt Pit prison in Afghanistan.[21]

One such prisoner is Gouled Hassan Dourad, or 'Hanat'. According to US military documentation, Hanat is a Somali citizen who was given asylum in Sweden in 1993 but returned to Somalia in 1996.[22] His Guantánamo Bay Detainee Assessment, made public by WikiLeaks, states that 'Djiboutian authorities captured detainee at his house in March 2004 for his involvement in terrorist activities and turned him over to US custody on an unknown date'.[23] Hanat disappears at this point, only resurfacing (along with thirteen other 'high-value detainees', or HVDs) with the announcement of his transfer to Guantánamo Bay on 6 September 2006.[24]

As of September 2018, Hanat remains in detention in Guantánamo, uncharged. There appears to have been little scope for the declassification of any statements Hanat may have made about his custody, nor has anyone who was held with him been in a position to speak publicly about his detention history. Scraps of information detailing his travels through the secret prison system include a leaked ICRC report, confirming what we know from his Detainee Assessment: that he was captured in Djibouti on 4 March 2004.[25] Investigations by journalist Adam Goldman (for the Associated Press) into the movements of high-value detainees suggest that, at some point soon after his capture, Hanat was held in a secret location at Guantánamo Bay, nicknamed 'Strawberry Fields' by the CIA, and at another secret prison in Morocco in the same month or later.[26] Although few details exist to bolster this sparse narrative, at least one potential transfer flight has come to light, which may well have taken Hanat out of Djibouti a few days after his capture—either to Afghanistan or onward to Morocco or Guantánamo.[27]

These scraps of information on Hanat's previous detention locations open the door onto a wider US secret prison system that has been partially publicly confirmed by media reports, documents released under the Freedom of Information Act in the US, and the unclassified summary of the Senate Select Committee on Intelligence's investigation into CIA detention.[28] It is now confirmed that between the years 2001 and 2006, CIA prisons operated in Thailand, Guantánamo Bay, Afghanistan, Poland, Romania, and Lithuania.[29] During this time, some CIA prisoners were also held in 'proxy detention' in foreign-run prisons for interrogation and often torture, whilst remaining under CIA control.[30] Other locations, such as Djibouti, appear to have functioned as stop-overs, or access points, where prisoners were held in temporary detention pending transfer to other destinations within the CIA's rendition spider's web.[31]

On 26 December 2003, several months after Suleiman Abdallah's capture in Somalia and about four months before Hanat was captured, Mohammed Abdullah Saleh al-Asad, a citizen of Yemen, was arrested in Dar es Salaam, Tanzania. At the time of his arrest, al-Asad was long settled in Tanzania with his family, having founded his own business: the al-Asad trading company. The family lived in a building owned by al-Asad, which also housed his company offices. Business was going well, and life was good, until 26 December 2003, when two Tanzanian policemen called at al-Asad's building, asking for him. He was summarily blindfolded, cuffed, put into a car, and driven to a safe house. There, he was interrogated until the early hours of the morning, when he was asked to sign an interrogation record without being given time to read it. He was then taken to an airport, restrained and blindfolded, and put onto a small plane. He was not told where he was going. A *habeas corpus* petition brought by al-Asad's father confirmed, via disclosures from the Tanzanian government, that al-Asad departed Tanzania on TanzanAir plane number 5H-TZE on 27 December 2003, bound for Djibouti. His family did not hear of him again for almost a year and a half.

In unclassified witness testimony given after his release from US detention, to his lawyer Meg Satterthwaite, at New York University, Al-Asad has said he spent around two weeks detained in an unknown location, questioned, he thinks, by Americans.[32] He described his interrogation room as having a picture of an official-looking African man on the wall; al-Asad believed it was a picture of the president of Djibouti, Ismaïl Omar Guelleh. Then, one evening, two guards entered al-Asad's cell after *maghrib*, the sunset prayer. He was blindfolded, put into a vehicle, and driven to an airport.

Al-Asad has described an assault at the airport, almost identical to the treatment of Suleiman Abdallah.

After riding in the car with these guards for about twenty or twenty-five minutes, we arrived at an airport, where I was assaulted and experienced very humiliating, painful and terrifying treatment. I was pulled roughly out of the car. I was lifted off the ground and my blindfold was ripped off. I saw about five black-clad individuals whose faces were concealed by balaclavas. They tore off all of my clothing. One shoved a finger into my rectum. They photographed me naked. Then they put a diaper on me and dressed me in a western-style dark-blue short-sleeved shirt, which seemed to have been cut or torn in the front. They also dressed me in dark-blue heavy-fabric calf-length trousers. They plugged my ears with cotton, placed headphones and a hood over my head, and securely taped the hood. They chained my hands, waist, and feet. I was blind, deaf, and could barely walk. I was in severe pain and felt deeply humiliated and weak.[33]

The transfer procedure was fairly standardised in most cases.[34] The detainee would be photographed, both clothed and naked prior to and again after transfer. A body cavity check (rectal examination) would be carried out and some detainees alleged that a suppository (the type and effect of the suppositories was unknown by the detainees) was also administered at that moment.

The detainee would be made to wear a diaper and dressed in a tracksuit. Earphones would be placed over his ears, through which music would sometimes be played. He could be blindfolded with at least a cloth tied around the head and black goggles.[35]

I half-walked and was half-carried onto a waiting plane by people holding me on both sides. I was forced to lie on my back on the floor, and then was strapped down around my legs and waist.

The flight lasts many hours. Every so often, a pulse oximeter—to measure the levels of oxygen in the blood—is clamped onto his finger.

Figure 2.1[36]

> There is no interaction with the HVD during this rendition movement except for periodic, discreet assessments by the on-board medical officer.

Over the following fourteen months, Mohammed al-Asad was held in two secret CIA facilities in Afghanistan. The first was almost certainly the Salt Pit—Suleiman Abdallah's second detention location. His transfer to the second facility involved long plane and helicopter flights, and, until his release in May 2005, did not know where he had been held after Djibouti. Subsequent research by his legal team led by Professor Margaret Satterthwaite at New York University suggests that in fact he has been held in Afghanistan, in a prison called 'Fernando'[37] or 'Orange'.[38] The long journey may therefore have been a deliberate attempt to disorientate him. 'Orange' was one of four CIA prisons in Afghanistan (Fig. 2.2).

Figure 2.2[39]

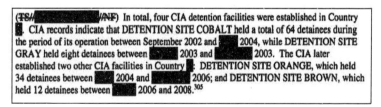

> (TS// [redacted] //NF) In total, four CIA detention facilities were established in Country [redacted]. CIA records indicate that DETENTION SITE COBALT held a total of 64 detainees during the period of its operation between September 2002 and [redacted] 2004, while DETENTION SITE GRAY held eight detainees between [redacted] 2003 and [redacted] 2003. The CIA later established two other CIA facilities in Country [redacted]: DETENTION SITE ORANGE, which held 34 detainees between [redacted] 2004 and [redacted] 2006; and DETENTION SITE BROWN, which held 12 detainees between [redacted] 2006 and 2008.[305]

Al-Asad and the other prisoners detained there rarely leave their cells, and seldom interact with anyone other than prison personnel.[40] Each cell has two double steel doors that are very close to each other; the interior of the door, facing into the cell, is made of thick metal with a small glass window at the bottom and a slot below the window through which food can be passed. The cells are windowless, with floor and walls painted in the same grey colour.[41] There is a stainless steel toilet and a washbasin. There are video cameras fixed to the walls, near the ceiling, a mesh-covered loudspeaker and a metal shackle close to the floor, attached to the wall below one of the cameras.[42] One prisoner notices a listening device built into the wall.[43]

Orange was supposed to be a replacement for, and a significant improvement on, the earlier facility (Fig. 2.3).

Figure 2.3[44]

> (TS//███████//NF) The first quarter 2003 review also found that conditions at DETENTION SITE COBALT satisfied the January 2003 guidance, citing "significant improvements" such as space heaters and weekly medical evaluations. The review noted that a new facility was under construction in Country █ to replace DETENTION SITE COBALT, and that this new detention facility, DETENTION SITE ORANGE, "will be a quantum leap forward" because "[it] will incorporate heating/air conditioning, conventional plumbing, appropriate lighting, shower, and laundry facilities."[310] DETENTION SITE ORANGE opened in ██ 2004. Although some of the cells at DETENTION SITE ORANGE included plumbing,

However, there were not enough interrogators (Fig. 2.4), and so the prisoners remained there in a kind of limbo, waiting for an end to their indefinite detention.

Figure 2.4[45]

> (TS//██████████//NF) A CIA OIG audit completed in June 2006 "found that personnel assigned to CIA-controlled detention facilities, for the most part, complied with the standards and guidelines in carrying out their duties and responsibilities." The OIG also found that, "except for the shortage of debriefers, the facilities were staffed with sufficient numbers and types of personnel." The lack of debriefers, however, was described as "an ongoing problem" for the program. According to the audit, there were extended periods in 2005 when the CIA's DETENTION SITE ORANGE in Country █ had either one or no debriefers. At least twice in the summer of 2005, the chief of Station in that country requested additional debriefers, warning that intelligence collection could suffer. Months later, in January 2006, the chief of Base at the detention site advised CIA Headquarters that "the facility still lacked debriefers to support intelligence collection requirements, that critical requirements were 'stacking up,' and that gaps in the debriefing of detainees were impacting the quantity and quality of intelligence reporting and would make the work of future debriefers more difficult."[873]

Mohammed al-Asad was held in Orange for approximately thirteen months, until his transfer back to Yemen on 5 May 2005. His transfer out of the system occurred during an apparent period of winding down activity. By this point, details of the CIA's detention system had leaked out into the media, and sustaining the prisons in their incarnation of that time was becoming increasingly untenable. Many prisoners were transferred back to their home states, or for further detention in US military prisons.

The prisons had ceased operating, at least temporarily, by 6 September 2006, when George W. Bush announced the transfer of Hanat and thirteen other high-value detainees to the US military prison at Guantánamo Bay:

> So I'm announcing today that Khalid Sheikh Mohammed, Abu Zubaydah, Ramzi bin al-Shibh, and eleven other terrorists in CIA custody have been transferred to the United States Naval Base at Guantánamo Bay.

They are being held in the custody of the Department of Defense.
The current transfers mean that there are now no terrorists in the CIA program. But as more high-ranking terrorists are captured, the need to obtain intelligence from them will remain critical, and having a CIA program for questioning terrorists will continue to be crucial to getting lifesaving information.'[46]

At the time of al-Asad's release, Suleiman Abdallah was being held at Bagram Airforce Base. In US extraterritorial prisons, innocence alone has never been sufficient for release—the process is far more political than legal. Suleiman was finally released in July 2008. What exactly prompted the decision to release him is unknown, but at that time the US government was busy arguing in court that, unlike prisoners at Guantánamo Bay, Bagram prisoners should continue to be denied access to lawyers and the right to challenge their detention in US courts.[47] The basis of the government's argument was that Bagram was a battlefield detention facility, holding only prisoners captured on the Afghan battlefield, and thus fundamentally different from Guantánamo Bay. Cases such as Suleiman's, where prisoners had been rendered to Afghanistan in order to be detained at Bagram, provided material for compelling counterarguments to this position. The timing of Suleiman's release suggests that it was most likely part of a wider effort by the US military to retain Bagram's status as a prison where detainees could be kept beyond the reach of the US federal courts, rather than a moment of justice.

After his release, Suleiman Abdallah was provided with no support—financial, psychological or otherwise—by the US or any other state involved in his detention. In the early days, he hardly slept. Walking along an empty Zanzibar beach with me, he described how he would wake up at night in a state of panic, fully believing that he was back at Bagram. The only way that he had found to ease his anxiety after such a flashback was to play with the baby rabbits his family kept in a hutch in the yard. Shrugging, Suleiman added that his family told him he was crazy for playing with rabbits in the middle of the night.

In the spring of 2010, Suleiman met with Kenyan and American medics who specialise in assessing and treating victims of torture. Suleiman had reached out in a plea for help to rebuild his life. The purpose of their trip was to conduct a medical evaluation and discuss his legal options. Sondra Crosby, a Boston-based doctor who works with Physicians for Human Rights, described the clinical evaluation as extremely harrowing, with both clinicians and Suleiman at times breaking down in tears.[48] The Kenyan clinician, Dr Joan Nyanyuki, a medic with long experience of treating victims of torture by East African governments, later commented that never, in all her hundreds of evaluations of victims of East African torture, had she met a victim who had been so thoroughly mentally unravelled in the course of his mistreatment. Whilst Dr Crosby had never previously evaluated a torture victim in East Africa, her experience as a US medic with top-secret security clearance treating US torture victims of various nationalities, held in locations as far apart as Guantánamo, Abu Ghraib and Afghanistan, enabled her to recognise clearly that Suleiman had been the victim of a peculiarly effective, pervasive, and distinctly American form of torture.[49] This was later confirmed by the Senate Intelligence Committee in the unclassified portion of its report into CIA detention, where Suleiman is listed as having been subjected to both authorised and unauthorised enhanced interrogation techniques.[50]

3

A GIANT FOOTPRINT
AND A STRING OF PEARLS

Diego Garcia, named after one of the Portuguese explorers who stumbled upon it in the early sixteenth century, is a 39-mile-long, footprint-shaped island with a natural deep-water port. It is right in the middle of the Indian Ocean, about 1,000 miles south of the Southern Indian coast and almost 2,000 miles from Madagascar. It is the largest of fifty-five islands that make up the Chagos Archipelago, and was first settled under French rule in the eighteenth century by African slaves and Indian contractors brought to work on coconut plantations. Captured by the British in 1810 during the Napoleonic Wars, and later officially ceded by France under the terms of the 1814 Peace Treaty of Paris, this tiny remote island has played a key role since the Cold War in British and American military strategy in the Indian Ocean region and beyond. This chapter takes as its focus the persistent rumours that US rendition flights and high-value prisoners held in the War on Terror have transited through and been detained on the island by the US, with British complicity.

In 1965, in anticipation of the independence of its Indian Ocean colonies, the United Kingdom separated the Chagos

Archipelago from Mauritius and combined it with three islands that had previously been part of the Seychelles to form the British Indian Ocean Territory (BIOT). The islands were formally established as an overseas territory of the United Kingdom on 8 November 1965. The following year, the British bought the privately-owned Copra plantations on Diego Garcia and, over the next five years, worked to forcibly remove the entire local community of around 2,000 Chagossians—descendants of the workers originally brought over by the French to farm the copra. Testament to the prevailing attitude within the British establishment toward the soon-to-be exiled Chagossians, D.A. Greenhill—then head of the British Diplomatic Service—wrote in a 1966 diplomatic cable that 'unfortunately along with the birds go some few Tarzans or Men Fridays whose origins are obscure who are being hopefully washed on to Mauritius etc.'[1] By 1971, UK's self-pledged deadline year for withdrawing all colonial presence from 'East of Suez', all of the resident Chagossians had finally been removed from Diego Garcia.

Peter Sand has written that the 'central geographical location in the maritime region between Africa, the Near East, South Asia and Australia gives the archipelago's largest island, Diego Garcia, a unique strategic importance: in the words of Admiral John S. McCain, "as Malta is to the Mediterranean, Diego Garcia is to the Indian Ocean—equidistant from all points".'[2] The strategic presence on Diego Garcia was thus protected. The removal of the Chagossians left the UK and US free to sign a treaty providing for the island's lease to the US, for the purpose of establishing a large joint US/UK military base.

During the 1960s, the prime focus of US naval policy in the Indian Ocean had involved supporting Iran, and maintaining a US naval presence in order to deter Russia from disrupting the flow of Persian Gulf oil to Europe and the United States. As Britain prepared to withdraw from 'East of Suez', the preparation of the military base at Diego Garcia was one element of an increasing militarisation of the Indian Ocean, as both the United States and Russia rushed to fill the power gap and steadily increase their presence in the region. Construction of the US Naval Communications Facility at Diego Garcia began in 1971. GlobalSecurity.org has noted that 'following the overthrow of the Shah of Iran in 1979, Diego Garcia saw the most dramatic build-up of any location since the Vietnam War era.'[3] By the 1980s, the communications facility was a major US fleet and armed forces base, becoming fully operational in 1986 with the completion of a $500 million construction programme.

Later, during the 1990 Gulf War, Diego Garcia

> achieved and maintained the highest degree of operational readiness achieved and provided levels of support which outstripped all contingency planning. As the base population doubled almost overnight [...] Diego Garcia became the only US Navy base that launched offensive air operations during Operation Desert Storm and Diego Garcia remains a vital link in the US defense structure.[4]

Regarding Diego Garcia's ongoing strategic significance in a region of increasing significance for US foreign policy, Green and Shearer have written that 'in the past few years, the Indian Ocean has emerged as a major center of geostrategic interest,'[5] identifying 'three clear and abiding US interests': securing the trade routes between Asia and the Persian Gulf, maintaining freedom of navigation through strategic chokepoints such as the South China Sea (increasingly under threat from Beijing and Tehran), and the Ocean's role as a 'secondary arena' in Asia's new great game, 'particularly between India and China.'[6]

Regarding Diego Garcia's role in this wider strategy, Erickson, Ladwig and Mikolay point out that in the Indian Ocean arena and in the global War on Terror, what the US needs is not 'large fixed military facilities' such as those built during the Cold War in Europe and East Asia, but 'a network of forward operating bases and small military facilities across the littoral region. The foremost among these is the American military base on the British island of Diego Garcia',[7] as 'the atoll abuts all major shipping lanes that reticulate the Indian Ocean.'[8] It is clear, then, that as Diego Garcia's lease to the US for military base use has just been renegotiated for a further twenty years (renewed in late 2016), Diego Garcia continues to be a site of key, possibly increasing, strategic importance for the US.[9]

Alongside this geopolitical grandstanding, the diminutive island has also been the focus of a persistent trickle of lawsuits and allegations relating to human rights abuses. The main set of lawsuits (see below) has involved the ongoing plight of the exiled Chagossians, whose interests have consistently been disregarded by the UK in its efforts to preserve the island as a US military base. In short, this matter, which has enormous implications for the execution of a 'covert war' on Diego Garcia, concerns the financial provisions for resettlement of the Chagossians under the 1965 UK-Mauritian agreement excising the Chagos Archipelago from Mauritian territory. After the British government formally detached it, the UN General Assembly stated that this was a violation of the principles of self-determination set out in Resolution 1514 on the Declaration on the Granting of Independence to Colonial Countries and Peoples.[10] Although the UK agreed in 1982 to pay a further £4 million in trust for the benefit of the Chagossians as 'full and final settlement' of any claims relating to the detachment,[11] a group of Chagossians initiated proceedings in the UK courts, seeking further compensation and the right to return to the Archipelago. These were all dismissed by domestic courts in England and Wales by June 2008.[12] On 11 December 2012, the European Court of Human Rights rejected the Chagossians' appeal, finding it inadmissible due to the earlier financial settlement.[13][14] In November 2016, it was again confirmed publicly by the UK, just prior to the renewal of the US lease for use of Diego Garcia as a military base, that the Chagossians would not be allowed to return 'on the grounds of feasibility, defence and security interests, and cost to the British taxpayer', but would receive a further £40 million in compensation, 'to be spent on projects to support the Chagossians over the next decade.'[15]

In addition to these justifications for denying the Chagossians' right of return, the UK has also invoked international environmental law to sidestep their ancestral claims to the island. A US Embassy cable, released by WikiLeaks, revealed the FCO's plans for 'a "marine park" or "reserve" providing comprehensive environmental protection to the reefs and waters of the British Indian Ocean Territory (BIOT)'. After reassuring the US that 'the establishment of a marine park—the world's largest—would in no way impinge on USG use of the BIOT, including Diego Garcia, for military purposes', the senior official in question added 'that the BIOT's former inhabitants would find it difficult, if not impossible, to pursue their claim for resettlement on the islands if the entire Chagos Archipelago were a marine reserve.'[16] Incidentally, Mauritius has claimed that these plans in themselves constitute a violation of international law, specifically the United Nations Convention on the Law of the Sea (UNCLOS), as well as agreements limiting the UK's jurisdiction over the location. It brought a complaint against the UK in 2010, asserting that '[i]t appears that the true purpose of the "MPA is not conservation but to prevent the right of return" of the Chagossians.'[17] On 18 March 2015, the tribunal ruled that the Chagos Marine Protected Area was 'not in accordance with the provisions of the Convention', declaring that in establishing the MPA surrounding the Archipelago the UK had breached its obligations under Articles 2(3), 56(2), and 194(4) of UNCLOS.[18]

The Chagossian question is of direct relevance to the US's alleged execution of War on Terror-related activities on Diego

Garcia. Put simply, the displacement of the Chagossians—now upheld by domestic and international courts—and the resulting 'unpopulated' status of the Archipelago has long been used by the UK to assert that the key human rights instruments protecting against torture—Convention Against Torture and the International Convention on Civil and Political Rights—do not apply on BIOT.[19] Yet, as we have seen, human life certainly exists on Diego Garcia—on the US military base. And alongside the Chagossian litigation have been persistent allegations, as yet unanswered, alleging that Diego Garcia has been used for CIA renditions and detentions.

The matter was first publicly raised in an open letter to then Prime Minister Tony Blair on 28 December 2002, when Human Rights Watch wrote:

> We [...] urge you to take steps to ensure that torture does not take place on British soil, including the islands that are part of British Indian Ocean Territory. According to press reports in the United States, U.S. forces are holding and interrogating suspected al-Qaeda detainees at a U.S. operated facility on the island of Diego Garcia. [...] The allegations [...], if true, would place the United States in violation of some of the most fundamental prohibitions of international human rights and humanitarian law. [...] The treatment of detainees on Diego Garcia also implicates the legal obligations of the British government. [...] We also urge you to request a commitment in writing from the U.S. government as a condition of continued use of the island that it will comply with international law governing the treatment of detainees.'[20]

In a subsequent series of parliamentary questions and answers from 2003 to 2008, the UK Government consistently denied that any detainees were on Diego Garcia, relying on the circular argument that the US would have to ask for UK permission to bring any detainees to the island, that the US had not asked for such permission, and that therefore nobody was being held on or near the island.[21] Aside from the dubious worth of this unquestioning acceptance of US assurances, in October 2003, *Time Magazine* published a report citing interrogation records from the US prisoner Hambali, who had reportedly been held on the island,[22] and in November 2003 the UK Bar Human Rights Committee wrote to then Foreign Secretary Jack Straw raising concerns about the use of the island as well as US ships off-shore (both within and beyond the 3-mile territorial limit), specifically including a reference to 'the transit of any detainees across UK territory, for example, by landing by air on the island of Diego Garcia before being transported [off-shore].'[23]

Over the following years, further allegations would appear in the international media citing various high-level sources in the US administration confirming detentions on the island of 'high-value' US prisoners including Abu Zubaydah, Ramzi Bin al-Shibh, Khaled Sheikh Mohammed, and Mustafa Setmariam Naser.[24] As of September 2018, all but one of these men is now being held at Guantánamo Bay, where any statements they make to their lawyers are subject to strict classification procedures, meaning that nothing they say about any alleged torture in secret prisons is likely to be permitted to reach the public domain. The last prisoner, Mustafa Setmariam Naser, is believed currently to be held incommunicado in a prison in Syria, by the Assad regime, following his capture and rendition there by US agents.[25]

Despite denials in private to British counterparts, US officials have elsewhere appeared publicly equivocal, and in some instances have casually confirmed that prisoners have been detained on Diego Garcia. At a Defense Department Operational Update Briefing on 14 July 2004, Principal Deputy Assistant Secretary of Defense Laurence Di Rita, when asked whether there were detainees at Diego Garcia, stated, 'I don't know. I simply don't know.'[26] General Barry McCaffrey, former head of Southcom, has now stated twice on US National Public Radio (NPR) that the US has used Diego Garcia to hold prisoners in the War on Terror. In an

MSNBC Tonight interview with Deborah Norville on 6 May 2004, McCaffrey stated, 'We're probably holding around 3,000 people, you know, Bagram Air Field, Diego Garcia, Guantánamo, sixteen camps throughout Iraq.'[27] And on 5 December 2006, he again referred to Diego Garcia in interview with Robert Siegel on NPR, when asked about terror suspects: 'They're behind bars, they're dead, they're apprehended. We've got them on Diego Garcia, in Bagram Airfield, in Guantánamo.'[28]

The presence of detainees on Diego Garcia has also been confirmed by international investigators connected to the Council of Europe and the United Nations. In his June 2007 report, Senator Dick Marty, rapporteur for the Council of Europe's investigation into illegal inter-state transfers involving Council of Europe member states wrote that

> we have received concurring confirmations that United States agencies have used the island territory of Diego Garcia, which is the international legal responsibility of the United Kingdom, in the 'processing' of high-value detainees. It is true that the UK Government has readily accepted 'assurances' from US authorities to the contrary, without ever independently or transparently inquiring into the allegations itself, or accounting to the public in a sufficiently thorough manner.[29]

In June 2008, the then UN special rapporteur on torture, Manfred Novak, spoke of 'very, very serious' allegations that the United States was secretly detaining terrorism suspects in various locations around the world, notably aboard prison ships in the vicinity of Diego Garcia.[30] The most recent set of allegations came in 2015 from Lawrence Wilkerson, Secretary of State Colin Powell's former chief of staff, who claimed to have confirmation from three intelligence sources that Diego Garcia was used as

> a transit site where people were temporarily housed, let us say, and interrogated from time to time. ... What I heard was more along the lines of using it as a transit location when perhaps other places were full

or other places were deemed too dangerous or insecure, or unavailable at the moment.[31]

One particularly compelling set of allegations—yet to be fully investigated—involves the Indonesian terror suspect Hambali, who was captured in Thailand on 11 August 2003.[32] Following his capture, Hambali disappeared into secret US detention, not officially reappearing again until 6 September 2006, when President George W. Bush announced that Hambali and thirteen other high-value detainees (HVDs) in the CIA prison system had been transferred to Guantánamo Bay. The location(s) of Hambali's detention for those three years before his transfer to Guantánamo Bay remain officially unconfirmed, and any statements made by Hambali in Guantánamo Bay will be subject to Top Secret classification. However, a leaked International Committee of the Red Cross (ICRC) report containing interviews with HVDs including Hambali after their arrival at Guantánamo Bay has confirmed that Hambali was held for three to four days in Thailand before being transferred around 15 August 2003 to Afghanistan, where he was held in Bagram Air Base for approximately four to six weeks. Hambali told ICRC personnel that he was starved of solid food and kept naked for most of his time in Afghanistan: 'Mr Hambali alleged that he was ... held for one week naked in Afghanistan. He was then provided with clothes, which were again removed after one week after which he remained naked for another month before clothes were finally provided.'[33] Regarding sustenance, the ICRC reports that 'during the two months he was detained in Afghanistan he received solid food irregularly, sometimes twice a day and sometimes only once in two or three days. Ensure [a nutritional drink] was provided throughout to supplement the lack of solid food.'[34] 'Provided' may here refer to the controversial tactic of forced 'rectal rehydration' practised on CIA prisoners during periods of interrogation.[35]

On 5 October 2003, *Time Magazine* cited a 'regional intelligence officer' claiming that Hambali 'is being interrogated at the joint British-American air base on the remote Indian Ocean island of Diego Garcia.'[36] The article also referred to interrogation records from 22 and 26 August 2003, which we now know relate to the time that the ICRC report has Hambali in detention in Afghanistan. As for information on Hambali's treatment whilst he may have been held on Diego Garcia, the only publicly available information comes again from the ICRC report, which states that in Hambali's 'third place of detention', he was 'threatened with a return to previous methods of ill-treatment'[37]— namely, having his head slammed against the wall by use of a collar. During his detention he was reportedly denied the opportunity to leave his cell for nine months.[38] About four days after his arrival he was provided with a Qu'ran, but Hambali recalls that a few days later 'the air conditioning was made very cold and everything was removed from my cell, including the Qu'ran. I was only left with a T-shirt and shorts.'[39]

UK officials have twice confirmed (once in 2004, and once in 2008) that there is a British-run prison on Diego Garcia. The first confirmation came by way of the then foreign secretary Jack Straw's answer to a parliamentary question from Menzies Campbell, inquiring as to whether Diego Garcia had 'any facilities for holding human beings against their will.' Straw responded that 'in exercise of powers conferred on him by the Prisons Ordinance 1981 of the British Indian Ocean Territory, the Commissioner for the Territory has declared certain specified premises in Diego Garcia to be a prison. This was done by orders made in February 1986 (which replaced an earlier order made in July 1982), July 1993 and December 2001.'[40] The second confirmation came from David Miliband, during his time as foreign secretary (2007–10), when he confirmed that 'In December 2001, the Commissioner declared that the fenced compound containing tended or other accommodation facilities, adjacent to the British Indian Ocean Territory Police Station on Diego Garcia, to be [sic] a prison.'[41] Since these disclosures, the British government has steadfastly refused to release any further data as to who has been held in this prison and why it was refurbished or expanded during a key early phase of the War on Terror in December 2001.

Despite the numerous allegations, the UK Government has consistently avoided opening an investigation, repeatedly referring only to US assurances. For example, in June 2004 then-Foreign Secretary Jack Straw stated: 'The United States authorities have repeatedly assured us that no detainees have at any time passed in transit through Diego Garcia or its territorial waters or have disembarked there and that the allegations to that effect are totally without foundation. The Government [is] satisfied that their assurances are correct.'[42] Similarly, in its inquiry into UK involvement in renditions of July 2007, the UK Intelligence and Security Committee relied on assurances from Washington, simply stating: '[T]he U.S. has given firm assurances that at no time have there been any detainees on Diego Garcia. Neither have they transited through the territorial seas or airspace surrounding Diego Garcia. These assurances were last given during talks between U.S. and UK officials in October 2006.'[43]

Why the UK has felt able to rely solely on US 'assurances' in this regard is not clear, since the 1976 Exchange of Notes between the UK and US Governments clearly requires that the UK must be informed of all intended movements of US ships and aircraft on or through BIOT territory, stating at paragraph 3: 'The US Commanding Officer and the Officer in Charge of the United Kingdom Service element shall inform each other of intended movements of ships and aircraft.'[44] Additionally, the UK Foreign Office has stated that the United States would need to ask the permission of the UK should it bring any prisoners onto the island.[45]

Furthermore, the UK has legal jurisdiction over the island, and a significant military and administrative presence on Diego Garcia. Section 4 of the 1965 BIOT Order creates a British commissioner who has, under Section 11, the power to legislate. BIOT Ordinance No. 3 for 1983 establishes an appellate structure, and, at Section 6, creates a Supreme Court, described as 'a superior court of record with unlimited jurisdiction to hear and determine any civil or criminal proceedings under any law and with all the powers, privileges and authority which is vested in or capable of being exercised by the High Court of Justice in England.' The BIOT Supreme Court may sit in Diego Garcia or London, and appeal lies with the BIOT Court of Appeal and from there the Privy Council. Diego Garcia has its own independent administration, run by the East Africa Desk of the Foreign and Commonwealth Office in London (FCO).

The senior UK official on the island is called the British representative, and he is there under the authority of the FCO. The British representative is the commanding officer of Diego Garcia's civil administration, known as 'Naval Party 1002' (NP 1002). The British representative is also the commander of the Royal Navy, the magistrate, the coroner, and the registrar of marriages. Approximately fifty further British Royal Navy and Marines personnel work for NP 1002, carrying our policing and customs duties. A detachment of Royal Marines carries out security for the entire Chagos Archipelago.[46] The FCO also oversees a fleet of patrol boats in BIOT waters, which regularly interdicts vessels suspected of illegally fishing for tuna and other marine life, forcibly seizing catches, ejecting foreign vessels from BIOT waters, and imposing fines. Presumably, therefore, the fleet would have been aware of the activities of US vessels in the area.

Another example of the UK's ultimate oversight regarding Diego Garcia is in the matter of conservation. According to the UK Joint Nature Conservation Committee, 'enforcement of conservation measures, such as for the existing bird sanctuaries, is the responsibility of the senior UK representative stationed on the island in his role as Magistrate.'[47] Indeed, the United States Navy boasts that 'all wildlife on Diego Garcia is protected by British law. Any detected harm, mistreatment, or harassment of any of the island's animals will result in punitive action.'[48] In principle, British responsibility extends far beyond the realm of wildlife protection; the US Navy's 'Integrated Natural Resources Management Plan' of 2005 makes it clear that: 'US federal policies and programs apply only to the extent that the UK agrees that they should be applicable and as they conform to British Indian Ocean Territory (BIOT) policies and programs. The full governmental and civilian judicial authority ... rests with the British Representative (BRITREP), a Senior Royal Navy Commander.'[49]

Two recent judgments at the European Court of Human Rights leave no doubt as to the UK's legal duty to investigate allegations of torture on the British territory of Diego Garcia, and the liability of the British government if it is found that the US has been detaining prisoners on, or rendering them through, Diego Garcia.[50] However, in their periodic reports to the UN Human Rights Committee (UNHRC), the UK has consistently refused to report on whether or not the UK has observed its obligations on Diego Garcia under the International Covenant on Civil and Political Rights (ICCPR), claiming that (following the forced removal of the indigenous Chagossians) the Archipelago is officially 'unpopulated'. The UK's position notwithstanding, the Committee's 2009 concluding observations on the UK stated unequivocally that the ICCPR does apply with respect to the UK in BIOT.

In its most recent Concluding Observations (30 July 2008), the UNHRC specifically 'regretted' the UK's view that the Conventions did not apply, again requested that the UK report on BIOT, and addressed both the situation of the Chagossians and the use of BIOT for renditions to torture.[51] Meanwhile, the United Nations Committee Against Torture (UNCAT), in its 2013 Concluding Observations with respect to the UK, left no doubt that UNCAT applies 'anywhere under the UK's jurisdiction' (i.e. regardless of whether or not the UK considers it to be officially populated): 'The State party reminds the State party of its obligations to take effective measures to prevent acts of torture "not only in its sovereign territory but also in any territory under its jurisdiction", including "all areas where the State party exercises, directly or indirectly, in whole or in part, de jure or de facto effective control, in accordance with international law".'[52]

Despite these legal obligations, no clarification was forthcoming. In July 2014, Andrew Tyrie MP once again revived the question of Diego Garcia's elusive flight logs, asking the government: 'Which Government Department or Office keeps a list of flights which passed through Diego Garcia from January 2002 to January 2009?' The response from Mark Simmonds of the FCO was that some records were kept on Diego Garcia itself, but were apparently incomplete:

> Records on flight departures and arrivals on Diego Garcia are held by the British Indian Ocean Territory immigration authorities. Daily occurrence logs, which record the flights landing and taking off, cover the period since 2003. Though there are some limited records from 2002, I understand they are incomplete due to water damage.[53]

Following this statement, *The Observer* published blow-ups of confidential emails snapped by a paparazzi photographer as an FCO mandarin left a government building; they revealed that in his parliamentary answer to Tyrie's question (described in the emails as an 'inspired question!'), Simmonds had only mentioned one form of flight log, whereas in fact both 'monthly log showing flight details' and 'daily records [obscured] month of alleged rendition' did exist. Neither form of log has yet been disclosed to lawyers or human rights groups,[54] despite follow-up parliamentary questions from David Davis on 15 and 21 July 2014.[55] Simmonds gave a particularly bizarre answer to Davis' question of 15 July inquiring after the 'status ... of the monthly flight logs of flights which have passed through Diego Garcia from January 2002 to January 2009,'[56] responding that

During routine work to add existing records to the store in Diego Garcia, BIOT immigration officials noted water damage to a small number of records, caused by a leaking roof. This is believed to have resulted from extremely heavy weather in June 2014. Although the extent of the damage was not clear on initial inspection at the time, as I said in my answer of 8 July 2014, *Official Report*, column 172W, records from 2002 appeared to be incomplete due to water damage.

However, since my answer of 8 July, BIOT immigration officials have conducted a fuller inspection, and previously wet paper records have been dried out. They report that no flight records have been lost as a result of the water damage. A small number of immigration arrival cards from 2004 have been damaged, but that information about those flights is still available in the daily occurrence logs and monthly statistics. These records provide dates of aircraft movements in the Territory, and passenger and crew numbers.

Following the incident, all hard copy records from the affected location are being transferred from the airport to a new location, and will be digitalised over the coming months.[57]

I have personally checked historical weather data, which showed that during the entire month of June 2014 on Diego Garcia there were no more than 5.8 inches of rain, and on any one day during that period there were no more than 12 milimetres of rain—in other words, a light sprinkle.[58] The government's response prompted a further question from Tyrie as to 'Where and on what dates the water damage occurred?' and 'What other files were lost in the same incident?'[59] The answers to Tyrie's questions (and to a similar question by Davis the previous day) merely referred to an answer given on 16 July 2014 to Paul Flynn

MP by Parliamentary Under-Secretary of State for Foreign and Commonwealth Affairs Tobias Ellwood, repeating the reference to 'heavy weather' and mentions of a leaking roof in June 2014.[60]

4

'WE FORGIVE YOU: JUST ACCEPT YOU MET OSAMA BIN LADEN'

Before the six-year wall of silence, on 21 February 2008 there was a concession to Parliament by then-Foreign Secretary David Miliband that, contrary to previous denials, two rendition flights carrying US prisoners had in fact stopped on Diego Garcia, in January and September 2002. By statement to Parliament, Miliband said,

> Contrary to earlier explicit assurances that Diego Garcia had not been used for rendition flights, recent US investigations have now revealed two occasions, both in 2002, when this had in fact occurred. An error in the earlier US records search meant that these cases did not come to light. In both cases a plane with a single detainee on board refuelled at the US facility in Diego Garcia. The detainees did not leave the plane, and the US government has assured us that no US detainees have ever been held on Diego Garcia or any other Overseas Territory or through the UK itself since then.[1]

In a statement to staff about the CIA's past use of Diego Garcia, CIA Director-General Michael Hayden said:

The refuelling, conducted more than five years ago, lasted just a short time. But it happened. That we found this mistake ourselves, and that we brought it to the attention of the British government, in no way changes or excuses the reality that we were in the wrong. An important part of intelligence work, inherently urgent, complex, and uncertain, is to take responsibility for errors and to learn from them. [...] Our government had told the British that there had been no rendition flights involving their soil or airspace since 9/11. That information, supplied in good faith, turned out to be wrong.[2]

In respect of the individuals on board, Miliband said in his statement:

The House will want to know what has become of the two individuals in question. There is a limit to what I can say, but I can tell the House the following. The US government has told us that neither of the men was a British national or a British resident. One is currently in Guantánamo Bay. The other has been released.[3]

In response to questions about why these two flights acknowledged by Miliband had taken so long to come to light, former Foreign Secretary Margaret Beckett (2006–7) said, 'It was very difficult for the government to go back and look at what had happened on previous occasions. There was not a clear, simple trace of record keeping. That may, I don't know, have been the case in the United States also.'

Nothing further was offered by way of clarification, save on 12 February 2009, when an FCO minister, Bill Rammell, responded to a parliamentary question from Andrew Tyrie, asking 'whether one of the detainees rendered through Diego Garcia is still being held in the Guantánamo Bay detention centre.' Rammell confirmed that, since that date, 'Both of the individuals rendered through Diego Garcia in 2002 have been returned to their countries of nationality.'[4]

However, the UK government then declined to conduct any investigation into these revelations. Rather, it invited NGOs and

MPs to submit questions regarding any further suspicious flights of which they were already aware. The result was inevitable: Foreign Secretary Miliband announced in July 2008 that the US had assured Britain that no further instances of rendition had been found. In the challenge to identify the two prisoners referred to in Miliband's statement, limited information was offered by the UK government. Using what information was available and a process of elimination, followed by investigative work, I and my then-colleagues at Reprieve were able to identify one individual, a Pakistani-Egyptian dual national named Mohammed Saad Iqbal Madni, whose case corresponded clearly with the data for one of the flights referred to by the British government.

Madni was detained in Jakarta on 9 January 2002, reportedly at the request of the CIA. According to *The Washington Post*, US authorities urged the Indonesians to apprehend him after they claimed to have discovered a link to Richard Reid, the so-called British 'shoe bomber'.[5] In a witness statement, Madni described being pushed aboard an unmarked, US-registered Gulfstream V jet at a military airport in Jakarta on 11 January 2002:

> The intelligence personnel covered my eyes with a hood, and pushed me aboard a jet aircraft. Then I was put in a coffin-shaped wooden box lying horizontally on the floor. The box was open but I was bound with plastic, with shackles wound so tightly all around my body that I was unable to move. A plastic sheet was then placed over the box. The plane took off around two hours later, I would estimate at around 10.00pm. As a result of the beating, I was bleeding from my nose, mouth and ears, and I later learned that there was blood in my urine.[6]

Madni was taken via a stop-over to Cairo, where he spent ninety-two torturous days before being taken to Bagram Air Base and then Guantánamo Bay, where he remained until his release in August 2008.[7]

The Guardian reported on Madni's case as early as March 2002, when he was still being tortured in Egypt: 'Madni was taken from Indonesia to Egypt on a US-registered Gulfstream jet without a court hearing after his name appeared on al-Qaeda documents. He remains in custody in Egypt and has been subjected to interrogation by intelligence agents.'[8] Of his time in Egypt, Madni's 2009 witness statement recalled:

> I was taken to an underground cell that was smaller than a grave ... It was completely dark, and I could not lie down straight in the cell, I had to bend my knees.

> On or around 11 or 12 January I was subject to intense interrogation sessions involving torture. During these sessions I was given high voltage electric shocks to my head and my knees, denied food and medicine for my bleeding. My interrogators were Egyptian but there were four US personnel in the room...

> On many other occasions, too many to count, my Egyptian torturers hung me from metal hooks from the ceiling and beat me. During my time in Egypt I regularly bled from my mouth, nose and ears as a result of my torture.[9]

Madni has consistently denied any connection with Richard Reid, and has never been put on trial in relation to any such allegations. In fact, his seven-year journey through the secret prison system appears to have been triggered by a single ill-advised comment, made privately on the telephone.[10] In his Combatant Status Review Tribunal at Guantánamo, Madni maintained that he was betrayed by one of four radical Islamists whom he had met by accident on a trip to Indonesia in November 2001, to deal with family business after his father's death: 'After I went to Indonesia, I got introduced to some people who were not good. They were bad people. Maybe I can say they were terrorists. When someone gets introduced to someone, it is not written on their foreheads that they are bad or good.'[11] This account was corroborated by the *Washington Post* investigation, which found that during his time in Jakarta Madni had spent 'hours on end watching television at a friend's house'; when he was not doing that, he was handing out business cards 'identifying him as a Koran reader for an Islamic radio station.'[12]

The New York Times reported in 2005 that the entire, embarrassing basis for Madni's capture, rendition and interrogation was that Madni, in the words of one of his uncles, was a young man with 'a childish habit of trying to portray himself as important', who had simply made something up—that bombs could be hidden in his shoes—to impress his new friends in Jakarta. According to the paper, the comment was picked up by Indonesian intelligence agents, who were monitoring the four men, and relayed to the CIA, who decided to pick up Madni a few weeks later, following Richard Reid's failed shoe bomb attack. A senior US official speaking to the paper confirmed Madni's uncle's account, calling Madni a 'blowhard' who 'wanted us to believe he was more important than he was.'[13]

According to *The Sunday Times*, the well-known rendition plane with tail-number N379P collected some Egyptian security personnel and flew them to Cairo to assist with Madni's rendition. The latter was seized in Jakarta at 4am on 9 January 2002 and bundled aboard a plane at an airport, taking off around 10pm the following evening.[14] After his 2008 release, Madni related the same circumstances both in his *New York Times* interview in January 2009, and in his witness statement of July 2009: that 'during the flight to Cairo, Mr. Iqbal [Madni] said he was bleeding from his nose, mouth and ears, and was unable to move because of shackles wound tightly around his body.'[15] Madni's witness statement also reported that the plane stopped more than once en route to Egypt, and that while he was hooded cameramen boarded the plane and took pictures of him. He remembers the camera flashes. He was never taken out of the plane:

> After several hours, the plane stopped. I could hear the sound of the plastic being uncovered. They opened my shackles so I could urinate into a bottle. I think they did this because they realized that I was bleed-

ing. One of the Egyptian officers told me that we had stopped for refueling. Later on the stopover after I was re-hooded, I was aware that some other people came onto the plane and took photographs of me. I was aware of the camera-flashes through my hood.[16]

Madni's recollection of being photographed during his rendition is consistent with the accounts of other rendition victims.[17]

Where did Madni's plane stop for refuelling between Indonesia and Cairo? The flight logs of European air traffic organisation Eurocontrol show N379P on a circuit without details for the leg of the journey wholly outside of Eurocontrol territory, so we cannot know for sure without further confirmation. However, Madni's testimony, and the data that is available, suggests that the plane may well have refuelled at Diego Garcia. The time taken from Jakarta to this stop-over location was about five to seven hours, and then it was another three or four hours to Cairo.[18] The distance from Jakarta to Diego Garcia is 3,797 km (2,359 miles or 2,050 nautical miles), and N379P had an average range of 5,800 nautical miles, cruising at between 459 and 585 knots.[19] At 470 knots, then, the flight duration is consistent with Madni's estimate that the first leg of the flight took five to seven hours.[20] The distance from Diego Garcia to Cairo is 6,032 km (3,748 miles, or 3,257 nautical miles). Madni's recollection of the second leg is that it took three to four hours, including a stop-over of around thirty minutes; this is also consistent with N379P's above-average cruising speed.

For the flight across the Indian Ocean from Jakarta to Cairo, a stop-over on Diego Garcia would be eminently logical. After all, as Admiral McCain put it, 'Diego Garcia is ... equidistant from all points' in the Indian Ocean.[21] Madni says he arrived in Egypt on 11 January 2002, at 11:30am. He was assigned a basement room like 'a grave'—about 6 feet by 4 feet—and was kept there for ninety-two days.[22] In his *New York Times* interview, Madni said that on 11, 12 and 20 January 2002, he was interrogated for twelve to fifteen hours on each occasion.[23] He described his interrogators as Egyptian, but also noted that there were other men in the room whose faces were covered and who did not speak, but who passed notes with questions to the Egyptians.[24]

The Eurocontrol flight logs show that N379P stopped over in Cairo for six days (likely after dropping Madni there) before returning to Washington via Prestwick, once again utilising UK territory (and once again raising the spectre of UK knowledge of or complicity in Madni's rendition). Given the lengthy stop-over in Cairo, it is possible therefore that the masked men Madni describes as present at the Egyptian interrogations on 11 and 12 January 2002 were members of the US rendition crew.

Madni told *The New York Times* that his Egyptian captors tried to torture a confession out of him, and that when he told them that he had never been to Afghanistan, nor had he met Osama bin Laden, they responded by giving him electric shocks and forcing him to take drugs: 'I cry and I yell,' he recalled. 'Also they gave my brain electric shocks.' Madni also claimed that he was forced to consume liquids laced with drugs, 'so you don't know what you are talking about.'[25]

One witness who may be able to corroborate Madni's account of what happened in Egypt is the Australian national Mamdouh Habib, who had been arrested on 5 October 2001 in Karachi. During October 2001, Habib was detained in Pakistan, beaten and humiliated by Pakistanis, and interrogated by Americans. In November 2001, Habib was then sent to Egypt for the next five months, a period which overlaps with most of the time that Madni spent in Egypt. Habib has alleged that his Egyptian captors shocked him with high-voltage wires, hung him from metal hooks on walls and beat him before he was eventually sent to Guantánamo Bay.[26] According to three British men who were in Guantánamo Bay, Rhuhel Ahmed, Asif Iqbal and Shafiq Rasul, Habib himself was in 'catastrophic shape' when he arrived at Guantánamo: most of his fingernails were missing, and, like Madni, when he slept he regularly bled from his nose, mouth and ears.[27]

In addition, a Russian prisoner released from Guantánamo in 2004, Rustam Akhmyarov, said that while they were detained together, Madni told him of his time 'in an underground cell in Egypt, where he never saw the sun and where he was tortured until he confessed to working with Osama bin Laden', and added that he 'recalled how he was interrogated by both Egyptian and US agents in Egypt and that he was blindfolded, tortured with electric shocks, beaten and hung from the ceiling.'[28]

Madni later described how, in April 2002, he was flown to the Bagram Air Base outside Kabul. Again, Eurocontrol flight logs (not publicly available) match Madni's recollections exactly. This time, Madni was flown via a joint US/German airbase near Tashkent, where he changed planes before being taken onto Bagram. Madni described his detention and interrogation there in his *New York Times* interview:

> He was held there for almost a year, at times shackled and handcuffed in a small cage with other detainees, and further interrogated, he said.
>
> 'A C.I.A. person said, "We forgive you; just accept you met Osama bin Laden." I said, "No, I'm not going to say that."' Even though polygraph tests showed that he was telling the truth, he said, he was shifted from cell to cell every few hours and deprived of sleep for six months.[29]

Madni would ultimately spend over seven years in US custody, in wretched conditions that brought him repeatedly to psychological breaking point. *The New York Times* reported in 2005 that Madni had told a military tribunal of one suicide attempt; Habib remembered in particular that Madni 'pleaded for human interaction' and had overheard him saying, 'Talk to me, please talk to me ... I feel depressed ... I want to talk to somebody ... Nobody trusts me.' On the 191st day of his incarceration, according to Madni's own account, he attempted to commit suicide.[30]

Habib told *The New York Times* in 2009 that Madni in fact tried to hang himself twice, and went on three hunger strikes.[31]

Madni arrived at Guantánamo on 23 March 2003. It is evident from accounts of fellow prisoners that he was in a particularly bad mental and physical state before and during his detention. Ahmed, Iqbal and Rasul, the three British citizens released in 2004, recalled that Madni 'had electrodes put on his knees', and 'something had happened to his bladder and he had problems going to the toilet.'[32] According to Rustam Akhmyarov, Madni was also 'passing blood in his faeces', and said he overheard US officials telling Madni, 'we will let you go if you tell the world everything was fine here.'[33]

A 2007 court filing at the Washington Court of Appeals by Dr Ronald L. Sollock, the commander of the naval hospital at Guantánamo Bay, revealed that from 2003 Madni was prescribed antibiotics, and that in April 2007 he was diagnosed with a perforated left eardrum, inflammation of the left external ear canal and inflammation of the left middle ear.[34] Madni would later testify that interrogators had told him he would not receive assistance unless he cooperated with them, in which case he would be 'first in line for medical treatment.'[35]

Never charged with any crime, Madni was able to return home to Pakistan in August 2008.[36] His *New York Times* interview recounted this journey:

> After Guantánamo, he was flown on an American military aircraft to Islamabad's airport, where, two American Embassy officers, First Lt. Brian Strait and Keith Easter, witnessed his release, according to a United States government document he displayed. He was admitted to a hospital in Islamabad for treatment, and questioned for three weeks at a safe house by Pakistani intelligence officers in what Mr. Iqbal described called friendly sessions. Pakistani security officers then drove him back to Lahore and his extended family. 'It was like a new life for me,' he said. 'I was born again. There is no word to explain.'

Since his release, Madni has been dogged by enduring health problems: he is now unable to walk unaided, and, according to Dr Mohammed Mujeeb, an ear, nose and throat specialist at the Services Hospital in Lahore, by the time he returned home to Pakistan he was both dependent on a 'long list of drugs', and suffering debilitative psychological scarring from his traumatic experience.[37]

As of April 2017, it has been impossible for Madni to gain any confirmation, let alone an explanation or apology, from the UK or US governments. A legal challenge by Madni in the UK failed when the UK government maintained its position of 'neither confirming nor denying' that Madni's plane had refuelled on Diego Garcia.[38]

The obfuscations about allegedly water-damaged records (see Chapter 3) were prompted by an April 2014 Al-Jazeera America report suggesting that the long-awaited US Senate Intelligence Committee report would confirm that

> the CIA detained some high-value suspects on Diego Garcia, an Indian Ocean island controlled by the United Kingdom and leased to the United States. The classified CIA documents say the black site arrangement at Diego Garcia was made with the "full cooperation" of the British government. That would confirm long-standing claims by human rights investigators and journalists, whose allegations—based on flight logs and unnamed government sources—have routinely been denied by the CIA.[39]

In the event, the unclassified (and heavily redacted) summary of the report—the only part that has been publicly released—made no mention of detainees being held on Diego Garcia. The public version of the summary was revised in December 2014, the same month it was released, suggesting that negotiations over what material should be included or omitted may have been substantial.[40] An FOIA request by Reprieve found that UK government ministers had met repeatedly with members of the Senate

Intelligence Committee in the months leading up to publication of the summary, and Foreign Secretary William Hague (2010–14) confirmed that the UK had lobbied the Committee about the contents of the public version.[41] Inevitably, like the alleged roof over the records on Diego Garcia, the truth will eventually leak. Whether this will happen in time for Mohammed Saad Iqbal Madni to receive justice is another matter.

5

GOODBYE AFRICA

The first known legal use of the word 'rendition' occurs in US law reports from the 1800s, dealing with the non-legal transfers of slaves escaped from their southern masters to the free northern states. When northern states refused to make it obligatory to return escaped slaves to the south, an industry developed around hunting them down. For a bounty, professional slave catchers would, at a southern slave owner's request, venture north and abduct slaves from their new-found freedom. 'Rendition' was the term used for the transfer across state borders of captured slaves, back to bondage in the south.

The term first became associated with counterterrorism and the non-legal transfer of terror suspects during the 1990s, under a programme authorised by then-US President Clinton, involving the capture and transfer of exiled Egyptian Islamists from locations around the world back to Egypt for torture, disappearance and often death. It is well documented that the US had a major hand in training and financing exiled Egyptian and other Arab Islamists as proxies opposing the Soviets in Afghanistan, from up to six months prior to the Soviet invasion.[1] After the withdrawal of Soviet troops from Afghanistan, many of these fighters then turned their focus to toppling the regimes of their citizenship, in particular Egypt. The US had helped to train and equip these dissidents; now, in an ill-fated attempt to return the mujahideen genie to its bottle, the US was actively supporting Egypt in eradicating the exiled opposition, by capturing and rendering members of opposition groups back to Egypt, where they then faced the prospect of torture and often death.

The 1998 bombings of the US embassies in Nairobi and Dar es Salaam can be partly understood as a revenge attack in response to American involvement in the rendition and torture of four members of Egyptian Islamic Jihad (EIJ). Talat Fu'ad Qassim and three others had been captured by the US in Albania two months prior to the Embassy bombings and rendered by American agents to Egypt for incommunicado detention at the hands of the Egyptian state, which was known to practise torture.[2]

In the aftermath of the explosions in August 1998, the US continued conducting its controversial rendition operations. During the second half of August 1998, two suspects later convicted of offences related to the Embassy bombings, Sadek Odeh and Mohammed al-Owahili, were held in extra-judicial FBI custody in Kenya, then transferred with no extradition or other judicial process from Kenya to the US mainland for prosecution. Former US Ambassador to Kenya Johnnie Carson commented:

> because of the close co-operation between US and Kenyan authorities, the Kenyan government did not seek to detain Sadek Odeh and al-Owahili or put them on trial in Kenya. Acting with virtually no legal precedent or formalities, Kenyan officials waived all local legal and extradition procedures and released the suspects directly into US custody. Fearful that Kenya might be subject to future terrorist reprisals, Kenyan officials agreed to turn the suspected terrorists over to American authorities to prevent Kenya from becoming involved in what would be a long, complex and sensitive judicial procedure.[3]

In other words, the US persuaded the Kenyan authorities to turn over the suspects, without extradition procedures or any other form of judicial oversight, in contravention of both Kenyan and international law. In this way, the seeds were sown of what has become a normalised practice: rendering terror suspects in and around East Africa.

The Embassy bombing renditions were probably authorised by Presidential Decision Directive (PDD) 39, issued by then-President Clinton in June 1995, which allowed for the 'return of suspects by force'. PDD 39 states that

> when terrorists wanted for violation of U.S. law are at large overseas, their return for prosecution shall be a matter of the highest priority. ... If we do not receive adequate cooperation from a state that harbors a terrorist whose extradition we are seeking, we shall take appropriate measures to induce cooperation. Return of suspects by force may be effected without the cooperation of the host government, consistent with the procedures outlined in NSD-77 [a Bush 41-era National Security Directive that remains classified], which shall remain in effect.[4]

This policy was confirmed and expanded in May 1998 with a new presidential directive. PDD 62 outlined ten policy programmes, the first of which was 'apprehension, extradition, rendition, and prosecution.'[5] Since 9/11, after which 'the gloves came off' with respect to US treatment of terror suspects,[6] the requirement of an end-point to the judicial process in the destination state, already inadequate, has been dropped entirely.

The CIA was thereby authorised to forcibly transfer individuals such as Mohammed Saad Iqbal Madni to foreign states for torture and indefinite detention. The CIA was also authorised to set up and operate its own indefinite detention programme outside mainland US territory (see Chapters 1 and 2).[7] The CIA's term for the means by which prisoners were shuttled around detention sites, run by either the CIA or complicit foreign governments, was 'extraordinary rendition'.[8] Unlike the earlier so-called 'renditions to justice' practised in relation to East Africa and Egypt, the full extent of the entire 'extraordinary rendition' programme has never been fully disclosed by the US. Thanks to a global mesh of national security and secrecy laws, those who have been subject to this procedure have not yet had their experiences fully and publicly confirmed in open court anywhere in the world.

East Africa fully entered the post-9/11 theatre of US operations when, following the November 2002 bombing of Mombasa's Kikambala Hotel and a failed attack on an El Al airliner at Mombasa's airport, the United States pledged considerable further funding, training and other support to urgently reform and boost Kenya's counterterrorism capacity. The State Department's Anti-Terrorism Assistance Program (ATA), in its report for the fiscal year 2004, stated that as a result of ATA-sponsored consultations and seminars, Kenya had already launched a joint terrorism task force, drafted a national counterterrorism strategy, convened a national security advisory committee, created a national counterterrorism centre, and established the Antiterrorism Police Unit (ATPU).[9]

In Kenya, investigations into the Kikambala Hotel attack were carried out in the context of these radical, US-led reforms to Kenya's national security structure, and in close operational partnership with US personnel. This was the first known post-9/11 example of a domestic East African counterterrorism investigation triangulating across regional borders and being carried out in association with US counterterrorism operations elsewhere in the world.

In 2005, Amnesty International documented at least thirty-four examples of serious pre-trial violations committed by both Kenyan and 'foreign' personnel in the course of the Kikambala investigation, including incommunicado detention and torture. Amnesty noted that

> while recognising Kenya's duty to ensure the security of its citizens and other persons within its territory and subject to its jurisdiction, Amnesty

International is concerned that the rule of law and respect for Kenya's obligations under international human rights law and standards were being disregarded as the country came to grips with how to counter 'terrorist' acts.[10]

As discussed elsewhere in this book, the Kikambala investigation was also conducted beyond Kenyan borders, involving abductions and detentions in Somalia and Djibouti, and reaching as far as US prisons in Afghanistan. As a result of the widespread abuses carried out by Kenyan police during the investigation, little admissible evidence was collected, and the 2006 attempt at a trial in Mombasa was an embarrassing flop, with no convictions. The prosecution case ultimately turned on one major piece of evidence: the confession of the lead defendant, Omar Said Omar. This confession was disallowed on the basis that it had not been made in accordance with a recent provision of Kenyan law requiring all confessions to be made before a magistrate.

It has been suggested that the confession was disallowed on the basis of a 'technicality'.[11] It may equally be argued that the provision was introduced precisely to restrict the likelihood of coerced confessions and other unreliable torture evidence being introduced into Kenyan trials. Both Omar's confession, and the trial, occurred after the law had been changed. Omar alleged that not only had his confession been made in the absence of a magistrate, it was also false, and coerced via torture; he claimed that he had been held incommunicado, threatened, beaten, and tied to a chair during interrogations. Later, Omar also alleged that, during his pre-trial detention, Kenyan interrogators had repeatedly attempted to coerce him into falsely implicating Tanzanian Suleiman Abdallah in the Kikambala bombings. This occurred during a period when, according to official US documentation, Suleiman Abdallah was being held incommunicado in secret US detention in Afghanistan, and subjected to abusive interrogations by US personnel.[12]

This pattern of triangulation between unlawful operations in Kenya, other regional states and further-flung territories continued when, in 2007–8, local and international NGOs documented a transnational rendition and detention operation (the 'Border Operation') involving Kenyan, Ethiopian, Somali, American, British and other European personnel working to capture, detain and interrogate people fleeing from the conflict in Somalia following the US/Ethiopian invasion in late 2007.[13] Many of these renditions followed the pattern of 'outsourcing' and 'working with host states' that appear to have become increasingly prevalent in US rendition operations, particularly under President Obama, after his well-publicised disbanding of the CIA prison system.

These cases show that in fact the strategy of working with foreign states to act both as formal custodians and in other logistical roles has been in use in the East and Horn of Africa since at least 2007, during the Bush administration. After the Ethiopian-led bombing of Mogadishu on 26 December 2006, US forces reportedly fired on a group of individuals fleeing towards the Kenyan border, claiming that senior al-Qaeda leaders were amongst the targeted group.[14] This was the beginning of an operation whereby at least eight-five individuals of nineteen different nationalities, including many women—some pregnant— and their children, were captured on the border of Kenya and Somalia, and brought to Nairobi for incommunicado detention.[15] The prisoners were a motley collection and included the wives and children of two well-known terror suspects, Comorian Fazul Mohamed, and Kenyan Swale Nabhan. The fugitives themselves, however, were nowhere to be found.[16]

Whilst being held in Nairobi, many prisoners reported being denied access to a lawyer or consular assistance while being interviewed repeatedly by their own national security personnel. For example, four British ex-prisoners alleged to me (as a representative of Reprieve) and to a researcher from the NGO Cageprisoners that they had been interrogated in Nairobi by people who told them they were MI5 agents, and who let it be known that they were only there for interrogations, not consular support, and that they could not inform their families of the detainees' whereabouts. Some of these prisoners also reported having their photographs and fingerprints taken by FBI agents, and being told that this data was being gathered for inclusion in a 'terrorist database'.[17] When one of the British detainees managed to call the outside world after bribing a guard for the use of his phone, the Foreign Office was brought in, and an official let slip that the FCO had known of the citizens' detention for over a week, but had not yet performed any consular activities or contacted family members in the UK to alert them of the situation. The first contact between the families of the four young men and officialdom occurred the morning after the Cageprisoners representative and I had first spoken to the Foreign Office, when counterterrorism officers carried out raids on the London family homes of all four detainees. Before being flown home to the UK, they were rendered by Kenya back into the Somali warzone, with UK government officials maintaining that they had no power to interfere with 'Kenyan sovereignty' and insist otherwise, even if it would risk UK citizens being exposed to war crimes.

On the basis of flight manifests produced by the Kenyan government in court, it was soon possible to establish that eighty-five prisoners were removed from Kenya to Somalia between January and March 2007, by Kenyan anti-terror police officers on private airplanes operated by the companies Bluebird Aviation and African Express Airways.[18] The Kenyan Department of Immigration later submitted in court that it had 'processed 96 deportation orders of persons who had fled from the Somali conflict of January–February 2007 on the recommendation of the Police.'[19] Based on credible information obtained by the Muslim Human Rights Forum, however, it is likely that the number of individuals ultimately rendered may be closer to 120.[20] Even this figure does not include large numbers of individuals arriving by boat and motor vehicle, who may have been summarily turned back by Kenyan military and police on the Somali-Kenyan border.

Many former prisoners have subsequently described being held in incommunicado conditions in Somalia before being rendered onward to Ethiopia, where they were again held incommunicado, and subjected to physical abuse by Ethiopian guards. A number of the female prisoners were pregnant, and some gave birth in Ethiopian detention. At least eleven of the prisoners rendered from Kenya to Ethiopia were reported to be children, one as young as six months old.[21] One Kenyan citizen captured around the same time was taken to Guantánamo Bay. In unclassified statements, Abdulmalik Mohammed has described in detail how he was captured by Kenyan anti-terror police in Mombasa in March 2007, and abusively interrogated for several weeks in Kenya before being handed to US forces for rendition to incommunicado detention and abuse in Djibouti, Afghanistan and finally Guantánamo Bay.[22]

Since the 'Border Operation' of 2007–8, there has been a steady stream of counterterrorism renditions in East Africa, albeit not on the scale of early 2007. These renditions have been harder to monitor as they have increasingly involved members of the Somali community in the Nairobi suburb of Eastleigh. As a result of widespread intimidation by Kenyan police, and a series of mass refoulements of Somali refugees from Kenya to Somalia, these individuals are increasingly fearful of sharing their experiences with human rights researchers.

At least three renditions from Kenya to Somalia were documented during 2009. Twenty-five-year-old Kenyan citizen Ahmed Abdullahi Hassan went missing from Eastleigh in July 2009. After his disappearance, Hassan's family filed a *habeas* petition on his behalf, and the Kenyan government responded that

Hassan was not being held in Kenya and that it had no knowledge of his whereabouts.[23]

Hassan's fate remained a mystery until April 2011, when a former prisoner told me that he had met Hassan in a secret underground prison in Mogadishu. Hassan had described to this source how Kenyan police had knocked down his door in July 2009, snatched him, and taken him to a secret location in Nairobi. The next night, Hassan had said, he was taken to Wilson Airport in Nairobi:

> They put a bag on my head, Guantánamo style. They tied my hands behind my back and put me on a plane. In the early hours we landed in Mogadishu. The way I realized I was in Mogadishu was because of the smell of the sea—the runway is just next to the seashore. The plane lands and touches the sea. They took me to this prison, where I have been up to now. I have been here for one year, seven months. I have been interrogated so many times. Interrogated by Somali men and white men. Every day. New faces show up. They have nothing on me. I have never seen a lawyer, never seen an outsider. Only other prisoners, interrogators, guards. Here there is no court or tribunal.[24]

According to Jeremy Scahill, writing for the US weekly *The Nation*, this secret prison is situated in the basement of the headquarters of the Somali National Security Agency, and run by the Somali Transitional Federal Government with a significant level of CIA access and control.[25] Hassan remained in incommunicado detention, without charge, in Mogadishu until his quiet release some time in 2013.

A Kenyan 'intelligence' report widely leaked to and reproduced by the Kenyan media in 2011 suggested that Hassan was believed to have been a close associate of Swale Nabhan, who was killed by a US drone strike in Somalia in September 2009, two months or less after Hassan's capture and whilst he was still in detention.

There are several more reports of renditions from Nairobi to the secret underground prison in Mogadishu. Khalif Abdi is a

Somali citizen who was held in pre-arraignment detention in the Ugandan capital Kampala in connection with the Kampala suicide bombings of July 2010, before being unconditionally released on 12 September 2011. Abdi reported to former fellow prisoners that he was captured by Kenyan security forces in Nairobi in July 2010. He was flown to Mogadishu, where he was held overnight in an underground prison, before being flown by military plane to Kampala, where he was held for over a year of pre-trial detention, before all charges against him were dropped and he was released. Abdi's description of the underground prison to former fellow prisoners, and a prisoner he met there, appears to match that of the secret prison underneath the Somali NSA's headquarters described by Hassan and reported in *The Nation*.[26]

Another case of disappearance and rendition in the summer of 2010 is that of Badrudin Mohamed Abdi, a 17-year-old Kenyan or Somali citizen. Abdi was last seen in Nairobi on 29 August 2010, where he was being held incommunicado in an underground prison by ATPU officers.[27] A Kenyan lawyer who heard of his detention from a former fellow prisoner (since freed) then telephoned ATPU headquarters enquiring after Abdi's whereabouts. The ATPU officers refused to disclose any information, and the former fellow prisoner subsequently received a threatening text message on his phone, warning him not to go back to his lawyer: '*Wewe endelea kwenda kwa lawyer tutakupata tena wewe endelea tu.*' (You continue going to the lawyer and we will get you again, just continue.)[28] Further investigations have since confirmed that Abdi was rendered to Somalia and detained incommunicado in a secret underground prison in Mogadishu.

Abdi's statements, made in these conditions, may have been used in triangulated interrogations of Kenyan and Ugandan prisoners held in Uganda on suspicion of involvement in the 2010 Kampala bombings. Like the earlier examples, underpinning that case was a complex, murky, transnational intelligence-gathering operation involving detentions, unlawful interrogations and renditions of suspects and witnesses. Above ground, the legal case, comprising a constitutional and a criminal element, has been the vehicle for legally sanctioning those renditions in East Africa that end in some form of legal process, however unsatisfactory the latter may be.

6

RULE BY LAW

THE KAMPALA BOMBINGS CASE

Khalif Abdi and Badrudin Mohammed Abdi were not the only suspects to be rendered to Somalia in the course of the 2010 Kampala bombings investigation—they were just two instances amongst a raft of abuses committed by regional security forces, in some cases with apparent complicity from the US and the UK. The case itself was a prime example of East African states' developing strategy of 'rule by law' in the counterterrorism context, whereby the separation of powers is collapsed, and legal institutions and laws become vehicles solely to carry out the will of the state, and to sanction the violation of due process and other rights. Clearly, those who commit acts of mass violence should be brought to account, and the public should be protected from further attacks. However, the accounting must be done in a way that is reliable, without giving way to prejudice, and in a way that respects the rule of law and due process. To do otherwise risks punishing the wrong people, thereby leaving the guilty at large, perpetuating social schisms, and inflaming target communities already being pushed towards the edge.

At the time of the bombings, counterterrorism-related abuses in East Africa had settled into a pattern of peaks and troughs. The last peak had occurred with the mass renditions and detentions described in Chapter 5, occurring just after the US-sponsored invasion of Mogadishu in early 2007. From around mid-2008 until the July 2010 attacks, there had been something of a lull, following the embarrassment of the 'Border Operation' and the near total exposure by human rights organisations of mass unlawful rendition and detention operations.

In Kenya at this time, the local human rights activists and lawyers working on this issue were a small group, notably the well-known human rights defender Al-Amin Kimathi and his Muslim Human Rights Forum, comprised mainly of a large cohort of volunteers, and Nairobi-based lawyer Mbugua Mureithi (who would later win a landmark legal case against the Kenyan government on behalf of eight Kenyan rendition victims transported from Kenya to Ethiopia during the Border Operation). They worked closely with a range of international groups, including Reprieve, Human Rights Watch and Amnesty International, bringing legal cases and publishing reports further exposing the unlawful excesses of East Africa's War on Terror.

In Uganda, against the backdrop of the Ugandan government's longstanding securitisation policies and a range of other concerns—such as rampant government-sponsored homophobia and the detention and torture of political dissidents—the global War on Terror almost failed to register as a distinct domestic human rights issue. But things were not quite as they seemed. Despite there having been no recent incidents of Islamist terrorism in Uganda, President Yoweri Museveni's government was already heavily embroiled in the Somali counterinsurgency, fighting Al-Shabaab and similar groups.

In March 2007, the first Ugandan troops participating in the African Union Mission to Somalia (AMISOM) had arrived on the ground, making Uganda the first state to deploy troops to Somalia under this mission. To date, Uganda's has also remained the largest contingent of troops; at the time of writing, 6,223 Ugandan troops are based in 'Sector 1', which is made up of Banadir (Mogadishu), Upper Shabelle, and Lower Shabelle provinces.

Uganda's motivation for entry into the Somali war were at least partly venal: clearly the Ugandan military presence in Somalia provided proxy US boots on the ground, conveniently filling a gap in Washington's Somalia policy (there being essentially no US ground troops there), for which the Ugandan government continues to be paid handsomely by way of considerable amounts of counterterrorism-related military aid and equipment from the United States.[1] There were also domestic dynamics at play. By the time of the AMISOM deployment, most troops had just returned from their 'adventures' in the Congo. John Njoroge, a Ugandan journalist, has pointed out that

> Uganda has never had a peaceful transition of power. Guns and soldiers have always been involved in a change of regime. The ruling NRM party does not want thousands of soldiers hanging around in barracks with time on their hands. And there is no work for them outside the army— unemployment is 50% here. President Museveni has been in power for almost 26 years and his popularity is waning. Military officers are already getting restless. From the government's point of view, far better for them to be fighting in Somalia.[2]

Whatever the combination of reasons, by 2010 Museveni had kingpin status in Somalia, and Al-Shabaab leaders had started making public threats that Uganda would be directly targeted if its military presence in Somalia continued. These threats were borne out on 11 July 2010, with Al-Shabaab's first bomb attack beyond Somali borders: during the South Africa-hosted World Cup final, bombs ripped through two crowded bars in Kampala in quick succession. The first attack hit a busy bar/restaurant called Ethiopian Village, in Kampala's Kabalagala neighbourhood, where many foreigners had congregated to watch the game. The second bombing was at Kyadondo Rugby Club Nakawa, where the match was being broadcast on a massive screen.

Of the seventy-four dead and seventy injured, most were Ugandans who had gathered to watch the football. From all reports, the attack appeared calculated and strategic in its execution. Choosing busy international bars showing the final combined the advantage of soft targets with maximum global impact and resonance. Although we may never know for certain whether the high-level fugitive Fazul Mohamed was the mastermind (there is currently no publicly-known evidence to confirm that he was), the style of the attacks echoed the 1998 Embassy bombings, combined with a good helping of pragmatism and an understanding of the modern media.

My focus, in this book and my wider research, is on human rights abuses perpetrated by governments. I have not, therefore, gone into the plight of the victims of this attack, or their families, in depth. This is not because this is not of the utmost importance: it is, and out of control, misguided counterterrorism operations are a common way in which the victims of terrorism are failed by the states whose role it is to protect them. Indeed, it is remarkable that as counterterrorism has developed as a global, multilateral, billion-dollar enterprise, no common approach to state compensation and reparations for terror victims has evolved. There are too many examples, within East Africa and beyond, where despite apparently huge budgets for carrying out investigations, victims and their families have effectively been abandoned without adequate state support. Uganda's approach to the Kampala bombing victims, who were reportedly speedily compensated by the government, initially appeared to be an exception.[3] Later reports, however, suggest that all was not as it seemed; as of January 2015, over 205 million Ugandan shillings channelled through the Office of the Prime Minister for families' compensation allegedly remained unaccounted for. A remaining 794 million shillings, which were forwarded to the Ministry of Internal Affairs for distribution to the families, cannot be confirmed by the Ugandan auditor general as having been used for the intended purpose, because 'no accountability documents were available for audit examination'.[4]

Following the Kampala attacks, the US and the UK pledged to assist the Ugandans with their investigation. A Metropolitan Police team was dispatched from London to assist with 'forensics', and over seventy FBI agents arrived in Kampala from the US. Despite, or possibly exacerbated by this international assistance, the subsequent investigation followed a similar pattern to that following the Kikambala bombing in Kenya in 2002—a botched investigation characterised by rampant human rights abuses, followed by a prosecution which managed to present fairly sparse evidence admissible in court. Unlike the Kikambala case, however, the Kampala bombings investigation did ultimately result in a series of convictions, albeit on somewhat shaky evidence and against a backdrop of worrying abuses (both legal and physical). Uganda's 'Rapid Response Unit' was primarily responsible for the investigation in its initial stages, until it was hurriedly disbanded following a damning 2011 Human Rights Watch report detailing routine torture and unlawful detention in a network of un-gazetted safehouses.[5] Credible rumour had it that, following this shut-down, the investigation file was mislaid. Indeed, the US appears to have had concerns at a fairly late stage about the strength of the prosecution case, as its Embassy in Kenya is reliably said to have secretly brought the Ugandan prosecutor to Nairobi to work on stitching the case together. Thus, the investigative methods and chain of custody of the evidence are questionable. The investigation also raised questions from an 'intelligence' perspective, with not only the legal validity but also the accuracy and even credibility of its sources remaining uncertain; regional security, and the situation in Somalia in particular, have both clearly deteriorated significantly in the years since the Kampala bombings.

In the days following the attacks, hundreds of people were rounded up and detained by Ugandan security forces, in particular by the Rapid Response Unit before its disbandment. In Kenya, the Anti-Terrorism Police Unit (ATPU) and the National Security and Intelligence Service were involved in further arrests, detentions, and rendition of suspects to Uganda. Abuses documented in the course of defence investigations (see notes below) suggest that between July and September 2010 at least eight Kenyan nationals, the two Somalis mentioned at the beginning of this chapter, and three Ugandan nationals were abducted by Kenyan security forces and unlawfully rendered to Somalia and Uganda.[6] Five of these Kenyan nationals—Habib Suleiman Njoroge, Omar Awadh Omar, Mohammed Hamid Suleiman, Hussein Hassan Agade, Idris Magondu—and Ugandan nationals Isa Ahmed Luyima, Hassan Harun Luyima and Abubakari Batematyo were ultimately amongst fourteen co-defendants taken to Kampala for trial.

A Kenyan, Mohammed Aden Abdow, and one of the Somalis, Khalif Abdi, were released on 12 September 2011. An eighth Kenyan national—Ismail Abubakr—was rendered twice from Kenya to Uganda, but was ultimately released, and was not amongst the defendants held in Kampala. Two of those who ultimately stood trial, Kenyan national Mohammed Ali Mohammed and Tanzanian national Yahya Mbuthia, were rendered from Tanzania to Uganda in 2011.

Each of these men reported being subjected to a range of serious human rights abuses by the various governments involved in their detention and transfer. Ill-treatment reported by seven of the eight during capture (no statement was taken from the eighth, Ismail Abubakr) includes excessive use of force, threats, and failure to show an arrest warrant or give reasons for arrest. All reported subsequent incommunicado detention, denial of food during detention in Kenya (ranging from several hours to three days), denial of access to a lawyer or family members, threats of rendition to Guantánamo and Uganda for torture and death, and threats of harm to family members. There were also unanimous reports of excessive use of force during rendition, shackling by hands and feet, hooding, and failure to provide an opportunity for judicial oversight to challenge their forced transfers to Uganda.[7] The renditions of the Kenyan nationals were widely reported at the time in Kenya, and *habeas corpus* proceedings were brought on behalf of several of the prisoners.

The public position of both the British Embassy and the Kenyan justice minister shortly after the renditions was to condemn them,[8] though this British position was somewhat undermined by subsequent allegations of UK security service involvement in the interrogations of some of the prisoners.[9] Two Kenyan High Court judges also condemned the renditions as an infringement of the victims' constitutional rights.[10] *Habeas* applications were filed for a number of the rendition victims, and a further application for an injunction was made for a detainee who was not ultimately transferred.[11] In the cases of two prisoners, Omar Awadh Omar and Habib Suleiman Njoroge, the Kenyan state has continued to deny any involvement in the transfer, despite overwhelming evidence to the contrary.[12]

With great difficulty (inhibited by many factors, including intimidation by Ugandan government personnel of defence lawyers and other observers, and denial of defence lawyers' access to their clients by prison authorities), a constitutional petition was lodged in Kampala in 2011, alleging that the treatment of the men—in particular the fact of their rendition—should bar their being brought before a Ugandan Court for trial. At this point, the trial, which the Ugandan government initially tried to rush through before any of the defendants had accessed adequate legal representation, was stayed pending outcome of the petition.

A full hearing of the petition was held in 2013 in the Kampala High Court. When the judgment was finally handed down over a year later, the applicants lost on every point, in an extraordinary ruling dismissing all allegations of human rights abuses.[13] A trial commenced in March 2015 but was adjourned before completion after the prosecutor dealing with the case was assassinated.[14] Eventually, in May 2016, seven of the fourteen accused were found guilty of involvement in the bombings. Two of these defendants were released unconditionally before trial; the remaining five were acquitted, but were not released, and days later were rearrested and charged with terrorism for allegedly plotting another attack whilst in prison in Uganda.[15] At the time of writing, they remain detained in Kampala.

Alongside these extrajudicial renditions and detentions came a general government crackdown on people working on protecting human rights in the national security context, and in particular a concerted attempt to intimidate, and limit the work of, human rights defenders who were investigating national security-related violations, especially on anything connected to the Kampala bombings case. During 2010 and 2011, over eleven human rights defenders working on national security matters were attacked by the governments of Kenya and Uganda. The first and most serious attack came in September 2010, when Al-Amin Kimathi, a well-known Kenyan human rights activist, and Mbugua Mureithi, the Kenyan lawyer of some of the Kenyan rendition victims in Kampala, were lured to a hotel and then detained incommunicado with their clients at the Ugandan Rapid Response Unit headquarters at Kireka, Central Uganda.

Mureithi reported first being detained at gunpoint by Rapid Response Unit officers on the night of 15 September 2010, without any reasons given or warrant shown. According to his account, he and Kimathi were hooded and their legs manacled, before being threatened with execution and accused of being terrorists. Mureithi was detained incommunicado for four days before being removed to Kenya, on 18 September 2010.[16] Kimathi was subjected to similar treatment, but rather than being released with Mureithi, he was taken to court and charged with the same offences as his clients—involvement in the Kampala bombings. Kimathi's detention was widely condemned by human rights organisations, and described by Human Rights Watch as an apparent attempt by the Ugandan government to 'muzzle a well-known critic.'[17] Kimathi was detained in Uganda for over a year, before all charges were dropped and he was unconditionally released in September 2011.

I also had first-hand experience of being attacked for working on this case. The first time was in December 2010, when I attempted to enter Uganda to observe a bail hearing for Al-Amin Kimathi. I was travelling with an American citizen; we were refused entry and detained overnight at Kampala Airport. I was told that I was to be 'taken to headquarters' in the morning, however by that time the British and American Embassies had intervened.

I offered to speak to an interrogator with a representative of the British Embassy present, however this offer was declined and I was eventually permitted to leave the country. Elements of the detention were farcical. A Human Rights Watch researcher attempted to visit us and was denied entry. In the morning, I was told someone from the British High Commission would attend. At this point, we were confined to the arrivals hall, watching trains of visitors queue up to enter the country. No British diplomat was in evidence until I received a call on my mobile phone. In a whisper, the caller explained that he was from the British High Commission, and he was in fact at that very moment sitting on an adjacent bench to me in the arrivals hall. He explained that he could not come any closer, or speak to me directly, as the Ugandans had forbidden him to talk to me. Eventually, in a suitably filmic manner, a man from the US Embassy stormed through the doorway into the arrivals hall and successfully insisted on our release (we left on the next UK-bound plane). A British official later suggested, off the record, that I was on a Ugandan government 'blacklist' because the Ugandan government had found emails on Al-Amin Kimathi's computer which showed that I had been assisting him with research into abuses of some of the Kampala rendition victims.

In a similar case, on 13 April 2011, four Kenyan members of a delegation travelling to meet the Ugandan attorney-general to discuss Mr Kimathi's case—Kenyan lawyer Samuel Mohochi, Director of Muslims for Human Rights Hussein Khalid, Chairman of the Supreme Council of Kenyan Muslims Muhdhar Khitamy, and Commissioner at the Kenya National Commission for Human Rights Hassan Omar Hassan (now an MP in Mombasa)—were refused entry to Uganda at Kampala Airport, and detained for six hours before being summarily deported back to Kenya.[18] Mohochi has since obtained a judgment at the East African Court of Justice, stating that Uganda acted in contravention of his rights by refusing him entry to Uganda and deporting him in this way.[19]

Finally, in June 2012, I was deported from Kenya after three months on and off in the region, investigating Al-Amin Kimathi's case and some of the other excessive abuses occurring in the Kampala bombings investigation. During my time in Kenya, like others working on this issue, I had felt increasingly under surveillance and had experienced very obvious efforts to curtail my work. For example, I had received unexpected visitors to hotel rooms who clearly had believed the room would be empty; phones I used would routinely make strange clicks and buzzes; and at least one witness was intimidated into not meeting with me, having received an anonymous call telling him not to talk to 'the white lady'. My air travel within East Africa was increasingly fraught, with high numbers of seemingly random searches and checks. At every opportunity I would be pulled aside and my bag turned upside down. I took to only travelling with hand luggage. At passport control, judging by the behaviour of immigration officials, something was popping up on the screen whenever I tendered my passport. I would be told to wait whilst the immigration officer went off to make a call or speak to a superior, then eventually waved on. It was anxiety-inducing, and clear that something wasn't right. But I hoped it would not escalate, and continued trying to do my work.

The final straw occurred towards the end of June 2011. I had decided to go down to Dar es Salaam to meet with a couple of key defence witnesses. These were Mohammed Ali Mohammed, a Kenyan citizen who was at that time being detained in Tanzania, resisting Uganda's extradition request to try him for involvement in the bombings (he would later be convicted in Kampala), and his wife Amina Saif, a Tanzanian citizen who was living with her relatives in Dar es Salaam. I had tried to persuade others to go to Tanzania to meet with these two, because I had been warned that if I went myself, it would probably tip the Kenyan government over the edge and push them to kick me out.

In the end, no one else was foolish enough to agree to go for the whole trip, so I travelled down with a Kenyan lawyer, who stayed for one day and met Mohammed's Tanzanian lawyers with me. He then returned, while I stayed on to meet the witnesses. Attempts to visit Mohammed in prison were blocked by Tanzanian prison authorities, so I decided to attempt a meeting when he was produced in court for an extradition hearing. After the hearing, I went to the cells to meet with him. We were sur-rounded at all times by four Tanzanian officers armed with machine guns—one sitting on either side and two standing in front, inches from us. I remember thinking that, on so many levels, this was not quite how I'd imagined human rights work when I was in law school. These were hardly conditions of confidentiality, but we were able to cover what we needed and establish that, contrary to the claims of the Ugandan government, Mohammed had never even met Al-Amin Kimathi in person.

Meanwhile, the home of Mohammed's wife Amina was under heavy surveillance by Ugandan agents. Inside, I met a frightened young woman who had been thoroughly unravelled by her treatment by Kenyan and Tanzanian agents. She and her mother explained how they had been abducted from their home by Tanzanian agents and held incommunicado in a police station. Her mother had been strip-searched, humiliated, and held for several days before being released. Amina had remained in detention, describing how at one point Kenyan agents took her over the border to Kenya, driving her around at night asking questions about buildings and locations. She was never given access to a lawyer. Amina, like her husband, stated that, contrary to prosecution allegations, she had never met Al-Amin Kimathi in person.

These were the two key witnesses in Kimathi's defence case, and their statements would later be instrumental in securing his unconditional release from Ugandan detention.

Before leaving for Nairobi, I also caught up with Suleiman Abdallah, the Tanzanian former ghost prisoner who had been rendered to Afghanistan and held for five years in secret US prisons. We wandered to the scraggy beach in Dar es Salaam and he updated me on his young daughter and wife, and his efforts to get hold of a boat so he could return to life as a fisherman. When I'd first met Suleiman in Zanzibar, he was a skinny, haunted figure who could hardly eat or sleep, and complained of almost constant flashbacks to his time in the Darkness and Bagram. Seeing Suleiman three years on, persistently piecing together a fragile yet functional life and beginning to look to the future with hope, was both uplifting and also, in the context of dealing with a whole new wave of the War on Terror, depressing.

Leaving Dar es Salaam that Sunday evening, I was again subject to every 'random' check possible, and as I arrived at Nairobi's Jomo Kenyatta Airport at around 9:30pm I had a strong sense that something choreographed was happening around me. I wondered if I was finally losing my grip on reality. Wandering through the arrivals section of the airport, I noticed several people who seemed to be observing me. When I got to passport control, I was asked to go and wait outside a little room, where someone was waiting for me with handcuffs. I can't remember exactly what the officer said whilst he dangled the cuffs in front of my face, apart from his unsuccessful attempts to insist that I hand over my two mobile phones (one Kenyan and one British).

The next sixteen hours were spent holed up in a cell in international arrivals. I was already exhausted and the experience was horrible, albeit cushioned by the knowledge that I had the statements from the two witnesses, something that no amount of intimidation could at that point undo. The following day, FCO officials reiterated that my name was on some sort of blacklist (although they have subsequently denied all knowledge of this), and I was then summarily deported from Kenya, the dates on the documents showing that they had been prepared by the Kenyan government several months earlier. The slim silver lining in the cloud of my deportation was that it provided eloquent testimony to persuade European governments that the Kenyan and Ugandan governments were not playing fair in the Kampala bombings investigation, and that Kimathi's defence team had not simply dreamt up the claim that human rights defenders were being unfairly attacked. With statements from the two witnesses in Tanzania, there remained no reliable evidence to justify Kimathi's continued detention. In September 2011, three months after my arrival back in the UK, and after hard work by others on Kimathi's legal team, he was unconditionally released at a court hearing in Kampala, alongside two other men, Khalif Abdi and Mohammed Aden Abdow.

7

EAST AFRICA'S 'PHOENIX PROGRAMME'

Djibouti, the tiny state at the tip of the Horn of Africa, is a major strategic and military hub for the United States in both its counterterrorism operations and other security and military operations, stretching far into the Indian Ocean. Sitting at the intersection of Somalia, Yemen, and one of the world's busiest shipping lanes, Djibouti has been the base of operations for the US military's Combined Joint Task Force—Horn of Africa (CJTF-HOA) since 2002. Since 2007, with the creation of the US Africa Command (AFRICOM), Djibouti has hosted the only de facto permanent US military base in Africa, at the former French Foreign Legion base of Camp Lemonnier.[1]

The inauguration of AFRICOM—whereby the whole of Africa, apart from Egypt, was for the first time united within one US military command—was announced by then-US Defense Secretary Donald Rumsfeld in 2007, during a visit to Camp Lemonnier. Prior to 2007, whilst Camp Lemonnier was being renovated, US operations in Djibouti were run out of a US military vessel in Djiboutian waters.[2] In the years since the creation of CJTF-HOA and then AFRICOM, the US presence in

Djibouti has taken on an increasingly permanent and multi-layered character, providing a foundation for complex multiagency operations stretching deep into the African continent, across to the Arabian Peninsula, and far into the Indian Ocean.[3] Over the past several years, the US has both significantly expanded its facilities at Camp Lemonnier and opened a new base and airstrip at Chabelley Airfield,[4] and there is strong evidence to suggest that Djibouti has acted as a hub for a number of CIA renditions, along with later US military rendition operations involving the East and Horn of Africa. This tiny state is also now reportedly the key base of operations for drone surveillance and targeted killings in East Africa and the Arabian Peninsula, as well as acting as a 'logistics hub' for anti-piracy and other multilateral military operations throughout East Africa and the Indian Ocean.

The focus of this chapter is the increasing appearance of these activities, from an operational perspective, as part of a holistic US counterterrorism strategy, and the extent to which Djibouti and East Africa may have been a test zone for a kind of modern day 'Phoenix Programme'. The Phoenix Program was the code name for a counterinsurgency programme adopted by the US during the Vietnam War, in which, as Seymour Hersh has described, 'Special Forces teams were sent out to capture or assassinate Vietnamese believed to be working with or sympathetic to the Vietcong. In choosing targets, the Americans relied on information supplied by South Vietnamese Army officers and village chiefs.' Today's version of this approach is carried out across national borders, and with the advantage of modern forms of technology.

Renditions involving Djibouti took off not long after 9/11. Some of the earlier cases likely to have been perpetrated by the CIA have been described in Chapters 1 and 2. In September 2006, President George W. Bush announced that there were no further 'high-value detainees' in CIA custody, suggesting at least a temporary cessation of CIA overseas detention and rendition operations.[5] In the Horn of Africa region, this cessation also coincided with the rise of the Union of Islamic Courts in Somalia, who, in their de facto reign over southern Somalia, displaced the Somali warlords who were the CIA's primary partners for capturing terror suspects in Somalia. All this notwithstanding, there is strong evidence to suggest that at least two further renditions from Djibouti—to Afghanistan and Guantánamo Bay respectively—occurred in 2007. There is no evidence to imply express CIA involvement in these cases, suggesting that following Bush's declaration, the US military or some other agency/agencies effectively took over at least the outward-facing aspects of the CIA's rendition activities in the region. Whichever arm of the US military or government was responsible for these two renditions, they demonstrate from this relatively early—pre-Obama—period an increased US reliance on partner states at all stages of the operation, from arrest through to detention as well as at least initial interrogations.

According to the US military's own records, publicly released via WikiLeaks, Kenyan citizen Mohammed Abdulmalik was captured by Kenyan police on 13 February 2007 and transferred to Guantánamo Bay on 23 March 2007.[6] I was in Kenya at the time of Abdulmalik's arrest, and tried unsuccessfully to visit him in detention in Nairobi myself. Abdulmalik's own unclassified statement, filed in *habeas corpus* court proceedings in Washington DC in November 2010, communicates in his own words an account of his arrest by Kenyan police in Mombasa in March 2007, and his interrogation by Kenyan personnel under the observation of 'three white men' whom he took to be US security personnel working in cooperation with the Kenyan interrogators.[7] After a day of abusive questioning, Abdulmalik reports being taken by plane to Nairobi, where his interrogations—still carried out by Kenyans, in the presence of non-Kenyan observers—continued.

Some time later, by his own reckoning around 25 or 26 February, Abdulmalik was flown on a US plane to a location he believes to be Djibouti.

In unclassified testimony, Abdulmalik has described his experience in this location in some detail, and the modus operandi of his rendition clearly echoes the known CIA routine from earlier years:

'*They stripped me naked, put me in a diaper and dressed me in a tracksuit. I was then shackled, with ear-mufflers, blindfolded, and put into a plane with about ten American soldiers.*

'*At one point, the soldiers took my hood off and took me to the open door of the plane and made as if they were going to throw me out. I thought I was going to die. They hauled me back in, put my hood back on and chained me to the floor of the cargo plane. My eyes, head and mouth stayed covered the whole time. I could hardly breathe.*

'*The flight took two to three hours and landed at what I believe to be a U.S. Air Base in Djibouti. At the air base, I was taken into a shipping container, and given some water that said 'Made in Djibouti' on the label. On the wall was a poster saying 'Reptiles of the Horn of Africa', with pictures of snakes, lizards, and maps of Somalia and Djibouti.*

'*I had my hands and feet shackled together, and a mask was put on my face. They took me to another room, and the interrogations began. There were four of them: two guards and two interrogators. They said I was connected to people from all over the world. Someone told me that I would be held there, in a cage, for 100 years, for the rest of my life, unless I "admitted" to what they told me I had done. A US interrogator told me, "'You were coming to Kenya to destroy the marathon!" But I knew nothing about the marathon, and I told the interrogators this.*

'*The American interrogators said to me: "You have two possible journeys: one back to your family, or another that is very, very long. If you don't tell us what we want to hear, you will have a long, long journey; you will spend your life in a cage." They accused me of say-ing goodbye to my wife and sending money to her because I wanted to be a suicide bomber. This was not true. I said goodbye because I did not know what would happen to me in captivity.*

'After a number of days, I was again taken on a plane. I was again stripped naked, put in a diaper and dressed in a tracksuit, shackled, with ear-mufflers, and blindfolded. I was put into a plane with American soldiers. I was shackled to the floor of the cargo plane for the duration of the journey, with my eyes, head and mouth covered. This time, the journey was longer, around 8–10 hours.[8]

The plane deposited Abdulmalik in a location that he believes, according to his unclassified statements, to have been in Afghanistan, where he reports having being held in two US-run sites—their names and locations are unconfirmed—before being flown to Guantánamo, where, as of July 2016, he remains, held without charge or trial.

The second rendition case that occurred in 2007, again shortly after President Bush claimed that the CIA secret prison system was empty, is that of Somalilander Ismail Mohamed (AKA Abdullahi Sudi Arale), who was reportedly arrested for alleged passport fraud by Djiboutian authorities whilst travelling through Djibouti on 31 May 2007 on his way to Eritrea. According to official US Department of Defense documentation released by WikiLeaks, he was then transferred to US control at Camp Lemonnier on about 3 June, before being transferred to Guantánamo on 5 June.[9] Mohamed has reported in unclassified statements made after his release that following his arrest he was taken by cab to a residential building, where he was held for three days and given no opportunity to contest his detention or access a lawyer. Then, Reprieve is reported to have explained, he was taken to another location, and detained and interrogated in something resembling a shipping container.[10] He was held at Guantánamo until 18 November 2009, when he was released without charge.

Not long after these two cases, under the new Obama presidency (2009–17), US-targeted killings of terror suspects began to ramp up throughout the Horn of Africa. Although targeted killings by drone were arguably 'the' signature feature of Obama's counterterrorism strategy, it is clear that lethal operations, and drones, have been a feature of the War on Terror since its earliest days.

The first reported US assassination of terror suspects by drone occurred many years before Obama took office, in 2002, when a car in the northern Yemeni province of Marib was hit by a hellfire missile fired from an unmanned Predator drone, flown out of Djibouti. Six men were killed in the attack, including the probable target, Qaed Salim Sinan al-Harethi, a suspect in the October 2000 attack on the *USS* Cole. Although the US did not formally admit responsibility for the attack, in an interview with CNN, then-US Deputy Defense Secretary Paul Wolfowitz called it 'a very successful tactical operation', explaining that 'we've just got to keep the pressure on everywhere we're able to, and we've got to deny the sanctuaries everywhere we're able to and we've got to put pressure on every government that is giving these people support to get out of that business.'[11]

James Bamford has described in *The Atlantic* how the operation to kill al-Harethi was coordinated between NSA analysts based at Fort Meade, Maryland, a 'Cryptological Support Group' based in Yemen, and a 'battery of unmanned Predator Drones, each armed with deadly Hellfire missiles, based across the Red Sea in Djibouti.'[12] A US citizen, Kamal Derwish/Ahmed Hijazi, was also killed in this attack, nine years before the controversial drone assassination of US citizen Anwar al-Awlaki in Yemen. Dana Priest, writing in *The Washington Post*, observed that 'it was unclear whether the CIA operatives who fired the missile from hundreds of miles away knew that an American citizen was among their targets. It also was unclear whether that would have made any difference.'[13]

The publicly-known cases from the early years of Obama's presidency do suggest that the key targeted killings in and around Somalia were not routinely conducted by drone. They were, however, representative of a tactical curve in US assassination strategy, with its origins in the Cold War. The 1975 US Senate Select Committee (chaired by Senator Frank Church) investigating Cold War-era assassination programmes found evidence of no fewer than eight CIA plots to assassinate Cuban President Fidel Castro, as well as plots to assassinate President Ngo Dinh Diem of South Vietnam, and Chile's General René Schneider.

In addition to plots to assassinate high-level foreign personnel, targeted killing was also carried out systematically by the US, on a mass scale, during the Vietnam War. Describing similar pitfalls to those the US is beginning to face in today's War on Terror, Seymour Hersh reported that

> the operation got out of control. According to official South Vietnamese statistics, Phoenix claimed nearly forty-one thousand victims between 1968 and 1972; the US counted more than twenty thousand in the same time span. Some of those assassinated had nothing to do with the war against America but were targeted because of private grievances. William E. Colby, the CIA officer who took charge of the Phoenix Program in 1968 (he eventually became CIA director), later acknowledged to Congress that 'a lot of things were done that should not have been done.'[14]

Following Frank Church's report, an executive order banning assassinations was issued. This order is essentially still in force today.[15] And whilst this has evidently not prevented the development of a new programme of targeted killing in counterterrorism operations, academics Gabriella Blum and Philip Keyman offer some fascinating analysis into how this historical background, and the East Africa region in particular, may provide some insight into the way the US has framed and justified its counterterrorism activities since the 1990s. Linking this historical background to early East African War on Terror operations, Blum and Heymann have described how,

> following the 1998 bombings of the American embassies in Kenya and Tanzania, and on the basis of a (secret) favourable legal opinion, President Bill Clinton issued a presidential finding (equivalent to an Executive Order) authorising the use of lethal force against al-Qaeda in Afghanistan. Shortly thereafter, seventy-five Tomahawk cruise missiles were launched at a site in Afghanistan where Osama Bin Laden was expecting to attend a summit meeting. Following the attacks of September 11, 2001, President George Bush reportedly made another finding that broadened the class of potential targets beyond the top leaders of al-Qaeda, and also beyond the boundaries of Afghanistan. Secretary of Defense Donald Rumsfeld ordered Special Operations units to prepare a plan for 'hunter killer teams', with the purpose of killing, not capturing, terrorist suspects. Using the war paradigm for counterterrorism enabled government lawyers to distinguish lethal attacks on terror suspects from prohibited assassinations and justify them as lawful battlefield operations against enemy combatants.[16]

Circling back to Somalia and the US hub of operations at Djibouti, a well-known and controversial assassination occurred in May 2008, when the Al-Shabaab leader Aden Hashi Ayro was killed in Dusa Marreb, central Somalia. The killing echoed the attack on bin Laden following the 1998 Embassy bombings, and was reportedly carried out using 'at least four Tomahawk cruise missiles fired from a Navy ship or submarine off the Somali coast'.[17] Unlike that attack, however, this operation reportedly claimed many casualties. Alongside Ayro, between five and ten civilians were also reported to have been killed, including his wife and children. When I visited Somaliland (where Ayro was born) in 2009, I heard a high level of criticism of the number of civilian deaths during this operation.

The 2009 assassination of another Al-Shabaab leader, Swale Ali Nabhan, reportedly involved fewer civilian deaths than Ayro's assassination, and was explained by Somalia analyst Rashid Abdi as representative of a wider move by the US to reduce civilian casualties in their operations in the region: 'this was a very well-planned operation, meticulous. ... That should help contain any backlash. The impact is much less than it would have been if bystanders were hit.'[18] The killing of Nabhan by US Special Forces is also notable because of its similarity to the later success-ful assassination of bin Laden in Pakistan. Nabhan and Al-Shabaab spokesman Sheikh Muyadin Omar were amongst a group of four people killed by Navy Seals in an operation code-named 'Celestial Balance', whilst travelling in a convoy from Barawe. US Special Forces reportedly launched helicopters from a US Navy vessel, whilst Nabhan and three companions had stopped for breakfast. According to National Public Radio, mis-siles were fired at the group and at least one helicopter landed so that the bodies of Nabhan and two other wounded militants could be brought back to the ship.[19] Some reports have sug-gested that Nabhan had been under surveillance for some time, and that this was the first opportunity to target him away from a civilian population.[20]

There is an interesting unanswered question here that might throw some light on developing US policy at that time: what, if any, assessment was made as to whether Nabhan could have been captured rather than killed during this operation?

There is also intriguing circumstantial evidence suggesting that intelligence for Nabhan's killing may have come from an individual rendered from Kenya to Somalia and detained in an ostensibly Somali-run secret prison in Mogadishu. As described earlier in this book, 25-year-old Kenyan citizen Ahmed Abdullahi Hassan went missing from Eastleigh, Nairobi, in July 2009.[21] Hassan's fate remained a mystery until April 2011, when a former prisoner told me that he had met Hassan in a secret underground prison in Mogadishu, and that Hassan had described his capture, incommunicado detention and interrogation by Somalis and Caucasians—according to Jeremy Scahill of *The Nation* (US), in the basement of Somali National Security and Intelligence Service headquarters, with a significant level of CIA access and control.[22] A Kenyan 'intelligence' report leaked to the Kenyan media in 2011 suggested that Hassan was believed to have been Nabhan's close associate. The US drone that killed the latter struck no more than two months after Hassan's capture, whilst he was in detention—raising the possibility that his interrogations in the secret Somali prison provided live intelligence then used in the targeted killing.

If this turns out to be the case, Nabhan's assassination may represent an early example of a more joined-up, databased approach to US counterterrorism operations in the region, first described by *The Washington Post* in its 'Disposition Matrix' reports, described later in this chapter.[23]

In the years following Nabhan's killing, Djibouti has played a central role in an accelerating number of US drone operations carried out in both Yemen and Somalia, despite these being part of a comparatively 'small footprint operation' with fewer drone attacks than in other regions strictly within conventional warzones, such as Afghanistan.[24] The dramatic increase in the use of targeted killing under Obama occurred in tandem with a scaling down of US overseas prisons, a policy shift that, as we have seen, began under George W. Bush. This shift was likely influenced by a range of factors, including the legal and political impasse surrounding the fate of prisoners at Guantánamo Bay, the administration's partial victory over lawyers' access to detainees at Bagram Air Base (on the basis that it was a true 'battlefield' facility and therefore no longer available to hold scores of people not captured in Afghanistan), and a succession of scandals over detainee treatment.

Unlike targeted killings, US extraterritorial detainee populations have not grown under Obama, though they've been 'outsourced'—and joint forms of detention are a different matter. The Bureau of Investigative Journalism, which monitors US covert actions in Pakistan, Yemen and Somalia, estimates that at least 350 drone strikes occurred in Pakistan during Obama's presidency (against a total of 50 strikes preceding this period), between 69 and 79 total strikes occurred in Yemen (only one of which preceded the Obama period), and 6–9 strikes in Somalia.[25]

In contrast to the singular 2002 strike described above, after and since Nabhan's death, most known drone operations from Djibouti have been carried out primarily by the Department of Defense rather than the CIA. The Pentagon's Joint Special Operations Command (JSOC) is apparently the 'lead agency' in Somalia's War on Terror at the time of writing, carrying out surveillance, reconnaissance, capture and assault operations. JSOC also has its own fleet of Reaper Drones, high-tech drones capable of firing multiple, laser-guided hellfire missiles. [26]

According to Craig Whitlock in *The Washington Post*, between 2010 and 2012 Camp Lemonnier became the largest Predator drone base (an earlier version of the Reaper) outside the Afghan warzone and, effectively, an experimental zone in which to develop new methods for carrying out the War on Terror:

> Increasingly, the orders to find, track or kill those people are delivered to Camp Lemonnier. Virtually the entire 500-acre camp is dedicated to counterterrorism, making it the only installation of its kind in the Pentagon's global network of bases. ... About 300 Special Operations personnel plan raids and coordinate drone flights from inside a high-security compound at Lemonnier that is dotted with satellite dishes and ringed by concertina wire. Most of the commandos work incognito, concealing their names even from conventional troops on the base.[27]

However, this expansion in Djibouti has created significant logistical challenges for the US. In 2013, media reported that 'at least five drones based in Djibouti have crashed since 2011',[28] and in February 2012, a US spy plane crashed near to Camp

Lemonnier, killing all four Special Operations personnel on board.[29] A *Washington Post* investigation, based on a dossier of official US government documents released through Freedom of Information requests, details how the skies above Lemonnier had, at the time of writing, 'become chronically dangerous, with pilots forced to rely on local air-traffic controllers who fall asleep on the job, commit errors at astronomical rates and are hostile to Americans.'[30] Craig Whitlock describes how 'The documents chronicle an ill-fated $7 million U.S. program in which former Federal Aviation Administration officials were tapped to retrain the Djiboutian air-traffic controllers in 2012 and 2013. The effort collapsed after the Djiboutians stopped showing up for classes and locked the American trainers out of the flight tower.'[31]

According to Nick Turse, writing in *The Intercept*, by late 2013 the hub of US drone operations in Africa had moved from Camp Lemonnier to a quieter nearby airfield, Chabelley.

> Africom failed to respond to questions about the number and types of drones based at Chabelley Airfield, but reporting by The Intercept, drawing on formerly secret documents, demonstrates that 10 MQ-1 Predators and four of their larger cousins, MQ-9 Reapers, were based at Lemonnier prior to the move to the more remote site. Neither the Pentagon nor Africom responded to repeated requests by The Intercept for comment on other aspects of drone operations at Chabelley Airfield or the transformation of the outpost into a more permanent facility. The reasons why aren't hard to fathom.[32]

In fact, Chabelley Airfield is not the only additional territory supporting US drone and airborne surveillance operations in Africa. A series of official documents leaked to *The Intercept* confirm that drone operations at Camp Lemonnier are supported by a web of airfields in Djibouti, Kenya and Ethiopia, alongside US Navy vessels in the Gulf of Aden.[33] *The Intercept's* research suggests that, between 2012 and 2015, fourteen locations in Africa and the Indian Ocean, including Djibouti, Ethiopia, Kenya,

Somalia, Uganda and the Seychelles, hosted nodes of the 'US drone and surveillance network'.[34]

How these operations have been carried out is explained in part by reporting in *The Washington Post*:

> In Washington, the Obama administration has taken a series of steps to sustain the drone campaign for another decade, developing an elaborate new targeting database, called the 'disposition matrix', and a classified 'playbook' to spell out how decisions on targeted killing are made. Djibouti is the clearest example of how the United States is laying the groundwork to carry out these operations overseas. ... Drones will continue to be in the forefront. In response to written questions from *The Post*, the U.S. military confirmed publicly for the first time the presence of remotely piloted aircraft—military parlance for drones—at Camp Lemonnier and said they support 'a wide variety of regional security missions.' Intelligence collected from drone and other surveillance missions 'is used to develop a full picture of the activities of violent extremist organizations and other activities of interest,' Africa Command, the arm of the U.S. military that oversees the camp, said in a statement. 'However, operational security considerations prevent us from commenting on specific missions.'[35]

A Pentagon study leaked to *The Intercept* confirms further how decisions to order drone strikes in Yemen and Somalia were made in 2011 and 2012. According to the study, 'intelligence personnel from JSOC's Task Force 48–4, working alongside other intelligence agencies, would build the case for action against an individual, eventually generating a "baseball card" on the target, which was "staffed up to higher echelons—ultimately to the president"' at the time of the study. With the president's approval, JSOC then had a 60-day window to hit a target. For an actual strike, the task force needed approval from the Geographic Combatant Command as well as the ambassador and CIA station chief in the country where the target was located.[36]

This reference to an enhanced bureaucracy and infrastructure, with a targeting database or 'Disposition Matrix' allows us to understand how targeted killings by drone have become both systemic, and part of a wider counterinsurgency strategy. Within the context of other well-rehearsed tactics such as rendition, detention, interrogations and surveillance, targeted killings are simply one available action within a set of interlinking counter-terrorism tactics.

Independent journalist Marcy Wheeler, on her blog *emptywheel*, has suggested that the 2012 detention and rendition of the young Brit Mahdi Hashi and two others from Djibouti to the US was a 'test-drive of the disposition process.'[37] Hashi had come to the UK from Somalia with his family in 1995, gaining British citizenship in 2004. Reports suggest that in 2010 he travelled back to Somalia, where he met and married his Somali wife, with whom he had a young child. In June 2012, Hashi's family in the UK received a letter from the UK Home Office, instructing them to inform Hashi that his British citizenship had been revoked on national security grounds. On the family's telling, they were unable to inform Hashi of this development—thus he was not able to challenge the revocation—because by this point he had disappeared.

Several months later, in August 2012, Hashi's family learned from a man who said he had recently been imprisoned with Hashi that the latter was being detained in Djibouti, and had been interrogated by white Westerners. On 18 October 2012, a grand jury in the US federal district of New York returned a sealed indictment against Hashi, and on 14 November 2012, shortly after Obama's re-election, the US government officially took custody of him, charging and holding him in secret for five weeks until 21 December, when he was arraigned in the Eastern District of New York. Hashi was subsequently charged with offences of 'material support' to Al-Shabaab. Eventually, he pleaded guilty and was sentenced to nine years in custody.

The timing of the revocation of Hashi's citizenship strongly suggests some form of coordination or intelligence sharing between the UK and the US. Whether one state's actions triggered the other's will probably never be publicly known. It is clear, however, that the revocation of Hashi's citizenship at that point in time certainly may not have left him officially stateless (it has been held by the UK that he retained a residual Somali citizenship), but he was nevertheless left without an effective government to advocate for his rights whilst he was being held in what turned out to be prolonged incommunicado detention in both Djibouti and the US. As of July 2016, proceedings in the UK to challenge the legality of the revocation of Hashi's citizenship are ongoing.

This case is significant, as are several cases—predating Hashi's—of British men killed by drones in Somalia, revocation of whose British citizenship may also have occurred in some form of concert with the US 'disposition' process.

Bilal Berjawi, a 27-year-old from North London, was reportedly killed after three missiles fired from a US drone hit the vehicle he was travelling in on the outskirts of Mogadishu. Around twelve months before his death, Berjawi had been stripped of his British citizenship under the Immigration and Nationality Act 2006, on the order of the home secretary. According to *The Guardian*, 'Berjawi is understood to have sought to appeal against the order, but lawyers representing his family were unable to take instructions from him amid concerns that any telephone contact could precipitate a drone attack.'[38] Berjawi was killed on 21 January 2012, shortly after making a telephone call to his wife, who had given birth to their child in a London hospital a few hours prior to the strike. This chain of events appears to be a coincidence rather than suggestive of British complicity in triggering the targeting, as according to a classified report on Berjawi's case leaked to *The Intercept*, the fatal drone strike was 'facilitated by cellphone surveillance' that had already located Berjawi by the time of that call.[39]

A disturbing propaganda film published by Al-Shabaab includes a confession by a Somali youth that he was being run as an agent by a group of Western spies, possibly including British and American men, when on their orders he placed a cellphone operating as a tracking device in Berjawi's vehicle.[40] Mohammed Sakr, a friend of Berjawi and another British national who had his citizenship revoked, was killed in a US drone attack in Somalia shortly after Berjawi, in February 2012.[41]

Parallel cases of rendition involving Djibouti illustrate the ongoing practice of rendition alongside targeted killings by the US, and the possible interplay of different tactics within the wider Disposition Matrix. Prior to 9/11, US renditions usually culminated in a form of judicial process, however unsatisfactory. The main feature of post-9/11 renditions, carried out under George W. Bush, was the discarding of this end-point of judicial process, with prisoners rendered for the purpose of interrogations, torture and arbitrary detention. Obama's rendition policy—essentially secret—appears to have reverted back to something like pre-9/11 operations, whereby prisoners were detained incommunicado for a shorter time, before being transferred to some kind of judicial process. Added to this was the Obama-era practice of detaining suspects in short-term, temporary situations (rather than long-term detention in overseas US facilities), or in the custody of foreign states.

Testament to this new approach is one case that was highlighted by US General Carter Ham in his March 2012 testimony to the Senate Armed Services Committee—that of Ahmed Abdulkadir Warsame. Warsame, reportedly a military commander for Al-Shabaab,[42] was captured by the US at sea, off the coast of Djibouti. According to the US Attorney's Office in the Southern District of New York:

> Warsame, a Somali national in his mid-20s, was captured in the Gulf of Aden between Somalia and Yemen by the U.S. military on April 19, 2011, and was questioned for intelligence purposes for more than two

months. Thereafter, Warsame was read his Miranda rights, and, after waiving those rights, he spoke to law enforcement agents for several days. Warsame arrived in the Southern District of New York on July 5, 2011.[43]

Although the precise circumstances of Warsame's two types of questioning between 19 April and 5 July are unknown, it is likely that this process was a version of the 'clean' and 'dirty' interrogation system that first became notorious at Guantánamo Bay during the George W. Bush presidency. In this system, a 'clean team' of agents and investigators purported to be conducting traditional law enforcement activity interviews a prisoner after they have already been subjected to mistreatment, or 'dirty' interrogation practices, resulting in testimony obtained without the direct use of coercion or abuse, and therefore admissible in court.

A senior US military official has disclosed that, after his capture, Warsame was held in the brig of an amphibious assault vessel, the *USS* Boxer. After the initial and longer period of interrogation 'for intelligence purposes', i.e. the 'dirty interrogation', the US reportedly eventually disclosed Warsame's presence on the ship to the International Committee of the Red Cross (ICRC), who sent a representative to *USS* Boxer to visit him. According to *The New York Times*, the administration timed this visit to 'emphasize that the second set of interrogators comprised different officials questioning him for a different purpose.'

At the start of this second period of interrogation, Warsame was read his rights, thus making any statements given in the second interrogation period judicially admissible.[44] Further explanation as to this twofold process was given by AFP and the UK's Channel 4 News:

Officials told reporters Warsame's detention was justified by the laws of war and that he was treated humanely.

A US official told reporters that Warsame's questioning was conducted under the rules of the US Army Field Manual, which places limits on interrogation techniques and complies with the Geneva Convention.

Members of the High Value Interrogation Group—comprised of [sic] CIA, FBI and Defence Department staff—interrogated him, an official told AFP on condition of anonymity.

Unnamed US officials told the New York Times that because interrogators were seeking military intelligence, Warsame was not given what is known as a 'Miranda warning', which would be obligatory for a suspect being questioned by US police. Failure to give a Miranda warning advising suspects of their rights to have a lawyer and to remain silent can make any testimony inadmissible as evidence.

But after two months in detention Warsame was questioned by a separate group of interrogators who did apparently deliver a Miranda warning. Warsame is reported to have waived his right to remain silent, meaning that his subsequent statements would likely be admissible in court.[45]

During Warsame's detention, the *USS* Boxer continued its exercises in the vicinity of Djibouti,[46] coinciding with several US drone strikes in Somalia.[47] At least two other lethal air operations took place during Warsame's detention in Somalia between April and July 2011. It remains officially unconfirmed whether these events were linked to Warsame's captivity for intelligence interrogations. Warsame's value as a source of intelligence to his US captors is partly explained by the set of drone programme-related classified documents leaked to *The Intercept*. According to the documents, 'the US military has faced "critical shortfalls" in the technology and intelligence it uses to find and kill suspected terrorists in Yemen and Somalia', due to the combined issues of lack of US presence there and the 'tyranny of distance', i.e. the remote and large geographical areas to be covered.[48] *The Intercept* reports that, as a result, the US has been 'overly reliant on signals intelligence from computers and cellphones, and the quality of those intercepts has been limited by constraints on surveillance in the region.'[49]

It is probable that Warsame was flown direct from Djibouti to New York, arriving there on 5 July 2011. Ultimately, he never stood trial: in 2013, it was confirmed that a secret plea deal had been struck in December 2011.[50] It remains officially unconfirmed whether the 'intelligence-focused' interrogations continued after Warsame's plea, or if he proved more compliant following the deal.

8

DEATH SQUADS

I met Makaburi, the Kenyan sheikh who warned of his own impending assassination, in Mombasa in 2007. I'd gone there to research the Border Operation renditions and detentions along the Somali-Kenyan border (see Chapter 5) following the US-Ethiopian invasion of Mogadishu in December 2006 to oust the Union of Islamic Courts.

My aim was to meet former prisoners and family members of prisoners, to try to understand what was going on. An imposing figure in a white robe and skullcap, Makaburi was very much present on the ground in Mombasa. His death came a little over seven years later, when he was gunned down as he left a court-house where he had been seeking to challenge his very inclusion on what he asserted was a Kenyan police death list.[1] Makaburi was the third high-profile Muslim cleric to be assassinated in Mombasa. There have been many similar deaths since.

These Kenyan killings of terror 'suspects' raise a clear concern that, as well as increasing direct funding and arming of regional counterterrorism partners such as Kenya, another factor of the US's War on Terror—its blatant exceptionalist approach to international human rights and humanitarian law—gives a political *carte blanche* to partner states (in particular those with an already weak rule of law and longstanding human rights concerns), to effectively carry out their own versions of US counterterrorism tactics and operations.

In parallel to President Obama's expansion of the drone pro-gramme in East Africa and beyond, Kenya has also seen an increase in extrajudicial killings—or assassinations—of those labelled as terror suspects by its own security forces. Whilst there is limited evidence of direct US or UK involvement in most of these killings, they are clearly being carried out in a context where foreign partners will be aware of the pattern of abuses, have long been supplying significant material and practical sup-port to Kenyan counterterrorism operations, and are therefore, in effect, tacitly supporting and condoning these killings carried out within the counterterrorism context.

Kenya itself has a longstanding problem with politically moti-vated extrajudicial killings, not restricted to the counterterrorism arena. In 2007, the Kenyan National Commission on Human Rights (KNCHR) published extensive investigations into police killings, documenting at least 500 disappearances or deaths at the hands of the police between June and October 2007. A police whistleblower, whose detailed testimony relating to the killings of fifty-eight people in police custody was published by the KNCHR, was murdered in October 2008. Earlier that year, in March, at least 200 people were killed or disappeared by forces acting on behalf of the state during a joint military-police opera-tion in the Mt Elgon district.

Phillip Alston, the UN special rapporteur on extrajudicial kill-ings, has stated that

> these abuses were not carried out by undisciplined military/police units, acting outside of their command structures. Rather, they were system-atic and organised. With the assistance of local informants, police and

military cordoned villages, detained and frequently beat the male residents, and took them to one of several temporary military bases, the largest of which was Kapkota military camp. There, men were stripped, tortured and interrogated. They were screened before local informants. Those identified as SLDF [the area's guerrilla militia] were taken to the local police station and charged, the others were let go. Those who died as a result of being tortured were dumped in the forests or taken to local mortuaries. The security forces kept detailed records of this operation, and have records on all the 3,265 people detained, as well as extensive photographic evidence of the occurrences at Kapkota camp. My efforts to obtain these records have, not surprisingly, been unsuccessful to date... In the forests of Mt Elgon there are mass graves and sites where bodies were simply dumped on the forest floor. It is likely that both victims of the SLDF and the military/police are contained in those sites. Government authorities have made no systematic attempts to protect these sites or have them examined by independent forensic experts. NGOs who have attempted to study the sites have received veiled threats and been prevented from doing so.[2]

Following an investigation conducted in Kenya in early 2009, Alston concluded that

perhaps the most surprising outcome of my visit was the extent to which I received overwhelming testimony of the existence of systematic, widespread, and carefully planned extrajudicial executions undertaken on a regular basis by the Kenyan police. The Police Commissioner in particular, along with various other senior officials, assured me that no such killings take place. But he and his colleagues appear to be the only people in the entire country who believe this claim.

He continued:

I have received detailed and convincing reports of countless individual killings. It is clear from the many interviews that I conducted that the police are free to kill at will. Sometimes they do so for reasons of a private or personal nature. Sometimes they kill in the context of extortion, or of a ransom demand. Often they kill in the name of crime control, but in circumstances where they could readily make an arrest. ... In addition to these everyday police killings, there is compelling and detailed evidence that police death squads operate, primarily in Nairobi and Central Province, with an explicit mandate to exterminate suspected Mungiki members. These are not 'rogue' squads, but are police who are acting on the explicit orders of their superiors. ... In short, the Kenyan police are a law unto themselves and they kill often and with impunity, except in those rare instances where their actions are caught on film or otherwise recorded by outsiders in ways that cannot be dismissed.[3]

These tactics have transferred very easily to the War on Terror, where anti-terrorism police have for many years been given paramilitary training and high-tech arms and equipment from various quarters, including the US and UK governments. Documentation showing unlawful operations by these police units goes back at least to 2005. More recently, rights groups have accused the Anti-Terrorism Police Force (ATPU) and other security organs of carrying out a campaign of extrajudicial killings. The first victims were prominent Muslim clerics. The killings then spread to include other Muslims, catalysed by the injection of foreign arms, money, and counterterrorism objectives imposed from abroad. This increase in police killings of Kenyan Muslims has coincided with Kenya's enhanced role in the Somali conflict, after Kenyan troops entered the Somali warzone in October 2011, under Operation Linda Nchi. The enduring Kenyan military presence in Somalia itself has triggered a massive increase in Al-Shabaab terrorist attacks within Kenyan borders in the years since 2011. These three elements—Kenyan military involvement in Somalia, Al-Shabaab attacks on Kenyan civilians, and unlawful security force crackdowns on Kenyan Muslims (including but not limited to targeted killings)—have interacted explosively, and increasingly define Kenya as an informal extension of the Somali warzone. In Kenya, the US doctrine of a boundless, endless, global warzone has, arguably, now become a reality.

Following Kenya's entry into the Somali conflict, Al-Shabaab instantly threatened retaliation, and on 22 October 2011 the US warned of 'imminent' terror attacks in Kenya. The first terrorist attack in Kenya after the commencement of Operation Linda Nchi occurred on 24 October, when a grenade hurled into Mwaura's bar in downtown Nairobi left one person dead and twenty wounded.[4] A second blast occurred later the same day at the Machakos bus terminus, when a grenade was hurled out of a moving vehicle. Five people were killed and sixty-four injured.[5]

In Kenya's volatile border region, two further attacks occurred in October 2011, as well as almost daily attacks around Garissa Town and the Mandera district throughout November and December 2011.[6] Targets included a United Nations convoy at the Ifo camp in the Dadaab complex of refugee camps, the district intelligence chief of Wajir, and the Florida Hotel in Garissa Town. On 29 December, a refugee leader and chair of the Community Peace and Security Team was killed by gunmen at the Hagadera refugee camp, also in the Dadaab complex.[7] Al-Shabaab's efforts to bring the Somali war home to ordinary Kenyans continued into early 2012, with February and March claiming the lives of one police officer and six civilians.[8]

It was in this context that the first high-profile Kenyan Muslims, Samir Hashim Khan and Mohammed Bekhit Kassim, were assassinated. According to the Open Society Justice Initiative and Muslims for Human Rights, Khan, a Muslim preacher, was killed by police on 13 April 2012 after being pulled off a public bus in Mombasa by ATPU officers. A few days later his remains were found in Tsavo National Park. ATPU had arrested Khan in 2010 on weapons charges and again in 2011, alleging that he was a member of Al-Shabaab. The cases against him were pending at the time of his second abduction and murder.[9] To date, there has been no human rights-compliant investigation by the Kenyan state into his death.

Kassim, Khan's friend, was pulled from the bus at the same time. Kassim had previously been abducted in 2011 and was told by his abductors at that time that they would come back for him.[10] At the time of his first abduction, ATPU apparently released a statement saying that it had arrested him, but later denied doing so. Some reports indicate that Kassim's where-abouts remain unknown. It has also been reported that his remains were found in a Kilifi mortuary.

The killings of Khan and Kassim were the first of many. The organisation leading the documentation and advocacy on this issue is a courageous Mombasa-based NGO named HAKI Africa. While HAKI Africa has focused its research primarily on the Coast of Kenya, other groups have documented similar cases elsewhere in Kenya, in particular, Nairobi.[11] HAKI Africa's research, as well as that of other NGOs and media sources, suggests that at least eighty-one extrajudicial killings and enforced disappearances of Muslims were carried out in Kenya between 2012 and 2014. This number is likely to be conservative; anec-dotal evidence suggests that many cases of unlawful killing and enforced disappearance go unreported due to the families' fear of reprisals from state security forces, as well as the stigmatising effect in the wider community of it being known that a relative has been targeted by police. Although most known victims are young, there have also been sheikhs, imams and preachers, some of them well over fifty years old. The identity of two victims remains unknown to date. In the vast majority of cases, the likely perpetrators are officers from counterterrorism or other special-ised police units. In particular, the Kenyan Anti-Terror Police Unit, a unit that operates outside regular police command hier-archies, is implicated. Despite clear domestic and international legal obligations, no proper investigation has yet been carried out by the Kenyan state into the vast majority of these killings.

An analysis of these eighty-one cases, carried out by HAKI Africa and my organisation, Justice Forum, has identified four distinct categories or scenarios amongst the killings.[12] The first category, numbering thirty-five cases, involves excessive use of force during operations such as arrests and policing of mass gatherings. In this category we also included twenty-four extrajudicial executions that were subsequently described by police as 'shoot-outs' in an attempt to justify their excessive use of force. There were, in addition, eleven confirmed deaths in police custody.

The twenty-four extrajudicial executions concern cases where the police—or unidentified assailants reasonably believed to have been acting on behalf of the state—have targeted particular individuals and carried out killings, without then bothering to stage it as an 'encounter killing' (see below). In other words, in these cases there is no official acknowledgement of involvement, and therefore no defence mounted in relation to the killing.

Secondly, eleven of the cases were enforced disappearances. These are cases where no body has been found and the victims were last seen in the custody of the police, or people reasonably believed to be other agents of the Kenyan state.

The third category is that of 'encounter killings'—cases where police admit an encounter between them and the victim, but dispute that the force used was unreasonable. In these twenty-four cases, there have been no official investigations that, as well as being required under law, could support the police's claims. Indeed, in many of these cases, investigations conducted by human rights organisations including HAKI Africa and Human Rights Watch have found no evidence of the shoot-out claimed by police. For example, Human Rights Watch has written that in the cases of Hassan Omondi Owiti, Shekha Wanjiru, and Lenox David Swalleh, ATPU 'claimed that the suspects were killed in a firefight. Human Rights Watch did not find evidence of a shootout, as witness descriptions pointed to a short-lived, targeted killing by security officers and the scene suggested the shooting was unidirectional without any damage to the surrounding buildings as ATPU had suggested.'[13]

According to Human Rights Watch,

In the case of Hassan Omondi Owiti and Shekha Wanjiru, for example, witnesses said that officers from the counterterrorism unit and the General Service Unit had surrounded their apartment block in Nairobi's Githurai Kimbo estate in the evening of May 18, 2013, then stormed their apartment and shot them dead without armed resistance.

In another example, Lenox David Swalleh and an unidentified person were shot on November 13, 2013, as they left a mosque after morning prayers in Nairobi's Eastleigh neighborhood. While police claimed that other people were killed while preparing to rob a bank, witnesses and family said the two were unarmed and were shot without warning. The men had been accused of involvement in a November 2012 grenade attack on the Hidaya mosque in Eastleigh that killed 6 and injured 15, but the two were being held at Industrial Area Remand Prison at the time of the attack and were only released on April 16, 2013.[14]

The killing of 26-year-old Idris Mohamed, a case documented by HAKI Africa, is eloquent testimony to the importance of the exercise of proportionality in the use of violence by police during routine operations. Mohamed is believed to have been killed by police in the early hours of 14 September 2014, in circumstances strongly suggestive of a case of mistaken identity. Kenyan police have not formally accepted responsibility for Mohamed's death; however, according to HAKI Africa, police officers brought his body to a mortuary and conceded that officers were present at the time of death, claiming that the victim was 'gunned down' by an unknown perpetrator (see the official post-mortem records obtained by HAKI Africa in Appendix 2).

Prior to the post-mortem, Mohamed's family and HAKI Africa personnel noticed that official papers brought to the mortuary by police incorrectly referred to the deceased as 'Ismael Mohamed alias Idris Mohamed.' Ismail and Idris Mohamed were in fact brothers, not the same person. This fact was brought to the attention of police in attendance at the post-mortem, with the family and HAKI Africa officials insisting that the papers be amended before continuing with the examination. The police officers then consulted with their seniors via phone and, upon orders, duly crossed out the name 'Ismail Mohamed' and signed next to the alteration (see Appendix 2). The police report provided for Mohamed's post-mortem states that 'police officers on a tip-off that there were gangsters within Bondeni area visited the scene and one of the suspects was gunned down who was later confirmed to have been a wanted criminal. ... and a warrant of arrest in force.'

It later emerged that Ismael Mohamed, the deceased's brother, was indeed involved in legal proceedings and had a live arrest warrant on him. Idris Mohamed, on the other hand, had no criminal record or outstanding warrant of arrest. The facts of this case strongly suggest a case of mistaken identity. Moreover, the police report provides no real explanation of how Mohamed was killed. HAKI Africa has on several occasions sought further information from police regarding this incident, but the response remains that 'the police have no leads', and the investigation files remain open. HAKI Africa has now referred this case to the Kenyan Independent Policing Oversight Authority and the United Nations Working Group on Enforced or Involuntary Disappearances.

Nine of the documented cases involved excessive use of force by police either during the policing of protests or while attending locations of religious assembly. Clearly, law enforcement agencies may find policing mass demonstrations or gatherings a challenge, yet the cases in this category suggest that anti-terrorism police in Kenya have resorted to the use of excessive force in circumstances where it has not, at least initially, been justified, and without following any prescribed procedures or using non-violent means first. Furthermore, the unlawful failure to conduct inquiries into these cases has served to foster a climate of impunity, increasing the likelihood that the use of unwarranted lethal force by Kenyan anti-terrorism police will continue uncontested in the future.

The most contentious example of these kinds of killings centres around the Masjid Musa Mosque raid in February 2014. Aram Alan Olch (Ali Chechniya), Abdul Rashid (Ndayayisenga), Omar Mustapha (Muadhin), Ramadhan Mwagudzi, Salim Khamis Mwamleo, Suleiman Ali and Fuad Abdallah Ali, all young Muslim men, were killed by police on 2 February 2014 when officers raided the mosque in Mombasa.

Research by HAKI Africa suggested that heavily armed counterterrorism police were dispatched to the mosque to confront a large and initially peaceful crowd who had gathered to hear talks and have lunch. According to eye-witnesses, police used non-lethal weapons and firearms arbitrarily, without initial warning or first using non-violent means, in an attempt to close down a gathering where there was no imminent threat of death or serious injury. By contrast, police subsequently claimed that the raid was carried out following reports that a 'radicalisation session' was taking place. Following the raid, Mombasa police chief Geoffrey Mayek told reporters that officers had recovered a pistol, eight grenades and a flag associated with Al-Shabaab, and that only one man had been shot dead, after he 'attempted to hurl' a hand grenade at police.[15]

Given the conflicting accounts of events inside Masjid Musa on 2 February 2014, many questions remain unanswered. The initial level of force used by ATPU officers from the outset was, according to HAKI Africa and witnesses inside the mosque, neither necessary nor proportionate, resulting in an escalation of violence, tens of injuries and at least eight deaths, including that of a policeman. As the incident escalated, it is at least arguable that some use of force by the police may have become unavoidable. At this point, without a full and independent inquiry into the incident, it cannot be determined what level of police force would have been justified. Indeed, it is not even known how many of the deaths have been conceded by the police to have been at their hands.

Like the Masjid Musa case, none of the cases documented here have been adequately investigated by the Kenyan authorities, despite the facts that accountability mechanisms do exist on paper and, in some cases, official figures have publicly acknowledged the need for an inquiry. After the killing of the cleric Sheikh Makaburi later in 2014, Cabinet Secretary for Internal Security Joseph Ole Lenku stated, 'Kenyans are concerned about their security and rightly so. The criminal or terrorist who injured Baby Satrin, orphaned him, is no different from that one who killed Makaburi. As a government, ours is to investigate and deal with the same according to the law.'[16] Baby Satrin was a one-year-old boy who was shot during the Likoni church terror attack on 23 March 2014. The bullet was later successfully removed from his head.

However, no such investigation took place. The taskforce charged with investigating the murder of another high-profile Muslim cleric, Sheikh Aboud Rogo, reported to the Kenyan director of public prosecutions in August 2013 that although it had 'no doubt' that Aboud Rogo had been murdered, a contaminated crime scene and witnesses' fear of giving evidence meant that the taskforce had failed to identify the killers. It instead recommended a public inquest to uncover the truth of what had happened to Aboud Rogo. To date, no such inquiry has been opened.

As well as being unlawful under domestic, regional and international law, the lack of adequate investigation by the authorities into the past several years' high incidence of killings of Muslims suggests a growing problem of impunity for those perpetrating Kenya's War on Terror. The Cambridge Centre for Human Rights and Governance has noted that impunity [is] a prevailing climate within a particular state or part of a state which takes hold when a particular form of violation is allowed to continue without state response. While not every case of a high incidence of killing necessarily implies a culture of impunity, it would suggest that the state's chosen response is ineffective and ought to be supplemented or revised. ... Because of the irreversible nature of a violation of the right to life, the state's protection role must very often be primarily through the means of strong accountability mechanisms.[17]

It is not difficult to find a connection between the US's exceptionalist attitude to international law in its global targeted killing programme and the development of domestic counterterrorism policies in Kenya, one of its most important partner states. It has been established that the US has long funded ATPU, as well as elements of Kenya's National Security and Intelligence Service. Furthermore, an Al-Jazeera documentary broadcast in December 2014 featured officers from four different units confirming that Kenyan police had killed over 500 terror suspects, and that targets were selected using training, equipment and intelligence from Western intelligence agencies, including those of Israel and the UK. However, the extent to which Western intelligence agencies are directly involved in Kenyan ATPU operations is not yet fully known.

Whether Kenya's increasingly central role in East Africa's War on Terror will amplify its problem with police killings and disappearances remains to be seen over the long term. However, what is clear already is that such killings are adding to an increased sense of grievance amongst Kenyan Muslim communities. That the extrajudicial killings have also demonstrably failed to reduce the number of terrorist attacks in Kenya is a simple matter of arithmetic.

The most serious attacks, occurring at the Westgate shopping centre in September 2013, in various locations in the Lamu region during 2014, and in April 2015 in the Garissa region, have occurred subsequent to the deaths of most of the key clerics. This may even suggest that, if anything, their influence may have had a restraining effect on an increasingly out-of-control situation. Indeed, well-informed commentators such as the Kenyan human rights defender Al-Amin Kimathi have suggested that the removal of some of these clerics has created a worrying vacuum of religious authority amongst some Kenyan youth. If this is accurate, it remains to be seen how that vacuum will ultimately be filled.

9

WHERE THERE IS A SEA

Anti-piracy operations are not formally conducted within the realm of counterterrorism. However, the international response to the problem of Somali piracy has been almost wholly military, and has been the primary justification for an intense securitisation and subsequent militarisation of the seas around Somalia and out into the Indian Ocean. National navies of states including the US, China and Russia function under a patchwork of both national and supranational mandates from NATO and the EU. American-led (unilateral, bilateral and NATO) anti-piracy infrastructure including prisons and ships has been used for the interdiction and detention of terrorism suspects. Like the American military's Africa Command (see Chapter 7), US and other states' antipiracy operations also pivot out from Djibouti, meaning that there is now a securitised zone and military presence stretching both far out into the Indian Ocean, and far across the Horn of Africa.

It is a matter of speculation how far the excessively securitised and militarised response to Somali piracy is motivated by geopolitical concerns to maintain a strong military presence in the Gulf of Aden (a chief oil transportation route), and in the Indian Ocean (where Russian and Chinese military also maintain a presence). The longstanding and circular problem of Somalia's maritime security as it affects the Somali people suggests at the very least that the international response of recent years has not been formulated with the needs of the Somali people in mind. In its latest iteration, some former pirates have reportedly now become mercenaries acting for the illegal international fishing trawlers whose activities they originally claimed to seek to curb. This state of affairs suggests that the 'root causes' of Somali piracy (unconfirmed, but surely including the flagrant impoverishment of opportunity in Somalia, pushing many to join the pirate boats) have not been adequately addressed by the expensive, securitised and far-reaching international response to piracy.

Somali piracy captured American military and popular attention following the April 2009 seizure of a US vessel—the MV Maersk Alabama—240 nautical miles off the coast of Eyl, an ancient port town in the semi-autonomous state of Puntland. Four teenage pirates boarded the ship, and in the resulting confrontation, the captain of the ship, Richard Phillips, was taken hostage. In the ensuing rescue effort, three of the pirates were killed and one—Abduwale Muse—was captured. Muse was held initially on the *USS* Bainbridge and then on the *USS* Boxer, a US Navy vessel that would also, in subsequent years, be used to detain several terror suspects captured in Somalia.[1] After several months of detention on US Navy vessels, Muse was transferred to the US mainland and brought before the District Court for the Southern District of New York, in New York City.

Media reports at the time suggested that the reason Muse was brought to this district is that the local FBI office had expertise in major East African counterterrorism operations dating back to the Embassy bombings investigation in the 1990s. Indeed, FBI personnel had dealt with the Maersk Alabama as a crime scene shortly after Muse's arrest. It is also likely that FBI personnel were involved in Muse's interrogations on the *USS* Bainbridge, but this is not publicly confirmed. Despite the fact that there is now a book and a Hollywood film about the incident, nearly all of Muse's statements and his legal team's pleadings remain classified and therefore inaccessible to the general public. Muse is said to have been the first person charged with piracy in a US federal court for over 100 years.

Standing at only 5 foot 3, the diminutive Somali was in fact captured by members of the Maersk Alabama crew *before* the kidnapping of the captain, when he was stabbed in the hand after boarding the vessel. Muse was reportedly then detained as a counter-hostage, tied up for twelve hours by the crew, and offered to the other pirates in exchange for the kidnapped captain. Testament to his low ranking within the pirate crew, Muse's co-pirates declined the offer, abandoning Muse to his fate.[2]

Leading up to Muse's trial in New York, there was considerable debate about Muse's age, with his mother claiming to the Associated Press that he was only sixteen years old. On 21 April 2009, US Magistrate Judge Peck found that Muse was over eighteen and could be tried as an adult, and on 18 May 2009, he pleaded guilty to eight counts involving hijacking, kidnapping and hostage taking. Two years later, in February 2010, Muse was sentenced to thirty-three years and nine months in a US federal prison.

The Maersk Alabama hijacking of 2009 occurred at a time when piracy incidents off the coast of Somalia were reaching something of a pinnacle. That year and the previous year, several multilateral initiatives to combat piracy were launched. Combined Task Force-150 (CTF-150), a multinational coalition naval task-force working on security and counterterrorism, established the 'Maritime Security Patrol Area' in 2008. Security operations were then further expanded with the launch of Combined Task Force-

151 in early 2009, joining the existing CTF-150 as part of the 'Combined Maritime Forces' (CMF). Complementing CTF-150's more general maritime security and counterterrorism mandate, CTF-151's mandate was specifically focused on counterpiracy.[3] An EU naval operation, EUNAVFOR—Operation ATALANTA, had also been launched in December 2008, again with a focus on counterpiracy operations.[4]

The Combined Maritime Task Force had its roots in counter-terrorism operations in the region. In early 2007, following the US-Ethiopian invasion of Mogadishu in December 2006, CTF-150 (then commanded by the UK) provided a maritime cordon to prevent fleeing members of the Union of Islamic Courts from escaping by sea. Men, women and children were funnelled into a tiny channel on the border of Kenya and Somalia. Some were then killed either in US airstrikes or by Ethiopian or Somali troops on the ground, while others were apprehended and detained (and many then rendered) in a joint operation by US, Kenyan and Ethiopian personnel. Following this incident, CTF-150 continued to maintain a strong presence off the coast of Somalia, interdicting and boarding vessels in the course of counterterrorism operations.[5] The establishment of the Maritime Security Patrol Area across the Gulf of Aden on 22 August 2008, and the addition of CTF-151 into what became the Combined Maritime Task Force, was therefore an expansion of existing maritime security operations, expressly to include a focus on counterpiracy alongside existing counterterrorism operations.

The origins narrative of modern Somali piracy is a highly contested tale. A trope described by Shashank Bengali as 'the pirates' creation myth'[6] holds that piracy in Somalia began as a form of vigilante militia activity by former fishermen seeking to protect their fish stock and oceans from foreign trawlers illegally plundering fish. Certainly, some of the names of pirate groupings, such as the National Volunteer Coastguard, could to the less cynical eye suggest a background motive involving law-enforce-ment or civic activity, rather than criminal enterprise. Proponents of this theory include President Abdirahman Mohamed Farole of Puntland, who told the 2011 London Conference on Somali Piracy that

> the violation of Somali waters by foreign trawlers triggered a reaction of armed resistance by Somali fishermen, whose livelihoods were disrupted by the illegal fishing fleets. ... Over time, payment of ransom by the foreign trawlers to the poor fishermen of Somalia encouraged the escala-tion of pirate attacks to current levels. Consequently, the illegal fishers linked themselves with local warlords for protection, placing armed militiamen on board the trawlers. The fishermen-turned-pirates then targeted unarmed commercial vessels, inhumanly taking hostages for ransom and disrupting international maritime trade routes.[7]

A 2009 survey by Wardheer News found that an overwhelming number of Somali people—70 per cent—supported piracy 'as a form of national defence of the country's territorial waters'. However, detractors suggest that this simple narrative is not sup-ported by fact. Somalia expert Stig Jarle Hansen suggests that claims that Somali piracy started as a form of coastguard enterprise to protect Somali fisheries are not backed by evidence, although unlawful fishing plays a key role in its contemporary justification, and that undermining these false narratives is necessary to tackle the problem effectively. A 2013 report from non-profit research and analysis organisation CNA concurs that 'the narratives that Somalis have used to explain (and in some cases, to justify) piracy, while widely accepted, are undercut by the evidence.'[8]

The background to the explosion of illegal fishing in Somali waters centres on the global crisis in fish stocks. Between 1960 and 2002, the global capture of wild fish for human consump-tion more than quadrupled, jumping from 20 million tonnes to 84.5 million tonnes per year, with an estimated 40 per cent of this product entering international trade.[9] In 2004, the UN

Food and Agriculture Organisation reported that in twelve of its sixteen statistical regions, at least 70 per cent of fish stocks were fully exploited or overexploited. In its 2009 report 'Closing the Net: Stopping Illegal Fishing on the High Seas', the World Commission on Protected Areas High Seas Task Force (HSTF)—a group comprising fisheries ministers from six governments, two NGOs and one university research unit—concluded that the current level of exploitation of fish resources was unsustainable, and that 'the gravity of the global fisheries problem should not be underestimated.'[10]

Large-scale illegal fishing (described in the development lexicon as IUU: illegal, unreported and unregulated fishing) is a creature of globalisation. High consumer demand for fish in northern states, and restrictions on fishing in certain well-governed (principally northern) areas of the ocean, for example those enforced by the EU, result in transnational criminal networks extending from these areas into less well-governed southern oceanic space, carrying out transnational, organised illegal fishing operations with the purpose of supplying the consumer demand in rich states. The HSTF has described how

> the focus of criminal activity is on inserting illegal product into the chain of supply that links producers, processors, retailers and final consumers. Within this chain may be identified activities such as the co-mingling of legal and illegal catches, the vertical integration of fishing businesses to facilitate money-laundering, the falsification of documentation and the bribery of officials. As usual where profits are high and risks low, specialists learn how to take advantage of paper controls and how to influence regulatory decisions to create loopholes that can then be profitably exploited. While these activities are loosely organised, there is rarely a single entity directing the work of a unified network. This poses considerable challenges for law enforcement agencies who have to put together a jigsaw of clues from widely dispersed activities that are closely merged with perfectly legal operations.'[11]

The fishing operations themselves typically involve large, continuously cruising 'freezer ships' which rarely dock (and so avoid a level of scrutiny), rotating crews, and transfers of catches between ships.

IUU fishing in Somali waters and its exclusive economic zone (EEZ) took off following the collapse of the Siad Barre regime, and Somalia's descent into civil war in 1991–2. By 2006, the HSTF estimated the global value of IUU catches at between US$4 and $9 billion, of which $1 billion per year (the equivalent of around a quarter of Sub-Saharan Africa's entire revenue from fish) came from Sub-Saharan Africa—in particular, Somalia.[12]

Somalia has the longest coastline in Africa, at over 3,300 kilometres. It has abundant marine resources, but since the civil war there has been effectively no state authority over its territorial waters. As the HSTF has explained:

> one of the consequences of this state of affairs is that for over a decade foreign fishing vessels have been able to plunder the seas off Somalia with impunity. It is estimated that some 700 foreign-owned vessels are engaged in unlicensed and unregulated fishing in Somali waters, exploiting high value species such as tuna, shark, lobster and deep-water shrimp. It is highly unlikely that these resources are being fished sustainably. Many of these foreign vessels are equipped with anti-aircraft cannon and machine guns to defend themselves against Somali pirates who patrol the coast, seizing vessels and kidnapping crews, for which they demand ransoms.[13]

The consequences of IUU fishing for Somalia and its surrounding waters have been devastating. In environmental terms, unsustainable pressure has been placed on fish stocks and marine ecosystems—for instance, Somali fishermen have long complained of IUU fishers using illegal dragnets with a fine mesh that catches everything, including tiny juvenile fish and dolphin swimming near schools of tuna. There has also been a serious economic impact, with implications for regional security.

Given its extraordinary coastline, Somalia could in principle, and should, benefit economically from fishing in its waters and develop an infrastructure and workforce to support the processing of foreign-caught fish. But IUU fishing, as well as depriving local artisan fishermen of their catch as a result of depleted fish stocks, typically excludes Somalis in favour of a network of foreign ships catching fish bound for foreign markets, laundering the catch through third-party states and rotating their crews. The ships therefore avoid entering local ports and markets, thus contributing to the loss of fishing opportunities for local people while bringing no economic benefit to the state whose waters have been plundered.[14]

Somalia's maritime insecurity, then, has complex global roots and implications. Out-of-control IUU fishing contributes to food insecurity and stunts the economy more generally. It is a form of globalised cartel fishing, carried out in an increasingly securitised ocean, essentially run by a mesh of foreign navies and their various groupings but excluding Somalis themselves. It is also connected to the issue of toxic waste dumping off the Somali coast, a phenomenon directly linked to the flow of illegal arms to the warlords in Somalia, who are key local partners of the CIA in its capture and rendition programme. Information on this dumping is sparse, but the few existing reports suggest it began during Somalia's years of dysfunctional rule under the 1969–91 Siad Barre regime (which, amongst other acts of negligence, failed to declare a Somali Exclusive Economic Zone), and developed later in conjunction with arms trafficking, in violation of the UN arms embargo on Somalia begun in 1992.

In 1997, Italian magazine *Famiglia Cristiana* published the results of a Greenpeace investigation into the dumping of toxic waste off Somalia, claiming that the practice started in the late 1980s with Swiss and Italian companies acting as brokers in concert with a company owned by the then-Somali government, transporting toxic waste from Europe to Somali waters. In a later report, published in 2010, Greenpeace alleged that:

> Between 1994 and 1995 [an Italian businessman] contacted at least six-teen African governments, including the Somali warlord Ali Mahdi [later interim president of Somalia], seeking authorisation to import radioactive waste to be disposed into the sub-seabed of their exclusive economic zone.[15]

The report also notes that

> in the 80s and 90s Switzerland, home to the secretive banks made infa-mous by spy-thriller films and books, was obviously on the forefront in arranging shipments of millions of tons of hazardous waste to developing countries. A number of Swiss lawyers, trustees, bankers and traders, contacted European industries to get their waste out of sight at the lowest price. Africa was the favourite destination. Most of the proposals were made on behalf of unknown beneficiaries using the skills of renowned Swiss offshore specialists to discretely handle the proceeds of a lucrative and relatively safe business. Two Liechenstein-registered and Swiss-managed companies were amongst the busiest entities seeking for the shipment of millions of tons of hazardous waste to Africa.[16]

Following the outbreak of civil war in Somalia in 1992, the business became even murkier, since the companies transporting the waste then had to negotiate with warlords, with arms being exchanged for the right to dump toxic waste. After dumping waste and handing out weapons, the ships sometimes then trawled for Somali tuna before leaving Somali waters. The stakes were high, with at least one investigative journalist who worked on the issue dying in suspicious circumstances. Chris Milton, writing in scientific journal *The Ecologist*, explained that:

> an investigation into the murder of the Italian journalist Ilaria Alpi [who was investigating toxic dumping and arms dealing] in Somalia in 1994 quotes the warlord Boqor Musa as saying, "It is evident those ships carried military equipment for different factions involved in the civil

war", and it is widely believed that Alpi was assassinated because she had incontrovertible evidence of the guns-for-waste trade.[17]

The effects of the toxic waste dumping are not yet fully known. Following the 2004 Indian Ocean tsunami, reports of radioactive and toxic waste appearing on Somali shores were carried across the international media. Nick Nuttal, United Nations Environment Programme (UNEP) spokesman, confirmed that the tsunami had shattered containers full of toxic waste, including chemicals and medical waste.[18] More recently, in 2008, the UN special envoy for Somalia, Ahmedou Ould Abdallah, claimed that he had 'reliable information' that European and Asian companies continued to dump waste, including nuclear waste, in Somali waters. No comprehensive investigation appears to have been carried out by the UN or any other international body. In 2006, an investigation by the Somali NGO Daryeel Bulsho Guud ('Hope For Somalia') identified fifteen containers of 'confirmed nuclear and chemical wastes' in eight different locations. Research by Zainab Hassan of the University of Minnesota and the Environmental Justice Advocates of Minnesota has, according to Chris Milton in *The Ecologist*:

> brought to light a whole range of chronic and acute illnesses suffered by Somalis. These include severe birth defects, such as the absence of limbs, and widespread cancers. One local doctor said he had treated more cases of cancer in one year than he had in his entire professional career before the tsunami.[19]

It is acknowledged in some quarters that there has been a long-term lack of effective support and political leadership to tackle the problems of toxic waste dumping and IUU fishing in Somali waters.[20] Mombasa-based consultant Mohamed Abshir Waldo has stated that 'Somali elders asked for NATO assistance in combating the illegal fishing and dumping, but were told there was no mandate for that.'[21] Regardless of whether Somali piracy emerged because of IUU fishing, available evidence suggests that IUU fishing did reduce in correlation with the spike in Somali piracy around 2008–9. In 2009, Channel 4 News reported that an 'unexpected advantage' of the increased levels of piracy off the Somali coast that year had been a massive increase in fish stocks in that part of the Indian Ocean, with local fishermen reporting 'bumper catches' of shark and shellfish, and catches of up to £200's worth of fish per day, in an area where the average daily earnings are less than £5.[22]

The following year, in April 2010, a CIA official alluded to possible covert and overt action against the pirates, saying in monthly magazine *Harper's* that:

> We need to deal with this problem from the beach side, in concert with the ocean side, but we don't have an embassy in Somalia and [have] limited, ineffective intelligence operations. We need to work in Somalia and in Lebanon, where a lot of the ransom money has changed hands. But our operations in Lebanon are a joke, and we have no presence at all in Somalia.[23]

Incidents of piracy increased year on year, until 2011 saw an all-time global spike in incidents of piracy, driven by a surge off the coast of Somalia.[24] The number of successful piracy incidents then dropped precipitously in 2012 and effectively ceased in 2013, correlating not with an increase in international naval presence, but rather with commercial ships' increased use of private security firms.[25] In its 2012 report, Oceans Beyond Piracy noted that 'May 10, 2013 marked one full year since a commercial vessel had been hijacked and held for ransom by Somali pirates.'[26] The report further stated that 'Fifty-seven hostages were released in 2012 and 2013. ... Despite these releases, at least 78 hostages continue to be held captive by Somali pirates. ... There were at least 851 seafarers attacked off the coast of Somalia ... in 2012.'[27] In 2013, the US Navy reported zero successful attacks and only nine suspected piracy attempts in the shipping lanes between Yemen and Somalia in 2013.[28]

One such private military company associated with the cessation of piracy attacks was the UK-based Typhon, which offered a convoy of three ships, creating a one kilometre 'exclusion zone' around cargo ships signed up for protection. Each of Typhon's three craft were reported to carry forty ex-British Royal Marines as security officers, and a crew of twenty.[29] The ships were fitted with machine guns, and the staff was given rifles.[30]

The increase in the use of private security personnel in 2012 also coincided with an alleged increase in non-reporting and under-reporting of incidents, raising the question of whether unlawful levels of force were being used to deter pirates by private companies unwilling to then report the incidents. The Oceans Beyond Piracy 2012 report stated that:

> one example of underreporting is a case in which a vessel was carrying Privately Contracted Armed Security Personnel (PCASP). In March 2012, a video was released of an incident, in which armed guards used significant force against a pirate skiff.[31] This incident was reported to the IMB as the firing of warning shots by the embarked security team, after which the pirates aborted the attack.[32] However, the video shows that while the words 'warning shots' are spoken, the actions of the private security team clearly indicate that the skiff and its occupants took heavy fire.[33]

The report continues:

> There has been frustration associated with the lack of reporting of incidents in the Gulf of Aden and the Indian Ocean. This frustration prompted the following announcement by the United Kingdom Maritime Trade Operation (UKMTO): 'It has come to our attention that some private military security companies are reporting suspicious incidents through their internal communication channels and then to their customers. It is in all seafarers' interest that any concerns are reported immediately by phone to UKMTO in accordance with BMP4.'[34]

Closing the circle with mercenaries and counterterrorism, the first private security firm to involve itself in counterpiracy operations appears to have been Blackwater, a company firmly embedded in the global military-security-industrial-complex and long associated with counterterrorism-related operations. In 2009 Blackwater obtained Djiboutian government permission to operate an armed ship to secure client vessels against pirate attacks by pirates. This granting of permission to operate in Djibouti followed a meeting between Blackwater's CEO Erik Prince, former CIA chief Cofer Black and the Djiboutian ambassador to the US, Robleh Olhaye. It was the first such deal that Blackwater had closed in the region, although according to a WikiLeaks embassy cable the company anticipated similar agreements being reached with Oman and Kenya. As the cable made clear,

> BW has no intention of taking any pirates into custody. While the French have previously put pirates ashore in Puntland, [Blackwater's Africa Development Manager, Robert E. Downey] said BW had no plans to do so, either in Somalia or Kenya (noting that Kenya's bilateral PUC agreements with the USG and HMG were government-to-government). BW will share its SOP [Standard Operating Procedure] with Embassies Djibouti and Nairobi once approved; SOP is currently under legal review, as there is 'no precedent for a paramilitary operation in a purely commercial environment.' While asserting that international maritime law allows the use of lethal force against pirates, BW also recognizes the need to respect international humanitarian obligations. Of concern, for example, is whether BW would be responsible for assisting injured pirates, if doing so endangered BW's ability to protect its client(s).

The US Embassy in Djibouti noted that, while this type of action by Blackwater might be unprecedented, it was consistent with Djibouti's recent endeavours to become a centre for anti-piracy operations:

> Djibouti's decision to permit Blackwater to begin counter-piracy operations follows ongoing GODJ efforts aimed at addressing the piracy

threat. Djibouti recently hosted an [International Maritime Organization] conference on Somali piracy that, inter alia, recommended Djibouti serve as a center for maritime training. Numerous foreign military counter-piracy operations are based in Djibouti—involving units from Spain, France, the UK, the Netherlands, and other EU members. Japan and Korea are also considering military deployments to Djibouti to support counter-piracy efforts. Djibouti is a founding member of the Contact Group on Piracy off the Coast of Somalia (CGPCS) and has offered to host the group's planned Counter-Piracy Coordination Cell.[35]

In the several years following this cable, regional states including the Seychelles, Kenya, Mauritius, Somaliland and Puntland were provided with funding by the UN and the international community to host prisons and courts for the transfer, detention and prosecution of pirates and suspected pirates captured by multilateral forces in the Gulf of Aden and Indian Ocean. A kind of parallel justice system emerged, whereby Somalis captured by Western navies were transferred, detained and sometimes prosecuted in Indian Ocean locations far from their home, in conditions distinct from those of the local prison population and in purported compliance with the transferring states' legal obligations—for example, not to transfer people to situations with a real risk of torture and/or inhuman and degrading treatment, although even the normal prison conditions of some receiving states could amount to this.

The few prosecutions that did occur were troubling and ad hoc, with minimal resources directed towards assisting the defendants in building their case. In at least one case that was prosecuted, an eleven-year-old Somali boy was captured by the British Navy, detained and transferred to the Seychelles where he was held for over one year of pre-trial detention before being released and transferred home. UN Office on Drugs and Crime (UNODC)-funded prisons were built in Somaliland and Puntland to hold convicted pirates in accordance with international legal standards. However, the prisoners transferred there following conviction abroad, in locations like the Seychelles and Mauritius, report being given the option for transfer only on condition that they effectively waive their right to an appeal (as prisoner transfer agreements require that cases be 'concluded' prior to any transfer). Equally troubling is the apparent fluidity between antipiracy infrastructure and counterterrorism operations. There are several cases of the US detaining terror suspects on board ships deployed on counterpiracy missions (including Abdulkadir Warsame—see Chapter 7), and of terror suspects being detained in unclear circumstances at UNODC-built counterpiracy prisons in Somalia.

Useful though this infrastructure may be for the US and its allies, the international community is still failing to address substantively the wider problems besetting the Somali oceans, and the tapestry of Somali piracy's possible root (if not necessarily individually operative) causes. Following the reduction in piracy as a result of international operations, illegal fishing has once again increased, even with international navies still on patrol in counterpiracy operations.

In March 2015, UN and Somali fishing officials warned that an increase in illegal fishing could cause a spike in piracy. The same month, in the first reported successful hijacking off the Somali coast in three years, Somali pirates seized an Iranian vessel declared by UNODC to have been fishing illegally in Somali waters.[36] In March 2017, Somali pirates reportedly demanded a ransom for the Sri Lankan crew of a Comoros-flagged vessel— the first reported Somali piracy incident in several years.[37]

In an ironic twist to this tale, in the years following the dramatic dip of 2012, as piracy became increasingly dangerous and unlikely to yield any benefits, former pirates have, according to the UN Monitoring Group on Somalia and Eritrea, turned to providing security and other forms of facilitation to ships engaged in illegal fishing. The Monitoring Group's July 2013 report on Somalia claims that hundreds of foreign vessels, from states including Iran, Yemen, China, Taiwan, Korea and some European states, are engaged in illegal trawling in Somali waters, and that fishermen in Puntland 'have confirmed that the private security teams on board such vessels are normally provided from pools of demobilised Somali pirates and coordinated by a ring of pirate leaders in Puntland, Somaliland, the United Arab Emirates (UAE), Oman, Yemen and Iran.'[38] Other reports suggest that former pirates are now also facilitating arms trafficking. The Associated Press interviewed pirate sources shortly after the publication of the Monitoring Group's report:

> One current pirate said he did not know about pirates providing protection to foreign fishing vessels, but he said some pirates are using Yemeni fishermen to smuggle weapons into Puntland. 'That's our current money-making business because ship hijackings have failed,' a pirate commander who goes by the name Bile Hussein said by phone from Garacad, a pirate lair in central Somalia. 'If you drop one business, you get an idea for another.'[39]

Some have argued that former pirates' engagement in facilitation of illegal fishing is further evidence against the 'creation myth' of Somali pirates as vigilante former fishermen seeking to protect Somalia's fish stock. It does seem to be accepted that increased Somali piracy increases fish stocks, as it reduces IUU fishing, but a direct causal link is neither generally accepted, nor proven by sufficient known evidence. In a way, the 'creation myth' question is less important than that of whether tackling IUU fishing around Somalia should be regarded as a core element of a sustainable and long-lasting counterpiracy strategy.

CNA's November 2013 report concludes that 'while illegal fishing had prompted some Somali fishers to take up arms against foreign commercial fishing vessels, the most important drivers of piracy have been weak government institutions, extreme underdevelopment, a lack of maritime law enforcement and presence, and onshore political instability.'[40] Clearly, not all current Somali pirates are former fishermen, and the international networks supporting their kidnapping and ransom-taking activities suggest high-level organised crime of a different order to disgruntled artisan fishermen taking the law into their own hands. However, by the same token, the nature of the international response to the piracy, and the wider context of other (related) serious and longstanding maritime security issues—the foreign violations of Somalia's seas through overfishing and toxic waste dumping—reveal multiple, complex layers of contest and dysfunction surrounding Somalia's resources, land and seas. This instability has conditioned a perpetuation of the current counter-insurgency in Somalia, creating the economic conditions whereby people accept governance by extreme and violent armed groups as an alternative to further chaos.

10

CIVIL SOCIETY STIFLED

Attacks on human rights defenders and the shrinking space for civil society are topics rarely talked about in the context of the fight against terrorism. Indeed, the received liberal wisdom that a vibrant civil society is key to the function of a healthy democracy continues to be peddled by Western governments in their stated foreign policies towards East African states. However, parallel to this, US counterterrorism policy has clearly, if indirectly, allowed for the instrumentalisation of counterterrorism laws and tactics by East African governments to crack down on democratic opposition and stifle civil society actors and wider democratic life.

The language of counterterrorism inherently lends itself to misuse because of the value-laden and vague meanings of key terms, and the climate of political fear within which this language tends to be deployed. Counterterrorism cooperation in practice and the prolific spread of a global counterterrorism lexicon—wherein words such as 'terrorist' and 'terror suspect' are used instrumentally, shifting their meanings and value according to political context and power relations—increasingly works to undermine the function of civil society and to further restrict the space within which dissent and criticism of governments can operate in East Africa.

Ethiopia remains ahead of regional partners in its thorough attempts to stub out all sparks of a civil society using the tools and strategies of counterterrorism. This approach became apparent in the drafting of Ethiopia's 2009 Counterterrorism Proclamation, a piece of legislation expressly drafted and passed in order to ensure compliance with post-9/11 United Nations requirements that terrorism be criminalised in all member states. The Proclamation preamble states that it was drafted in order to 'enforce agreements that have been entered into under the United Nations and the African Union.'[1] UN Security Council Resolution 1373, which was adopted in the wake of the 9/11 attacks, amongst other provisions, required all states to criminalise activities in support of terrorism, and to share information relating to possible terrorist attacks. Resolution 1624, adopted in September 2005, related to prohibiting incitement to commit acts of terrorism, and stressed that states had to comply with international human rights instruments in the war against terror.

Whilst still in draft, the Proclamation was widely criticised by international human rights organisations. The devil is in the detail, and critics pointed out that the document had an extremely, dangerously wide definition of terrorism—encompassing, for example, forms of non-violent protest—and that it criminalised speech 'encouraging', 'advancing' or 'supporting' such acts. Indeed, the draft Proclamation provided for detention without charge of terror suspects for up to four months, and contained a massive expansion of police powers to search, arrest and destroy property with no judicial oversight. It also allowed for un-sourced intelligence reports to be admitted as evidence in court (thereby effectively providing a route in for evidence derived from torture to be introduced, effectively beyond legal challenge), and approved the death penalty for a range of crimes, both serious and non-serious.[2]

The Counterterrorism Proclamation was adopted on 7 July 2009, and came into force when it was published in the official Gazette of the Federal Democratic Republic of Ethiopia (*Negarit Gazeta*) on 29 August 2009.[3] In its final form, the Proclamation retained all of the major flaws highlighted by critics, including the highly vague and broad definitions of both 'terrorism' and 'support' for it. For instance, giving 'moral support' to a person committing an act of terrorism (which, under the act, could be in the form of a non-violent protest) was criminalised; provision was made for the wide use of secret evidence, entailing the possibility of conviction without the defendant being informed of the full allegations and evidence against them; and scope was created for the admission of torture evidence to a prosecution, via intelligence reports with unverified sources.[4]

This Proclamation, and the Charities and Societies Proclamation that followed, are clear examples of ways in which the War on Terror framework provided for an expansion of the Ethiopian government's authoritarian 'rule by law', whereby unfair and mutable laws were drafted and then used to enforce the government's power in order to crush its opponents and those holding it to account, first labelling them terrorists, then removing their rights and denying them access to basic due process—which is easy, because due process simply does not exist in Ethiopia.

Whilst the Ethiopian government was pushing through the Counterterrorism Proclamation, in a pincer attack, it was also working on the euphemistically-titled Charities and Societies Proclamation. The draft proclamation sought to impose strict controls on the activities of all civil society organisations, including those promoting human rights. It restricted international organisations from working on a range of human rights and democracy issues in Ethiopia without special permission, and barred local organisations from working on human rights activities if they received more than 10 per cent of their income from foreign sources. This formula effectively shut down the possibility of domestic organisations being able to operate independently of the Ethiopian government, and of international organisations being able to effectively monitor government violations inside Ethiopia.

To impose these provisions, the Proclamation established a Charities and Societies Agency with broad discretionary power, including powers of surveillance and interference in the management and operations of local organisations.[5] In 2009, Amnesty International commented:

> The new law, expected to be implemented in early January 2010, puts at serious risk the ability of local and international organizations to monitor, report and advocate against human rights violations in Ethiopia. Some human rights groups scaled back their operations in the interim. Re-registration of local organizations under the new law began in October.[6]

Initially, the prime focus of both of these Proclamations appeared to be a wide sweep of civil society actors, rather than those groups traditionally treated as War on Terror targets. Amnesty International reported that during 2010, after the passing of the Proclamation, 'human rights defenders chose to limit their own activities and journalists to self-censor in a climate of heightened anxiety over repression', and that 'an increasing number of prominent opposition figures fled Ethiopia. These included human rights defenders and journalists who were harassed and intimidated by the authorities, leading them to believe that their arrest and detention could be imminent.'[7]

Several months after the adoption of the Counterterrorism Proclamation, the legislation was used by the Ethiopian government against the major Ethiopian publishing company, Addis Neger, which it threatened with closure. In November and December 2010, several of Addis Neger's reporters were threatened with arrest, and by the end of the year, a number of Addis Neger journalists had fled the country.[8] In 2010, the 2009 Charities and Societies Proclamation also took effect. As a result, some Ethiopian human rights defenders fled abroad, and other organisations 'significantly altered their mandates and ceased their work on human rights'. Despite successfully re-registering with the Charities and Societies Agency, one of the few remaining Ethiopian organisations working on human rights, the Ethiopian Human Rights Council (EHRCO), had its bank accounts frozen in 2009.[9] In February 2012, the Board of the Charities and Societies Agency upheld this decision, which was appealed to the High Court; in October of that year, the High Court also upheld the decision.

With these and several other draconian laws in place in the name of counterterrorism, 2011–12 saw a major crackdown on freedom of expression in Ethiopia, with high numbers of journalists and political opposition members being arrested and charged with terrorism, treason and other offences, and printing houses coming under threat. Amnesty International has noted that

> the authorities used criminal charges and accusations of terrorism to silence dissent. Large numbers of independent journalists and members of political opposition parties were arrested on suspicion of committing terrorist offences, many after writing articles critical of the government, calling for reform or applying for demonstration permits. Detainees were denied full and prompt access to lawyers and family members.

By November 2011, 107 journalists and opposition members had been charged with terrorism-related crimes. Six more journalists, two opposition members and one human rights defender—all in exile—were charged in absentia. Human Rights Watch and Amnesty have both commented that the prosecutions appear to have been politically motivated, and a result of the victims' peaceful and legitimate activities. A large number of the 107 people prosecuted complained of torture or other serious ill treatment whilst held at Maikelawi detention centre, including 'beatings with pieces of wire, metal and furniture; suspension by the wrists; sleep deprivation; and being held in isolation and in complete darkness for prolonged periods. Many reported being forced to sign confessions and other documents that would be presented against them as evidence.'[10]

Amongst the accused were notable journalists: on 2 May 2013, the Ethiopian Supreme Court upheld Eskinder Nega Fenta's eighteen-year sentence under the anti-terrorism law. Fenta is a veteran journalist who was awarded the 2012 PEN Freedom to Write Award. The UN Working Group on Arbitrary Detention has found that his imprisonment was arbitrary and 'a result of his peaceful exercise of the right to freedom of expression.' Other Ethiopian journalists currently serving sentences under the Counterterrorism Proclamation include Woubshet Taye Abebe, a winner of the 2012 Hellman-Hammett Award, and Reeyot Alemu Gobebo, a journalist for *Feteh* and winner of the 2013 UNESCO/ Guillermo Cano World Press Freedom Prize. Two Swedish journalists were also convicted under the Proclamation: Martin Schibbye and Johan Persson were accused of 'rendering support to terrorism' and entering the country illegally 'to commit an act that is a threat to the well-being of the people of Ethiopia', after entering the country without a visa to document human rights abuses in Ethiopia's eastern region. They were pardoned and released in September 2012 after more than a year in prison.[11]

Alongside events in Ethiopia, in 2010, both Kenya and Uganda saw major crackdowns on human rights defenders working in the national security sphere. As we saw in Chapter 6, at that time there was, in particular, a concerted attempt to intimidate and limit the work of human rights defenders who were exposing governments excesses in the Kampala Bombings investigation— including Al-Amin Kimathi, Mbugua Mureithi and myself. Since Uhuru Kenyatta won the Kenyan presidential election in

2013, there has been a series of wider threats to human rights defenders working in the country, initially focusing on individuals and organisations working with the International Criminal Court (ICC) in relation to Kenya's 2007 post-election violence. In September 2013, the Kenyan police confirmed that a gang calling itself Nyaribo Support Group had threatened to burn down the home of Maina Kiai, the UN special rapporteur on the rights to freedom of peaceful assembly and of association, and former chairman of the Kenya National Commission on Human Rights. The threats reportedly came in response to erroneous claims on blogs that Kiai had travelled to The Hague to testify against Kenyatta at the ICC. The following month, Human Rights Watch noted that 'attacks and threats against human rights defenders are on the rise in Kenya. ... Harassment of people perceived to support the International Criminal Court (ICC) cases ... has been particularly acute', adding that,

> beyond the ICC issue, the broader environment for human rights defenders also appears to have worsened. In the last two months, a prominent human rights lawyer in the western town of Bungoma and a human rights activist in Moyale in Kenya's North Eastern region were shot dead by unidentified assailants, with preliminary evidence indicating they were shot because of their human rights work.[12]

In late October 2013, the Kenyan government sought to rush through legislation similar to the Ethiopian Proclamations that would radically reduce foreign funding for Kenyan civil society organisations, without notice or debate. The Miscellaneous Amendment Bill of 2013 sought to cap and control levels of foreign funding. Such restrictions would result in the severe hobbling of Kenyan civil society organisations, most of whose existence depends on foreign funding, particularly to give them the independence needed to challenge the Kenyan government. Threatening a fate similar to that of Ethiopian civil society, these kinds of measures would be devastating if carried out in Kenya.

This effort was temporarily blocked after successful resistance from civil society, but it came within a wider government strategy to stifle the work of organisations holding it to account, often through the misuse of counterterrorism legislation and the freezing of bank accounts under terrorism and anti-corruption financial provisions. Since 2014, reportedly more than 1,000 Kenyan NGOs have been forced to close or threatened with deregistration on the basis of financial violations or alleged links with terrorist organisations.[13] In 2014, 510 Kenyan NGOs were deregistered, including fifteen accused of terrorist links.[14]

Critics claim that the proposed deregistration in October 2015 of 959 Kenyan NGOs by the NGO Coordination Board was, in some instances, an attempt at harassment of legitimate NGOs, such as the Kenyan Commission for Human Rights, and an 'attack on the key players working on governance in [Kenya].'[15] One of the groups deregistered in 2014 on so-called terrorist grounds was the Mombasa-based HAKI Africa, whose work documenting the extrajudicial killings of Kenyan Muslims in the coastal region (see Chapter 8) brought them to the state's attention. Its deregistration reflected the Kenyan authorities' course of conduct by, throughout 2013–14, attempting to silence critics of their increasingly out-of-control counterterrorism operations.

At the same time as the government began an unprecedented and widely criticised security operation against Somali refugees (see Chapter 5), human rights defenders were publicly threatened and warned off documenting possible police violations in Nairobi. Inspector General of Police David Kimaiyo reportedly stated, 'I want to tell our Muslim brothers and activists to keep off Eastleigh operations otherwise we shall get them out of the way by force.'[16] Kimaiyo has not to date been investigated in relation to this alleged comment, nor has he made a statement to retract or qualify it.

During the second week of April 2014, Kenyan human rights defender Al-Amin Kimathi, who had previously been detained and falsely accused in Uganda as he worked defending Kenyan rendition victims during the Kampala bombings investigation (see Chapter 6), learned via security sources that his life was at risk. Following the high-profile killing in Mombasa of Sheikh Makaburi on 1 April (see Chapter 8), multiple credible sources, including from within the security services, warned Kimathi that he was on the 'kill list' of high-profile Muslims slated for extrajudicial execution. If accurate, this suggests that the Kenyan state was failing to recognise the rule of law on several points: not only with respect to meting out extrajudicial executions, but also by treating human rights defenders working on counterterrorism issues as associates of terror suspects or terror suspects themselves, simply by virtue of their work.

Another Muslim organisation that came under threat during this time was the Mombasa-based Muslims for Human Rights (MUHURI). Rapid Response Officer Francis Auma has reported that in November and December 2013, following the publication of a report documenting violations by the Kenyan Anti-Terror Police Unit (ATPU), he began being trailed in his car by a suspicious vehicle, and followed and watched in his home by people he strongly believed to be plain-clothes government agents. Auma said that he and his family felt intimidated and threatened by this ostentatious monitoring and that it restricted his ability to conduct his work, as he did not want to bring vulnerable individuals to the attention of Kenyan government agencies by meeting with them while under surveillance.

In March 2014, further concerns were raised as to the misapplication of administrative provisions in order to harass and restrict human rights work, when Mombasa County Commissioner Nelson Marwa, now also supported by Awiti Bolo (one of Mombasa's MPs), announced that Kenyan state security should investigate MUHURI and HAKI Africa for alleged incitement of youths to terrorism. Both organisations had recently been at the forefront of documenting violations committed in the national security context, and denied the allegations. The call for an investigation came to nothing, and appeared to be little more than a politically-motivated attack to undermine these civil society organisations seeking to hold security forces to account for a year of systemic human rights violations carried out in counterterrorism operations in Mombasa, as well as an attempt to deflect attention from the government's own rapidly unravelling security strategy.[17]

Following the massacre of university students in Garissa in April 2015, the Kenyan government, coming under further pressure over its responsibility for the security vacuum, once again turned on civil society. The government released a list of over seventy NGOs and individuals, including MUHURI and HAKI Africa, whose bank accounts were to be frozen over un-evidenced suspicions of links to terror. HAKI Africa's office was raided and all of its human rights documentation, including hundreds of sensitive and confidential case files on vulnerable victims alleging police abuse, was seized. The state's attempts at HAKI's deregistration and freezing of assets has now been successfully challenged in court, but the impact on the organisation's work has been significant. At the time of writing, over a year since this attempted crackdown, the property taken in the raid has still not been returned—including the confidential case files.

11

MOTIFS OF EXCLUSION

SECURITISATION AND COLLECTIVE PUNISHMENT IN KENYAN COUNTERTERRORISM OPERATIONS

People of Somali ethnicity have historically dominated Kenya's North Eastern Province (NEP), an arid, dusty place carved out of Southern Somalia during the colonial era and, at least nominally, part of Kenya ever since. In the years since Somalia succumbed to civil war in 1991–2, increasing numbers of Somali refugees have crossed the border into Kenya. Somalis with citizenship and residency status make up a significant portion of Kenyan residents (approximately 2.5 million, according to the 2009 census),[1] with almost half a million registered Somali refugees,[2] and an unknown number of undocumented Somalis.

Despite being a distinct ethnic group within Kenya's territory since its birth as a nation, ethnic Somalis of Kenyan nationality have long been systematically discriminated against and politically excluded in Kenya. On a functional level, many elements of this exclusion are underpinned by a relatively simple tactic, whereby Kenyan Somalis, with the right to Kenyan citizenship, are routinely denied practical access to basic identity and citizenship documentation, which makes them vulnerable to further violations, often underpinned by a de-facto denial of citizenship rights by the state. 'Somalis in Kenya are second-class citizens', one Somali-Kenyan told me.

> Whereas some other Kenyans, for instance those from the Kikuyu ethnic group, will find it very easy to get their identity documents, we have to produce papers going back to our grandparents' birth certificates. Even if we have been Kenyan for generations, it is assumed that we are not, truly, Kenyan.

Alongside this treatment of Kenyan Somalis as 'the other within', refugee and asylum-seeking Somalis fleeing war in Somalia—'Somali Somalis'—have also long faced denial of their basic rights under international human rights and humanitarian and refugee law.

One longstanding aspect of this discrimination involves systemic unlawful deferrals of considering right to asylum, and the indefinite postponement of integration of refugee communities by confining them to camps such as the sprawling Northern Kenyan camp at Dadaab, a practice now a quarter-century old. By 2011, the camp, designed to hold 90,000 refugees fleeing the Somali civil war in 1991, held almost half a million Somali refugees.

In February 2007 I travelled to Dadaab with the area's then-MP, to meet with a delegation of community leaders who were all long-standing refugees. We travelled via the northern town of Garissa. At the time, Ethiopian troops were pummelling the remnants of the Union of Islamic Courts just over the Somali border, and military and counterterrorism personnel of at least five different nations swarmed the area. Hot, dusty Garissa, or 'Little Mogadishu' as some people call it, was teeming with activity. On the terrace of the one international standard hotel, aid workers delivering a long-scheduled 'gender awareness' conference sat shoulder to shoulder with CIA agents taking in the scene from behind their Ray-Bans. The road to the camp looked as though it was in Somalia, and the camp itself was a sea of Somali-style benders patched together with colourful rags and used food bags, store rooms built from empty World Food Programme oil-cans, and flocks of huge white storks, silhouetted against the sky as they perched atop tottering piles of rubbish.

After a tour, we were brought to a covered meeting place where around thirty long-standing refugees sat on carpets, waiting to address us. As we settled in, rare clouds appeared in the sky outside and it began to rain thick, heavy drops, which turned the red dust outside to a dense brown mud. As the rain drummed on the corrugated roof, the delegation patiently explained that most of them had been there since the outbreak of the civil war sixteen years before. They felt like prisoners, and many of the children of the camp had been born there. They had nowhere to go. The camp was their home and their permanent reality. One refugee eloquently explained to us that their situation—effectively indefinite detention under a cloud of suspicion purely because they were Somalis—was like being in Guantánamo Bay.

Kenya's disregard for its legal obligations towards Somali refugees, and discrimination against Somalis more generally, long predates the War on Terror. However, over the past ten years, funding, tactics and a framework taken from America's War on Terror have merged with a set of particular local dynamics in this region to generate an environment permissive of abuses against ethnic Somalis (in particular Somali asylum seekers and refugees), which increasingly singles them out for a form of collective punishment in retaliation for Al-Shabaab terrorist attacks carried out in Kenya.

A particularly egregious, foundational and benchmark example of this is Operation Usalama Watch. This internal security operation, carried out between March and May 2014, was launched by the Kenyan state following a series of grenade and gun attacks in Nairobi and Mombasa. According to Human Rights Watch:

Kenyan police and military deployed about 5,000 security officers to Eastleigh over several weeks. The forces raided homes, buildings, and shops, extorted massive sums, and harassed and detained an estimated 4,000 people—including journalists, registered refugees, Kenyan citizens, and international aid workers—without charge, and in appalling conditions for periods well beyond the 24-hour legal limit.[3]

During this operation, thousands of Somali refugees and asylum seekers were detained in the Kasarani Sports Stadium Complex in Nairobi. Detainees were subsequently either released without charge, charged with unlawful presence, made to relocate to refugee camps, deported, or released after payment and on condition that they return to Somalia as soon as possible. Over 5,000 such individuals were forcibly relocated to refugee camps in northern Kenya, and at least 359 others were formally expelled back to Somalia, with an unknown number of individuals informally expelled.[4]

In 2015 my organisation, Justice Forum, interviewed a set of individuals who were sent back, or 'refouled', to Somalia in this operation. One such Somali arrested in this sweep, thirty-eight-year-old 'Farah',[5] offered a fairly typical narrative. When she was returned to Somalia, Farah and her family were the holders of UNCHR letters certifying the bearers as refugees, and of a Republic of Kenya Refugee Certificate for the household. Farah told us how in 2008 she had fled by car from Mogadishu to Kenya with her husband, their seven children and several nieces. Farah and her family then spent time in refugee camps in northern Kenya, and in 2011 moved to Eastleigh, Nairobi to escape the extreme chaos and high levels of gender-based violence in the Dadaab camps.

In Nairobi, the family were given refugee documents and ID cards by the office of the United Nations High Commission for Refugees (UNHCR). The family received support from relatives, and the children began to attend school. However, on 28 May

2014, Farah reports that members of the Kenyan Administrative Police forcibly entered her house and arrested her, alongside ten members of her family. Farah told us that she and her family were detained at Kasarani Sports Stadium until relatives paid Kenyan police a total of 350,000 Kenyan shillings (roughly £2,500) for their release. Upon release, they were 'advised' by the police to leave Kenya for Somalia in order to avoid the risk of being arrested again. Farah went to the Somali Embassy in Nairobi for assistance in returning to Mogadishu. In an operation coordinated by the Kenyan and Somali governments, and, unforgivably, sanctioned by the UNHCR, she was given papers, and plane tickets to Somalia were arranged. Farah told us that she was terrified of further arrest and detention whilst she was waiting in Nairobi for her flight back to Somalia.

Back in Mogadishu, Farah and her family were living in the city's Wadajir district. Life was extremely difficult. Alongside the conditions of generalised violence, there was insufficient food and water, overcrowded living conditions, and no schools for the children. Farah said that she was also forced to leave behind two of her daughters and her nieces in Kenya.

In total, Justice Forum interviewed nine people like Farah who were forcibly returned to Somalia. All of our interviewees held refugee certification documents, and none of them described what could credibly be considered a voluntary (non-coerced) return. These enforced transfers to Somalia, with no judicial oversight, breached the principle of non-refoulement, a cornerstone principle of both the 1951 Refugee Convention and the 1969 Organisation of African Unity Convention Governing the Specific Aspects of Refugee Problems in Africa.[6] Regarding the involuntary nature of the returns, Kenya was clearly in breach of domestic, regional and international legal obligations, as well as the 2013 tripartite agreement with Somalia and the UNHCR whereby Kenya undertook to continue providing protection and assistance to all refugees. Expulsion or forced repatriation of

Somali refugees is in direct contradiction of this agreement to 'facilitate [their] *voluntary* repatriation and reintegration' on a mutually agreed upon ... basis.[7]

No other organisation has tracked returnees to Somalia. However, the conditions of confinement and ill-treatment described by the Somali refugees whilst they were still in Kenya have been well documented by international human rights organisations and other bodies including the Independent Police Oversight Authority (IPOA), who sent a team of monitors and investigators to various police stations, including the Kasarani Sport Complex and Jomo Kenyatta International Airport detention centres. The IPOA indicated that the police operations in Kenya could 'engender a feeling of ethnic profiling',[8] and reported violations of human rights including discriminatory policing practices (with Somali refugees overrepresented amongst those detained and expelled during the operation); unconstitutional detention conditions (with detainees placed in overcrowded, unsanitary conditions and denied basic rights); and children routinely being detained with adults.[9]

While the US-led War on Terror has provided the current framework within which this treatment of Somalis can be meted out, neither the nature nor the fact of these violations is novel; indeed, they represent in many respects the continuity of several long-standing dynamics. The ideological foundation of the contemporary operations involves an ill-founded and unlawful conflation of all Somalis and Somali refugees with terrorism and a threat to national security. Yet the nature of the operations has its roots both in colonial history—in particular, tactics used by the British—and in the post-independence Kenyan treatment of ethnic Somalis. Hannah Whittaker wrote in the *Journal of Imperial and Commonwealth History*:

> For many Kenyan Somalis, especially those living in the border region of the NEP, the targeting of their community since 2012 is little surprising,

and the approach adopted by Kenyan security forces during Operation Usalama Watch nothing new. Just after Kenya gained independence in December 1963, the Kenyan government waged a four-year counterinsurgency campaign against Somali separatists operating in NEP. The security forces used indiscriminate violence against the local Somali population in the name of 'collective responsibility' ... Although the conflict officially came to an end in November 1967, the region remained subject to emergency rule until 1991 [with] numerous incidents of state-sponsored violence and intimidation against Somalis living in NEP, including two massacres ... as well as a nationwide 'screening' of all ethnic Somalis residing in Kenya during 1989 and 1990 ... these measures have led to instances of rape, beatings, stock seizures, detentions and potentially thousands of deaths that have yet to be officially recognized.[10]

Thus, the War on Terror framework can here be regarded as providing a contemporary justification for perpetuating a long-established dynamic of exclusion and discrimination. Regarding the deeper, colonial roots of the use of collective punishment, Whittaker writes:

At the same time, the use of collective punishment in NEP connects with Kenya's deeper colonial history ... it is a strategy that is as old as effective administration in Kenya's arid and sparsely populated northern frontier, and it was at the heart of British counterinsurgency during the 1952–60 Mau Mau emergency. Speaking in the aftermath of Operation Usalama Watch, Raila Odinga, the leader of the Kenyan opposition, urged the government to halt 'the indiscriminate harassment of a particular community', which reminded him of 'the Mau Mau days, when then British handled the Kenyans in the most brutal and inhumane manner imaginable'.[11]

This history has served as a foundation not only for the smooth integration of Somali refugee matters into Kenyan counterterrorism strategy. It has also influenced the wider Kenyan counterterrorism repertoire. The cultural and political 'othering' of Somali refugees and asylum seekers in Kenya is now both facilitated and normalised by a systemic denial of access to basic identity documentation and the de facto denial of access to certain legal rights, such as the right to have one's case assessed in a timely manner before a competent tribunal. The core resonance of this approach with broader Kenyan approaches to counterterrorism is supported by several significant counterterrorism cases involving non-Somali Muslims in Kenya, in which these tactics of denying basic documentation have served as a precursor to further abuses. The later massive increase in targeted killings and disappearances of Muslims in Kenya, explored later in this book, may be regarded as a further development in the same direction.

One such example is that of Mohammed Abdulmalik (see Chapter 7), a Kenyan citizen of Luo ethnicity captured in Mombasa in 2007 by the Kenyan Anti-Terrorism Police Unit (ATPU) who was mistreated in several detention locations in Kenya before being handed with no judicial process to US personnel who rendered him to Guantánamo Bay via Djibouti and Afghanistan. In Kenyan parliamentary debates and government disclosures in the context of a *habeas* petition and then a constitutional petition in the Kenyan courts, the Kenyan government repeatedly denied that Abdulmalik was a Kenyan citizen, taking various conflicting positions including that he was a Somali or a Ugandan, that he had been released in Kenya, and also that he had been 'returned' to Somalia. The truth of his rendition without judicial oversight into US custody and then out of the country emerged in a series of unclassified official US government documents disclosed during Abdulmalik's US *habeas* litigation.

Another example is that of Salim Awadh, a Kenyan citizen of coastal descent who had been living in Somalia but had fled back to Kenya after the December 2006 Ethiopian invasion of Mogadishu. Awadh was apprehended in early 2007 at the Kenyan-Somali border where, he reports, all of his Kenyan citizenship and identity documentation was confiscated by Kenyan

security personnel. Awadh was then held in various police stations in Nairobi, without access to a lawyer and purportedly
under immigration powers, before being rendered back into the
Somali warzone, and eventually to Ethiopia, where he was
detained incommunicado and abused for over a year. The Kenyan
government then used Awadh's lack of documentation to deny
any responsibility towards him for over a year whilst he was held
in Ethiopia, as they attempted to claim that he was not a Kenyan
citizen. After Awadh's eventual release, his legal case for damages
against the Kenyan government was hindered by the state continuing to dispute his nationality. He was, eventually, the lead
claimant in a group of eight Kenyans who successfully won damages from the government in 2013 for their unlawful detention
and rendition to Ethiopia.[12]

There were many other cases of refoulement of Somali refugees attempting to flee over the border to seek asylum in Kenya
in early 2007. Because the Somali-Kenyan border was so heavily
militarised, no human rights organisations were able to document comprehensively the returns of these Somalis. However,
credible witnesses spoke of Kenyan forces at the border summarily turning back lorry-loads of asylum seekers at the border, on
more than one occasion. The deputy mayor of the Kenyan border
village of Kiunga described to me how, one morning in early
2007, boatloads of Somali refugees had arrived on their crescent
beach, before being removed by Kenyan security forces to an
unknown location—presumably back over the border in Somalia.

As counterterrorism concerns in Kenya have increased in the
years since 2007, so too has systemic discrimination by the
Kenyan government against the Somali refugee population, cul-
minating in Operation Usalama Watch and related activities.
Amnesty International has noted that, prior to Operation
Usalama Watch, on the basis of alleged counterterrorism concerns, registration of Somali refugees in Kenya had been 'largely

halted since 2011, preventing many who should qualify for refugee status from obtaining papers.'[13]

Anecdotal evidence suggests that hundreds of such Somalis were unlawfully returned to Somalia from Kenya, both during the several years when Kenya was making an effort to document urban refugees, and after the registration efforts ceased. This has been impossible to substantively document due to fear of speaking out among the Kenyan Somali community and the difficulties of tracing transferees already returned to Somalia.

In the build-up to Operation Usalama Watch, in December 2012, citing security concerns over a recent series of terrorist attacks in Nairobi as a justification, the Government of Kenya announced a directive that would force all refugees living in cities to relocate to camps, and shut down all registration and service provision to urban-dwelling refugees and asylum seekers. Refugees International explained that 'this directive caused severe harm even without being implemented. [It] effectively empowered Kenyan security services to unleash a wave of abuse against refugees. Many refugees felt forced to leave Nairobi following severe harassment.' Its research suggests that following the issuance of this directive (before it was ever implemented), unlawful abuses against refugees by Kenyan security forces increased massively:

> Members of the security services treated refugees brutally during house-to-house searches and round-ups of individuals. Several refugees informed the RI team that they had been hit in the face by officers, and that large amounts of money and property were taken from them. There were many second-hand accounts of refugees being forced to pay bribes of up to 200,000 Kenyan shillings ($2,200) to secure the release of family members from police custody. Prior to the directive, such bribes were also commonplace, but usually only amounted to 500–2,000 shillings. There have been at least three allegations of rape made by refugees against members of the security services since the directive was issued. Refugees also stated that identity documents issued to them by UNHCR and by the Kenyan government are being disregarded, confiscated, or

destroyed by the security services, stripping them of vital legal protections. In fact, several refugees told RI that they feel as though they have no international protection now, and are only protected by the bribes they pay to police.[14]

The humanitarian organisation also noted that, since the issuance of the directive, the Kenyan government had ceased registering new refugees arriving in urban areas, a policy that wholly undermined the directive's stated goal, to improve security, since registration would give the government and the UNHCR the opportunity to identify those refugees who might actually pose a threat. Reports also suggested that many refugees, including families, without the means to flee elsewhere were forced to live in effective hiding within Kenya, principally in Nairobi. Refugee community leaders feared reprisals if they complained to the authorities, community meetings could not be held, and children were not able to attend school. This situation continued, without the directive actually being implemented, for over a year.

On 19 January 2013, a letter from the Ministry of Provincial Administration and Internal Security was leaked to the Kenyan media, pre-warning of Operation Usalama Watch and stating that the government intended to round up 18,000 refugees and hold them in Thika Municipal Stadium before moving them to refugee camps. This scenario was temporarily averted as a result of objections from some international organisations and donor states, but the UNHCR controversially stated that it was focusing on maintaining a good line of communication with the Kenyan government in an attempt to avoid the 'worst case scenario' of a militarised round-up of refugees. The directive was ultimately quashed in the Kenyan High Court in July 2013. These two small victories for international law, however, were only a temporary cessation in state attacks on Somali refugees.

The government's subsequent retraction of the directive was triggered by a massacre—in which no Somali refugees are believed to have been involved—raising many questions about the conduct of Kenyan intelligence and security forces. On 21 September 2013, unidentified gunmen attacked the popular Westgate Shopping Centre in the upmarket Nairobi area of Westlands. The resulting siege lasted until 24 September, and resulted in sixty-seven deaths and over 175 wounded. Al-Shabaab quickly claimed responsibility for the attack, stating that it was carried out in retaliation for Kenya's military deployment in Somalia (Operation Linda Nchi). The Kenyan government's immediate security response was bungled, with the siege lasting for three days. Afterwards, there followed several controversial security incidents including mass round-ups, disappearances of Muslims and a siege of a mosque, despite which even the most basic facts of the attack still appear to be unknown—for instance, at the time of writing it remains unclear whether the key attackers were killed in the siege, or escaped.

It was in this context that, on 25 March 2014, Cabinet Secretary for Interior and Coordination of National Government Joseph Ole Lenku issued a renewed directive, ordering all refugees living in urban centres to return to designated camps, stating that this was being done in a bid to address the increasing threat of terrorism. Under the terms of the directive, all urban refugees were to be relocated to camps unless they agreed to a 'voluntary' return, an arrangement sanctioned—incredibly—by the UNHCR. The directive was combined on 2 April 2014 with the launch of Operation Rudisha Usalama.

Anecdotal evidence and media reports suggest that, as a result of these government efforts to confine and remove Somalis, xenophobic attacks against Somalis in Kenya are on the increase. Since the launch of the operation there has been a spate of incidents involving Somali Kenyans being pushed off *matatus* (small private minibuses) by other passengers. One such example is Kenyan citizen Adan Mohammed, who explained how, in early

May 2014, he boarded a Number 48 *matatu* at the Odeon bus terminal in Nairobi—the seven passengers already onboard alighted and collectively stared at him. Adan said,

> I was dressed in a simple shirt and tie, I was not wearing a Kanzu or any other attire. But when I entered the *matatu* the other passengers came down. I immediately remembered the bus bombings in Nairobi and Mombasa over the weekend and my mind clicked on what they must have been thinking. So I alighted. I was afraid they might lynch me or steal my valuables because I was carrying my laptop in a bag. I left and walked some distance, when I looked back everyone entered the *matatu*. So I took a taxi to the office.'[15]

Somalis in Kenya report feeling as though they are constantly under suspicion, and the UK immigration courts now recognise that Kenyans of Somali ethnicity face a real risk on return to Kenya, solely as a result of their ethnicity.

Quite where this trajectory will lead depends very much on the future of the War on Terror and the priorities of the key donor states currently supporting its perpetration in East Africa. Whilst Somalia remains an effective warzone, and Kenya remains a key frontline state in the current execution of the US's War on Terror, it is hard to see how the securitisation of Somali refugee matters, the 'othering' of Somali Kenyans, and the gradual extension of this dynamic to the wider Kenyan Muslim population can be prevented. The War on Terror's motifs of violent exclusion and exceptionalism to international law have found a natural home in this East African political environment, intermixing with systemic violations being carried out against 'othered' ethnic, religious and political groups in the name of national security.

12

CYBER WARS

We live in the digital age, where high-level information and communications technology and software-based systems are fundamental to the functioning of modern society. On 17 January 2012, the US military announced that the United States intended to treat cyberspace as a military battleground alongside the air, land and sea: 'Disrupting the enemy will require the full inclusion of space and cyberspace operations into the traditional air-land-sea battle space. [They have] critical importance for the projection of military force. Arguably, this emergence is the most important and fundamental change ... over the past several decades.'[1]

Maintaining control over flows of information via computer networks and information infrastructure, and disrupting those of the enemy are therefore increasingly regarded as activities central to national security. It thus becomes clear exactly why organisations like WikiLeaks are regarded by the US government as such a threat to national security. Rather than conceptualising the conflict as one between ideals of privacy and freedom of information (with WikiLeaks taking, at least with regard to its publication of US government leaks, a position of radical freedom, i.e.

that all information should be freely available to all), the true nature of the conflict turns on a fight for control of information. WikiLeaks offends the US administration because it seeks to liberate information that the US has designated as not to be shared. It undermines the administration's control over that information. Thus, too, we may make sense of President Obama's policy of pursuing prosecution of those involved in 'unauthorised' leaks. Unofficially 'authorised' or sanctioned leaks, such as those relating to the official narrative of the death of Osama bin Laden, are acceptable because they occur within a context of official control over previously classified information. 'Unauthorised' leaks violate this understanding.

Following 9/11, in addition to its more outward-facing activities, such as the wars in Afghanistan and Iraq, and the transfers of hundreds of prisoners to Guantánamo Bay, the US was also shoring up an unprecedented system of global information control and surveillance that is only now becoming publicly understood. In June 2013, the first in a series of classified US documents leaked by the former CIA security contractor Edward Snowden were published by *The Washington Post* and *The Guardian*.[2] The documents detailed how telecom company Verizon had been clandestinely complying with secret court orders to provide the US National Security Agency (NSA) with the phone records of nearly all of its customers.

Subsequent documents revealed that Verizon was not the only corporation implicated in this mass, systematic privacy breach— nearly all American telecom corporations were doing the same thing. Over the following months, thousands more US intelligence documents were published, revealing further details of secret surveillance programmes operated around the world by the US and its allies. The number of documents released by Snowden is still unknown, although estimates proffered by various government sources suggest at least 15,000 Australian files, at least 58,000 British files, and about 1.7 million US intelligence files.[3]

The day after the Verizon disclosures, further leaks revealed the existence of PRISM, a secret programme whereby tech giants such as Apple, Microsoft and Facebook were being compelled to supply the NSA with private user data, without users even being aware of the 'request'.

The Snowden documents have great significance for people living beyond the United States, including those living in the East and Horn of Africa. In March 2014, the German media outlet *Der Spiegel* revealed that some of Snowden's NSA data showed that the British government's intelligence hub GCHQ had hacked into the networks of at least three German telecom companies (Stellar, Cetel and IABG), and that the NSA had collected and stored information about German Chancellor Angela Merkel, along with at least 121 other world leaders (East Africans included).[4]

The Tempora programme is a joint operation between the NSA and GCHQ, supported by private companies including British Telecoms, Vodafone Cable, Global Crossing, Level 3, Viatel and Interoute, to intercept fibre optic cables travelling all over the world in order to collect vast amounts of 'metadata'—i.e. descriptors of content rather than the content itself—relating to people's Internet usage. In May 2014, *The Intercept* reported on another NSA programme—MYSTIC—involving the secret monitoring of the telecommunications of several states, including Kenya. This operation in Kenya, 'sponsored by the CIA', was called DUSKPALLET, described in secret internal documents as 'a program for embedded collection systems overtly installed on target networks, predominantly for the collection and processing of wireless/mobile communications networks.' At the time that these classified source documents emerged, the programme was collecting only metadata, although there was the 'potential for [collecting] content at a later date.'[5]

This potential had, according to *The Intercept*, already been realised in NSA operations in the Bahamas and another unnamed country (later revealed by WikiLeaks to be Afghanistan).[6] *The Intercept* has described MYSTIC (known to be operational in Kenya) and SOMALGET (the enhanced content-gathering operations used in the Bahamas and Afghanistan, which could be rolled out in MYSTIC states such as Kenya), thus:

> If an entire nation's cell-phone calls were a menu of TV shows, MYSTIC would be a cable programming guide showing which channels offer which shows, and when. SOMALGET would be the DVR that automatically records every show on every channel and stores them for a month. MYSTIC provides the access; SOMALGET provides the massive amounts of storage needed to archive all those calls so that analysts can listen to them at will after the fact. According to one NSA document, SOMALGET is 'deployed against entire networks' in the Bahamas and the second country, and processes 'over 100 million call events per day'.

> SOMALGET's capabilities are further detailed in a May 2012 memo written by an official in the NSA's International Crime and Narcotics division. The memo hails the 'great success' the NSA's drugs and crime unit has enjoyed through its use of the program, and boasts about how 'beneficial' the collection and recording of every phone call in a given nation can be to intelligence analysts.

> Rather than simply making 'tentative analytic conclusions derived from metadata,' the memo notes, analysts can follow up on hunches by going back in time and listening to phone calls recorded during the previous month. Such 'retrospective retrieval' means that analysts can figure out what targets were saying even when the calls occurred before the targets were identified. '[W]e buffer certain calls that MAY be of foreign intelligence value for a sufficient period to permit a well-informed decision on whether to retrieve and return specific audio content,' the NSA official reported.[7]

Regarding any role played by the government of Kenya in this data snatch from its citizens, London-based watchdog Privacy International has pointed out that

> in some of the other countries where MYSTIC is implemented (the Bahamas, Mexico and the Philippines), MYSTIC required 'contracted

services for its "operational sustainment"'; this is not the case for Kenya however. It is unclear what if any role the government of Kenya as well as telecommunication and communication providers played in the deployment of MYSTIC.[8]

What is the significance of this for Kenyan residents and citizens? Kenyan Internet and smartphone usage has mushroomed over the past several years. The Communications Commission of Kenya (CCK) reported that, as of June 2015, 83.9 per cent of Kenyan residents had access to a mobile phone, while 69 per cent of the population (29.6 million users in total) had access to the Internet. Kenya was the first country in the world with a commonly-used mobile system of money transfers (M-Pesa). This capability allowed many low-waged and slum-dwelling Kenyans to effectively function as though they had a bank account; access to the Internet via smartphones has therefore become an economic necessity for many Kenyans, placing within their reach wider economic opportunities previously denied them. In terms of social and political engagement, Privacy International notes that

> social media is widely used in Kenya. According to a June 2015 report by the Bloggers Association of Kenya (BAKE), social media platforms such as blogs, Twitter and Facebook have 'become an effective tool through which Kenyans can write on topics of interest to them as well as exercise their freedom to free speech.' Popular platforms include Twitter and Facebook, which had 4 million Kenyan users in June 2015. Kenya had over 700,000 confirmed monthly active users on Twitter, the majority of which [sic] accessed Twitter on a daily basis.[9]

The Internet is therefore an increasingly important space for Kenyans economically, politically and socially. Foreign government access to Kenyan citizens' metadata, and potentially to the content of their online communications, is therefore a highly concerning issue that ought at the very least to be a matter of informed public debate in Kenya.

Alongside the US's ability to spy on Kenyan citizens, the Kenyan government's own capacity to directly monitor Kenyans' private online and telecommunications activity is steadily increasing. As with 'securitised' policing and the abuses it can entail (see Chapter 8), the over-reaching US attitude in this respect has created the conditions for key War on Terror allies such as Kenya to enhance their own surveillance and monitoring capacity. The developing capacity of Kenyan and other East African states to monitor their citizens' telecom activities is certainly no less than the capacities we now know the NSA and GCHQ to possess, and in some cases is enshrined in law. Article 31 of the Constitution of Kenya, for instance, enshrines the qualified right to privacy in Kenyan domestic law. However, several Acts of Parliament provide for these qualifications, in the shape of express provisions for counterterrorism-related monitoring of communications and other Internet-related activities. Under s36(1) Prevention of Terrorism Act 2012, a chief inspector of police may apply to court for an Interception or Communications Order either requiring a service provider to intercept and retain specified communications, or to enter any premises and install interception devices to access specified communications. Concerns with these provisions of the Prevention of Terrorism Act 2012 include the lack of definition within the Act; the lack of time limits on surveillance operations; the lack of requirement of a reasonable suspicion that interception will yield evidence in relation to the commission of an offence; and its overall broad and vague definition of the term 'terrorist act'.

The National Intelligence Service Act 2012 also includes a wide provision for surveillance of communications and extraction of records. Under Section 43 of this Act, application for such a warrant can be made for any reason that might 'enable the Service to investigate any threat to national security or to perform any of its functions.' An s43 warrant has a time limit of one month, but is renewable indefinitely.

Following the deaths of sixty-seven people in the 2013 attack on the Westgate Shopping Centre, attributed to Al-Shabaab, a significant expansion of the Kenyan National Intelligence Service's powers was proposed in the Security Laws (Amendment) Bill. Privacy International has commented that 'specifically, [the bill] weakens the legal safeguards pertaining to the interception of communications by police, increases the purposes for which surveillance may be undertaken, and provides for broad powers for the otherwise undefined "National Security Organs" to intercept communications.'[10] In January 2015, several clauses in the bill were struck down by the High Court, and a watered-down version has now been passed into Kenyan law.[11] There is, conversely, currently no data protection legislation in Kenya, the draft Data Protection Bill 2012 not having come into force at the time of writing.

Alongside any activities conducted under the above powers, the Kenyan government is also reportedly engaged in broader monitoring of email traffic, on an unclear legal basis. In March 2012, the Communications Commission of Kenya (CCK) announced the Network Early Warning System (NEWS) operation to monitor incoming and outgoing email traffic. Since May 2011, the National Cohesion and Integration Commission (NCIC) has been working with mobile providers and security agencies to monitor text messages and social networks, ostensibly to reduce hate speech. In the summer of 2014, Safaricom Ltd— 60 per cent government-owned and running mainly on infrastructure provided by Chinese telecommunications company Huawei—was awarded a contract to coordinate emergency responses for a National Surveillance, Communication Command and Control System. Privacy International has commented on this highly concerning scheme:

> while the system, set to be completed in 2016, is billed as a secure way
> for law enforcement to communicate, it will include additional, and

potentially worrying, surveillance capabilities such as video surveillance technology that allows for face recognition and a centralized database to perform analytic and cross-referencing on the images captured.

Privacy International went on to explain that

While the command and control centre is not a communications interception project per se, it is highly problematic from a privacy perspective.

According to the project specifications, the system is a way for police officers to securely communicate and process their responses to incidents with various technical barriers to prevent the interception of law enforcement's communications. The system will run on an independent 4G network, separate from the normal Safaricom network with 80 Base stations (60 in Nairobi, 20 in Mombasa). According to Safaricom, 'it will run on a standalone independent IP network... that will deliver high speed video, voice and data [to] a wide ranging number of secure device[s].' The surveillance network will consist of various types of cameras that will be networked to a central point from which analytics and other functions can be carried out by the National Police Service. Additional capabilities include geolocation through GPS of personnel in the field, an Automatic Vehicle Location System and [sic] 'IP-based video surveillance system on a proposed network for aiding visual surveillance' for law and order, crime control and 'special events like public gatherings, processions etc'.

Police would be able to pick out criminals from the crowd 'with a simple camera image grab.' Without strong safeguards, picking out criminals can quickly turn to politically motivated profiling. Face recognition facilitates religious or ethnic profiling and has in some cases led to the false identification of innocent persons. The temptation to place entire communities and neighbourhoods under potentially disproportionate surveillance subtly reverses the presumption of innocence. In light of episodic roundups of Somali Kenyans and other Muslim communities it is not a remote possibility that even this seemingly benign surveillance technology will be exploited beyond its legal mandate.[12]

Privacy is a qualified rather than an absolute right. Where a state has a set of powers for surveillance entailing the deprivation of a person's right to privacy, the only way to ensure lawfulness and observation of rights is in the proportionate exercise of the corresponding powers. This is different from, and more complex to implement than, the protection of absolute rights such as the right to freedom from torture, where there is no possible defence that could justify any degree of torture. Questions around what this proportionality assessment should comprise (for example: who ought to make it—politicians, spies, police, judges, or a combination of the above? How secret should the deliberations be?) form the core of debates about the proper use of surveillance in societies the world over. In a state like Kenya, and most other East African states, with high levels of corruption and a correspondingly weak rule of law, a further problem lies in how to ensure that such a system, even if it is provided for, could possibly work in the intended way.[13]

There is some evidence among cases discussed earlier in this book that surveillance of Internet-related activities may already have triggered targeting and extrajudicial violations on the part of Kenyan security personnel. One example (see Chapter 8) is the disappearance and extrajudicial execution of Samir Hashim Khan in 2012 (before the Prevention of Terrorism Act came into force). At the time of his death he was facing several charges, including possession of items suggesting support for an organised criminal group, due to his allegedly having downloaded a terrorism-related document onto his mobile phone. Similarly, the storming of the Masjid Musa mosque in November 2014 (see Chapter 8) offered a rather blunt example of Kenyan police techniques for online surveillance: individuals arrested during that incident reported to HAKI Africa that during interrogations at police stations they were forced to supply details of their email accounts, including passwords.

Concerns over the Kenyan government's powers to compel production of private data from telecom companies can also be linked to the Kampala (Uganda) bombings of July 2010. A third unexploded bomb was found in Kampala, in a bag with a mobile phone found, on investigation, to have been used frequently to call a phone belonging to a young man, Mohamed. Mohamed was arrested in the middle of the night by members of the Kenyan Anti-Terror Police Unit (ATPU) and taken to its head-quarters. He was interrogated about the phone, which he maintained he had bought second hand from a dealer in Eastleigh just a couple of weeks previously. He was then forced to point out the phone dealer to his captors and the two men were rendered without judicial process to Kampala, where they were abusively interrogated for over a year about mobile phone records for a period that they both maintained to be before either of them had come into contact with the phone in question. This explanation appears eventually to have been accepted, since both men were unconditionally released in September 2012.[14]

There are also examples of surveillance powers being used against civil society more widely. Then-International Criminal Court Chief Prosecutor Luis Moreno Ocampo and key prosecution witnesses in the ICC prosecution of multiple Kenyan politicians claimed that their computers were hacked, resulting in several witnesses being threatened and intimidated into withdrawing their evidence—a significant factor in the eventual collapse of the prosecution's case.[15] Other human rights groups have also complained of unlawful surveillance of human rights defenders carrying out their activities. Peace Brigades International stated in 2012 that 'incidences of surveillance by state and non-state actors have been reported. Offices have been raided or burgled and computers hacked, and several organisations suspected that their phones were being tapped.'[16]

Regarding practical capabilities, hacking tools manufactured and sold by private European companies are believed by researchers to be in the hands of the Kenyan state. In July 2015, WikiLeaks published documents taken from the networks of the Italian malware company Hacking Team, revealing that Kenyan agents had been liaising with the company in 2014 over possible procurement of its 'Remote Control System', a piece of equipment that allows a user to remotely penetrate and control a target's computer or phone, access all their files, and commandeer the microphone and camera so as to use the device as a bug. In this instance, Kenya did not purchase anything from Hacking Team, but during the negotiations Kenyan officers did, on the off chance, ask Hacking Team to demonstrate their hacking credentials by shutting down *Kahawa Tungu*, a blog highlighting corruption and other wrongdoings by the Kenyan government. Hacking Team refused.[17]

As it turned out, this may well have been an attempt to get some free aid, with no intention of taking the contract forward: subsequent investigations by the University of Toronto's Citizen Lab showed that at around this time Kenya did in fact purchase a similar piece of equipment, the powerful surveillance software FinFisher, from Hacking Team's rivals, Gamma International.[18]

Gamma International is a corporation with branches in Andover, Britain and Munich, Germany. It is also a subsidiary of the Gamma Group, a shadowy group of companies that specialises in manufacturing surveillance and monitoring equipment, registered in the British Virgin Islands, and owned by a British man with Lebanese connections called William Louthean Nelson. The group's spokesman is one Martin Muensch, a German former hacker. According to *The Guardian*,

Nelson set up a UK company in 2007 on an Andover industrial estate to make and sell Finfisher—a so-called Trojan which can remotely spy on a victim's computer by pretending to be a routine software update. He set up a parallel, more covert company with a similar name, registered in the BVI, via an agency in Singapore, using his father's address at

Winterbourne Earls, near Andover. He also sells to the Middle East via premises in Beirut. He ran into controversy last year when secret police in Egypt and Bahrain were alleged to have obtained Finfisher, which he denies knowingly supplying to them.[19]

This has been Gamma's greatest achievement: knowingly or unknowingly, to endow governments, law enforcement agencies and security forces around the world, many with questionable human rights records, with powers normally reserved for the American NSA, and Britain's GCHQ.

13

BIG BROTHER INC.

When I first saw the FinFisher promotional videos, I laughed incredulously and at the same time felt very, very scared. Now all over YouTube following WikiLeaks's publication of brochures from the product's developers, Gamma International, these films are at once terrifying and absolutely ridiculous.[1] Ridiculous because the terrible electronic background music and the strange, geeky graphics appear like some kind of lo-fi bedroom creation of a teenager with a morbid imagination and too much time on his hands. Terrifying because these products actually exist, and are sold to any government or law enforcement agency willing to pay. Gamma's FinFisher Suite is one of many similar sets of intrusive surveillance products that have appeared on the open market during the 2010s.

According to contemporary definitions, FinFisher is a cyber weapon, meaning it contains 'computer code that is used, or designed to be used, with the aim of threatening or causing physical, functional, or mental harm to structures, systems, or living beings.'[2] What I learned from the FinFisher promotional videos and from subsequent conversations with researchers who have studied the product closely is that this technology acts like a kind of controlled Trojan virus. Once it has gained access to a target's computer or phone, that machine is essentially owned by the person or government who sent it. The microphone and camera are commandeered so that the machine acts like a kind of bugging device carried around willingly (yet unknowingly) by the target. All content on the machine becomes fully accessible, and the product enables those surveilling to monitor live keystrokes, meaning that encryption technologies can be bypassed either through recording the original keystrokes prior to encryption, or by gaining access to passwords.

Other technologies similar to FinFisher include a suite of products from the Italian outfit Hacking Team. Research groups such as the University of Toronto's Citizen Lab and Privacy International have carried out groundbreaking research to help us understand this industry's value and the extent of its global reach. However, the industry is constantly changing, and continues to operate largely in the shadows, so it is impossible fully to know its true reach. The explosion of this shadowy business is a direct result of the increasing securitisation of the Internet and of cyber space. This development of a global 'cyber-industrial complex' has been led in conceptual and strategic terms by the United States, and has strong interlinkages with the development of the global War on Terror.

Since FinFisher's public exposure in 2011, it has been mired in controversy. Writing in *The Verge*, Amar Toor and Russell Brandon explain that 'FinFisher had become a kind of bogeyman in the security community since brochures advertising the software's capabilities popped up in a Wikileaks drop in December of 2011.' As explained in Chapter 12, Finfisher is a powerful tool sold by Gamma International that allows for users to carry out invasive digital intrusion techniques. The company maintains that it only supplies to legitimate governments and law enforcement agencies, and does not support human rights abuses. However, FinFisher has been implicated in several high-profile cases of purported misuse by states with weak rule of law and bad human rights records. In 2012, an investigation by researchers from various organisations found FinFisher to have penetrated the computers of Bahrain's top law firms, journalists, and democracy activists based both in Bahrain and the UK between 2010 and 2012.[3] Further research by Citizen Lab has identified FinFisher servers in states around the world including Ethiopia, a case-study of which provides perhaps the best evidence for why such technology should not be in the hands of dictatorships and other undemocratic regimes.[4]

In 2014, Citizen Lab research revealed the targeting, using FinFisher, of a group of diaspora Ethiopian political dissidents who had been granted asylum in locations around the world following their criminalisation under Ethiopia's Anti-Terrorism Proclamation and subsequent persecution.[5] The Electronic Frontier Foundation, who filed a lawsuit for one of the victims, one 'Mr Kidane', reported on their website that 'an American citizen living in Maryland has sued the Ethiopian government for infecting his computer with secret spyware, wiretapping his private Skype calls, and monitoring his entire family's every use of the computer for a period of months.'

According to the foundation, their client had fled to the US from Ethiopia more than twenty years previously. Mr Kidane's computer was hacked after he was sent a fake email with an infected Word attachment. When he clicked on the attachment, FinSpy (a component of the FinFisher suite) 'was surreptitiously downloaded onto his computer from a server located at an Ethiopian IP address.' The programme then took control of his computer to record everything that happened on it, and sent copies of communications and content, including Skype calls, 'to a command and control server located in Ethiopia and controlled by the government.'[6]

Subsequent research has identified at least two further Ethiopian dissidents whose devices were infected with FinFisher by the Ethiopian government, in locations around the world. One victim I interviewed in London, Tadesse Kersmo, eloquently described his sense of violation when he learned that the government from which he had fled had commandeered his computer and had been using it to spy on him and his family in his new home in London. However disturbing that sense of intrusion was for Tadesse, it did not compare to his sense of fear and guilt that his hacked communications may have been used to target vulnerable activists still in Ethiopia.[7] According to Human Rights Watch,

> Information gleaned from telecom and Internet sources is regularly used against Ethiopians arrested for alleged anti-government activities. During interrogations, police show suspects lists of phone calls and are questioned about the identity of callers, particularly foreign callers. They play recorded phone conversations with friends and family members. The information is routinely obtained without judicial warrants. While this electronic 'evidence' appears to be used mostly to compel suspects to confess or to provide information, some recorded emails and phone calls have been submitted as evidence in trials under the repressive Anti-Terrorism Proclamation.[8]

It is publicly known that FinFisher and Hacking Team's Remote Control suite have been used to attack Ethiopian civil society activists since at least 2013. Despite this negative publicity and analysis of the human rights costs by groups such as Human Rights Watch, these hacking activities have not ceased, and manufacturers appear to be continuing to sell their wares to the Ethiopian government. On 9 March 2015, Citizen Lab published a report suggesting that new attempts had been made by Ethiopia to hack into the computers of employees of the independent Ethiopian Satellite Television (ESAT), based in the United States.[9]

Ethiopia and Kenya are not the only East African states known to have been buying surveillance capabilities on the open market. In October 2015, Privacy International revealed that in December 2011 Gamma Group reportedly trained four Ugandan agents to use FinFisher. On 19 and 20 January 2012, the Privacy International report claimed, two Gamma officials had met with senior intelligence officials in Kampala and briefed them on FinFisher's capabilities in an 'IT Intrusion Seminar'.

FinFisher was the 'backbone' of a secret operation to spy on leading opposition members, activists, elected officials, intelligence insiders and journalists following the 2011 election, which President Museveni [won] following evidence of vote-buying and misuse of state funds.

The Police and military deployed the spyware specifically to 'crush...civil disobedience' and 'cra[ck] down [on] the rising influence of the opposition' by 'blackmailing them', according a secret briefing document prepared for President Museveni.

[...]

On 13 January 2012, President Museveni launched Operation Fungua Macho ('open your eyes') by military radio message, according to the documents.

Covert FinFisher 'access points' were installed within Parliament and key government institutions. Actual and suspected government opponents were targeted in their homes. Hotels in Kampala, Entebbe and Masaka were also compromised to facilitate infection of targets' devices. The CMI solicited state funds to 'bribe' collaborators to facilitate infections and intended to use collected information to 'blackmail' targets.

At the same time, the report noted, the Ugandan government had been inviting tenders for the development of its own communications monitoring centre:

In 2013, the inter-agency Joint Security/ICT Technical committee invited bids for the project from seven technology companies based in

China, Israel, Italy, Poland and the United Kingdom, in another government briefing document from another source.

Some familiar names were on the shortlist to supply the monitoring centre—Huawei and ZTE, NICE and Verint—and some less well known contenders—Macro System and RESI Group. And, of course, Gamma Group International. Later in 2013, Gamma's representative in Munich, Stephan Oelkers, returned to Kampala at least three times.

Fast forward two years. The Ugandan Government appears closer to finalising plans to purchase a monitoring centre. According to internal emails of surveillance technology company Hacking Team, NICE Systems was one of the frontrunners for the project. The Uganda Police was also looking to buy Hacking Team's intrusion malware through a trusted contact—a former Presidential IT advisor and, worryingly, an important media mogul.[10]

Uganda was apparently not the only East African state trying to access Hacking Team's products via local moguls, as evidenced in a series of emails released by WikiLeaks on 8 July 2015. The emails show an exchange in October and November 2012 between Ismail Dualeh, 'chief technical officer' at Somtel, the main Somali telecom provider. Dualeh writes that he was given the Hacking Team contact information by Hagai Frenkel of NICE Systems, stating,

> we have request from our government to check emails in case they suspect any users and we have advised them we can support them with trojan horses therefore we need to add this capability our the network we are currently testing various solutions and we want to evaluate your solution as well [sic].'[11]

Hacking Team's email response further illuminates the capabilities of its tools, the mode of cooperation with potential clients, and its policy of selling to 'government, law enforcement and security organisations only':

> 'Dear Mr. Dualeh,
>
> Many thanks for contacting us and for the interest in our technology.

RCS is designed to attack, infect and monitor target PCs and Smart-phones in a stealth way, including its location.

Once a target is infected, RCS allows you to access a variety of information, including:

Skype traffic (VoIP, chat), keystrokes (all Unicode languages), mails, messages, target positioning, files, screenshots, microphone eavesdropped data, camera snapshots, etc.

Supported PC platforms are: Windows XP/Vista/7 (32 & 64 bit) and Mac-OS.

The Smartphones' platforms are Windows Mobile, iPhone, Symbian, Blackberry and Android.

Would you mind having a look at the two RCS videos on our website? http://www.hackingteam.it/index.php/remote-control-system

As you can imagine, our policy allows us to sell the product to Government, Law Enforcement and Security Organizations only.

Regarding your enquiry, please note that we do not provide geographical representation; our approach is to work side by side with a local partner (like you) on every specific deal.

This means that, if you have a potential business opportunity, we will give you protection on such client for 1 year.

Obviously, in order to understand, if we can move on, we need to know which agency we are talking about.

If everything is positive, we will proceed with the signature of our Non Disclosure Agreement and we'll organize a meeting with the potential client.'[12]

Ismail Duale's response the following day confirms that 'we play as security organization for the government, when they need any security we provide it to them. Therefore I hope we will be able to sign the NDA and have trial of the RCS [sic].'[13]

There is no publicly-known information detailing the operational use of these tools in Somalia. In Ethiopia and Uganda, however, their deployment clearly corresponds at least in part to wider attempts to limit political dissent, stifle the free media and curtail free speech. In Ethiopia, the technologies have also been used to persecute those who have fled Ethiopia and become refugees elsewhere, and to carry out politically-motivated prosecutions of civil society actors under domestic counterterrorism legislation.[14] Both Uganda's and Ethiopia's use of FinFisher, Hacking Team, and other forms of surveillance and telecoms monitoring evidently go far beyond the terms of the War on Terror as it is normally envisaged by its architects and proponents in the United States, and such technology is being used by autocratic governments worldwide to maintain control by directly stifling democratic freedoms and attacking human rights. Dominant US security narratives, known practices relating to global surveillance activities, and extensive counterterrorism funding to these states, all provide a clear *carte blanche* for partner states to deploy their powers in a discriminatory fashion, within a legislative framework of unfair security and counterterrorism laws.

14

BETWEEN TWO FIRES

It's a July afternoon in 2016 and I am in Amsterdam, sitting in a café by a canal just around the corner from the house where Anne Frank spent her years in hiding from the Nazis and where she wrote her famous diary. A teenaged Jewish diarist with aspirations of becoming a journalist, Anne spent two years in a tiny hidden apartment on Prinsengracht in central Amsterdam. After Anne and her family were betrayed by an unknown informant, the apartment was raided and they were taken into custody. Anne died in the Bergen-Belsen concentration camp in February or March 1945, just a month or two before its liberation by the Americans in April 1945.

Being in Anne Frank's neighbourhood in Amsterdam on this glorious day, every detail—light glancing off the canal water, bicycle bells, boats chugging through the water and the low buzz of conversation, smoke from my neighbour's cigarette and the taste of my fish soup—appears heightened and precious. I imagine how beside herself Anne would have been given the opportunity to be part of such a scene just minutes from her place of hiding. And I imagine what that dark period in Amsterdam's history must have felt like to her.

Anne Frank has been on my mind of late because, for over a year, I've been helping another family in hiding, the Mumins. This family is not Jewish; they're Somali, and they're in hiding in Nairobi. The Kenyan government is demonstrably not comparable to a Nazi administration, yet as we have seen (see Chapter 11), Nairobi is increasingly a deeply hostile and frightening place for ethnic Somalis, who are liable to be ethnically profiled, arbitrarily arrested, detained and sometimes flown back to an uncertain fate in Somalia.

In addition to this peril facing all Somalis in Kenya, the Mumin family faces another imminent danger: Al-Shabaab operatives in Kenya. Abdalle Mumin is a well-known Somali journalist who regularly worked with international media such as *The Wall Street Journal*, *The Guardian* and Al-Jazeera. After he covered a series of stories relating to Al-Shabaab, he received death threats and attempts on his life, forcing him to flee Mogadishu for Nairobi, where he was eventually able to bring his wife and children, ranging in age from a young baby to a twelve-year-old daughter, to join him.[1] But Al-Shabaab has a strong presence in Kenya, and the threats eventually caught up with Abdalle in Nairobi. The entire family had to go into hiding and have since had to move locations several times due to fears that their cover had been blown.

For the past ten months or so, I've been in touch with Abdalle almost every day. A few months ago, he and his wife went out for provisions for the family, and were nearly arrested by Kenyan police in a random sweep of Somalis. They had to run and hide until the police had gone. Whilst in hiding, the family have also had to get to medical assessments and appointments to progress their resettlement application, but don't have anyone they could trust to be a driver. They've had to find funds to pay the rent on their safe-house, as well as for food, urgent medical services, and transport to their appointments. They're completely isolated because they are caught between two fires: the increasing xeno-phobia of many Kenyans towards Somalis, and a threat that comes from within the Somali community itself—Al-Shabaab. They are citizens of a state with no ability to protect them.

I cannot imagine what this experience is like for Abdalle and his family. For me, it is both frustrating and sobering. I am almost completely powerless to protect them from those who wish them harm—I can only help with the day-to-day problems, and try in some way to be there for them. I hope that this sup-port, and the knowledge that someone cares, will help them to endure their situation. As the days pass, a positive resolution that first appeared to be slowly materialising now seems further away than ever.

Back in Amsterdam, I've come to Anne Frank's house directly from the International Criminal Court in The Hague. Although it's fairly new, the ICC is emblematic of a decades-long journey involving the creation of a set of international human rights and humanitarian institutions and standards, whose foundations rose from the carnage of the Second World War. The word 'geno-cide' was coined by a Jewish jurist grappling to find the lan-guage, and help sketch a legal framework, to do justice to the magnitude of what had just happened to Anne Frank and approximately six million other European Jews.

Comparing genocides, especially when one remains only a possibility, is a doomed exercise on many levels. However, it is not an exaggeration to say that the situation for many Somalis in East Africa is increasingly catastrophic.

Somalis as an ethnic group—particularly in Kenya, where many of them are citizens and have lived for generations—are now so othered by mainstream politics, the media, and in turn by many other Kenyans that their daily existence is fraught with danger. Somalis are often discriminated against by the police, disappeared, arbitrarily detained and extorted. They are now routinely coerced into leaving Kenya for an unknown future in Somalia, the broken state from which many of those without Kenyan citizenship originally fled. Meanwhile, those who are Kenyan citizens of Somali ethnicity are, routinely, denied their citizenship papers by the Kenyan authorities, and then de facto denied many of the rights that would otherwise naturally flow from being able to demonstrate that citizenship.

The irony of Abdalle's situation is that one limb of the danger he faces in Nairobi—the risk of arbitrary arrest, detention, extortion and possible return to Somalia by Kenyan police and other authorities—comes as a direct result of the Kenyan government's out-of-control counterterrorism policies, thuggishly turning its attention to Somali refugees and apparently meting out a form of misguided collective punishment against this group in retaliation for a string of terror attacks carried out by Al-Shabaab on Kenyan territory. Yet Abdalle only found himself in Kenya because Al-Shabaab wants his head—precisely as a result of his courageous reporting as a member of the free global media, extending his journalism to objectively cover the organisation's workings despite the personal risks this entailed.

Thus, Abdalle and his family are at an intersection of a set of problems that flow directly from the region's increasing state of securitisation. The risk to them in Kenya is heightened by their Somali ethnicity, meaning they are more at risk of xenophobic and discriminatory attacks by Kenyan authorities carried out in the name of counterterrorism. But that is by no means the whole story. Securitisation and the shrinking space for human rights are long-standing themes of the War on Terror. The threats do not wholly emanate from groups like Al-Shabaab, but also from the governments and security forces that ought to be protecting these rights and principles—whose entire rationale for waging the War on Terror revolves around protecting such rights and freedoms.

Abdalle described his own situation as a reporter working in Somalia in a blog post published in May 2015, during his first stint of hiding, entitled 'Somalia: A Threat By Any Name'. He explained how the independent media in Somalia is in an impossible situation, with the Somali government on the one side, and Al-Shabaab on the other. Both sides are attempting to control the media, giving instructions that compromise independent reporting and place journalists in danger. For example, at one point, Abdalle reports, Somali authorities issued an edict to media houses ordering that Al-Shabaab be referred to as UGUS, an acronym for a Somali phrase that translates as 'the group that massacres Somali people'. Al-Shabaab then issued a counter-edict ordering journalists to refer to the Somali government as UGUS, an acronym for an adaptation of the original phrase, altered by Al-Shabaab to mean 'the group that humiliates Somali people'.[2]

In Abdalle's case, the United States, specifically the State Department, was initially responsive, and he and his family applied for resettlement in the US, via the US embassy, in 2016. By the second half of 2016, they appeared to have been provisionally approved for resettlement, and were undergoing security and other checks. This hope was dashed on 30 January 2017, with President Trump's issuance of the now famous 'refugee travel ban'—an executive order suspending the entry of all refugees into the United States, purportedly for reasons of national security. At the same time, Trump issued another executive order banning entry to the US by citizens of seven states, including Somalia. With a couple of signatures, President Trump abandoned the US's status as the most welcome of all nations to refugees, and adopted an approach akin to that of Kenya, described earlier, which problematises entire groups, particularly refugees, on spurious national security grounds. Abdalle and his family were issued a double whammy: banned because of both their refugee status, and their Somali nationality.

Abdalle Mumin's case is perhaps 'the' counter-example to President Trump's claim that these bans were necessary for US national security. The facts present a painful absurdity: a journalist who had become a refugee as a direct result of his courageous reporting on Al-Shabaab in the international media, and who was objectively assessed to be at serious risk of assassination by the terrorist group, has been denied safety as a direct result of US counterterrorism policy.

The 'refugee travel ban' was subsequently lifted by a federal court. At the time of writing, there have been several rounds of bans and court orders, leading to continued uncertainty over US policy; in the meantime, no refugees in the US resettlement system are currently being transferred to the US unless their case was fully approved before the first travel ban came into force. Abdalle Mumin's case has joined the queue of thousands of 'urgent' resettlement cases for which the UNHCR has been trying to find some kind of alternative solution. These developments in US policy mirror the worrying securitisation of refugee issues in East Africa, and suggest the formalisation of a kind of blunt, collective punishment approach to counterterrorism that has arguably characterised some earlier US tactics but has never before been systematised.

As well as the refugee issues, the US's past actions and policies in the wider War on Terror have arguably set the scene for both narrowing and making increasingly dangerous the space within which journalists like Abdalle are able to operate. The US has helped to create a culture in which representatives of the free press can be attacked and undermined from all sides in the name of security, indeed one in which the securitisation of geographic, conceptual and cyber space increasingly precludes the possibility of a truly free and independent media.

An early indicator of this trend came with US attacks on Al-Jazeera journalists and infrastructure, apparently in response to the station's coverage of the US invasion of Afghanistan, where Al-Jazeera was not embedded with the US military. On

13 November 2001, a US missile hit the Al-Jazeera office in Kabul, destroying the building, although no staff were injured or killed in the attack.[3] This was swiftly followed by the arrest and detention of Sudanese Al-Jazeera journalist Sami al-Hajj. He was eventually represented by Clive Stafford Smith at Reprieve, who characterised his detention as part of a wider strategy to undermine Al-Jazeera; the lawyer has stated that in over 100 interrogation sessions, the US military focused not on the allegations against him, but rather on turning him into an informant against Al-Jazeera.[4]

By his own account, al-Hajj had been arrested on 15 December whilst crossing the Pakistani-Afghan border at Quetta, en route to cover the Afghanistan conflict for Al-Jazeera. He was detained for twenty-three days at the border before being taken to US prisons at Bagram Airforce Base and Kandahar, where he was interrogated about his work for Al-Jazeera and falsely accused of having interviewed Osama bin Laden. Eventually he was transferred to Guantánamo Bay. He was released without charge on 1 May 2008, after spending 480 days on hunger strike.[5]

Al-Jazeera was publicly attacked by high-level figures in the US administration during the Bush Jr era, and former British Home Secretary David Blunkett has claimed in memoirs published in 2006 that in late March 2003 he advised then-Prime Minister Tony Blair to bomb Al-Jazeera's transmitter in Baghdad. In the event, on 8 April 2003, an electricity generator in the Al-Jazeera office in Baghdad was struck by a US missile. Reporter Tareq Ayyoub was killed and another staff member wounded in the ensuing fire. On the same day, a US tank shelled the Palestine Hotel, which was 'home and office to more than 100 unembedded international journalists operating in Baghdad at the time.' The shell killed two cameramen: Taras Protsyuk of Reuters and Jose Couso of Spain's Telecinco.

Al-Jazeera noted that 'in a chilling statement at the end of that bloody day in Iraq, then-Pentagon spokesperson Victoria Clarke spelled out the Pentagon's policy on journalists who were not embedded with US troops when she warned them that Baghdad "is not a safe place. You should not be there.'" These words proved prescient. The Al-Jazeera report cited research by the Committee to Protect Journalists (CPJ) suggesting that 'at least 150 journalists and 54 media support workers were killed in Iraq from the US-led invasion in March 2003 to the declared end of the war in December 2011', making the nine-year US invasion and occupation the 'deadliest war for journalists in recorded history.'[6]

In the years since the US occupation ended, the Iraqi government has failed to investigate any deaths of journalists during the war years, meaning that the rate of impunity in Iraq for attacks on journalists stands at 100 per cent. It is against this historical backdrop that Islamic State has carried out its own high-profile assault on the media within its territory. As of June 2017, twenty-nine journalists have reportedly been killed in Iraq since 2013, most of them in the city of Mosul.[7] According to the CPJ, 'dozens more journalists are missing in areas of Syria and Iraq that are controlled by Islamic State. They are likely held captive by the militants, but their fates are unknown.'[8]

The US government's attitude to national security journalists closer to home demonstrates a continued belief that purported national security concerns trump journalists' first amendment rights to protect their sources. The Obama administration, in the words of Jack Shafer in *POLITICO Magazine*, pursued national security leaks 'with a vehemence unmatched by any previous administration, using the Espionage Act to prosecute whistleblowers who leak to journalists more times than all previous administrations combined. ... He claims to helm "the most transparent administration in history" while bending government policies and practices towards secrecy.'[9]

From 2009 to July 2013, six US government employees and two contractors were charged or convicted under the 1917 Espionage Act following unauthorised leaks or whistleblowing activities.

Some of these cases were opened under the Bush administration, but the Obama administration chose to continue all of them.[10] The Obama-era crackdown also targeted journalists:

> Reporters' phone logs and e-mails were secretly subpoenaed and seized by the Justice Department in two of the investigations, and a Fox News reporter was accused in an affidavit for one of those subpoenas of being 'an aider, abettor and/or conspirator' of an indicted leak defendant, exposing [the reporter] to possible prosecution for doing his job as a journalist.[11]

Veteran *New York Times* reporter James Risen was also ordered by a federal appeals court to testify against CIA whistleblower defendant Jeffrey Sterling or face being sent to jail, in lengthy proceedings spanning the Bush and Obama administrations.[12]

In June 2013, McClatchy reported on a secretive US government initiative called the Insider Threat Program that equated media leaks with espionage. The programme was reportedly launched by the Obama administration in October 2011, after Bradley (now Chelsea) Manning downloaded hundreds of thousands of US government documents from a classified network and sent them to WikiLeaks. The Insider Threat Program, McClatchy reported, was essentially an internal surveillance operation amounting to 'a government-wide crackdown on security threats that requires federal employees to keep closer tabs on their co-workers and exhorts managers to punish those who fail to report their suspicions.' It extended 'beyond the US national security bureaucracies to most federal departments and agencies nationwide, including the Peace Corps, the Social Security Administration and the Education and Agriculture departments.' The programme reportedly relies partly on 'behavior profiles'; employees and contractors are compelled to turn themselves and others in for infractions, and urged to look out for 'high-risk persons or behaviors' among their colleagues. Penalties for failing to report can include criminal charges.[13]

Leonard Downie Jr, writing for the Committee to Protect Journalists, cites prominent transparency advocate Steven Aftergood as stating that the Insider Threat Program has 'already created internal surveillance, heightened a degree of paranoia in government and made people conscious of contacts with the public, advocates, and the press.' He continues,

> none of these measures is anything like the government controls, censorship, repression, physical danger, and even death that journalists and their sources face daily in many countries throughout the world ... but the United States, with its unique constitutional guarantees of free speech and a free press—essential to its tradition of government accountability—is not any other country.[14]

As we have seen, during its wars in Iraq and Afghanistan, for foreign journalists beyond the reach of its constitution, the United States demonstrably created just these conditions for continuing government controls, censorship, repression and physical imperilment of journalists. Regarding Somalia, where Abdalle Mumin lived and worked, the connection is not quite so direct. Long-standing US policy on Somalia has meant fewer US boots on the ground and more covert operations relying on local partners. There has never been a US occupation of Somalia, and successive Somali governments have therefore been key counter-terrorism partners, receiving funding and support for carrying out counterterrorism activities in coordination with various foreign and multilateral forces and agencies. In his blog, Abdalle noted that 'propaganda has been part of the war between al-Shabaab and the Somali government for years', as the two parties vie to control the media.[15]

In 2011, I met another Somali journalist, who had been detained in the Mogadishu secret prison documented by *The Nation* (see Chapter 5). He, too, was a Somali journalist forced, in the quest for journalistic integrity, to navigate between the twin threats of the Somali authorities and Al-Shabaab. In May

2016, Human Rights Watch released a seventy-four-page report detailing killings, threats and detentions of journalists in Somalia since 2014. The report states that

> both the Somali government and the Islamist armed group Al-Shabaab are using abusive tactics to sway media coverage[,] including arrests and forced closures of media outlets, threats, and occasionally, criminal charges. Al-Shabaab has targeted journalists as part of its campaign against the Somali government and for reporting deemed unfavorable. Government authorities have failed to adequately investigate and prosecute those responsible for abuses, leaving journalists to live in fear. ... Each side has pressured journalists about their reporting, manipulated casualty figures, and obstructed reporting, greatly affecting the media environment. Dozens of journalists have fled into exile over the last decade.[16]

It is easy to see that the Somali government's 'with us or against us' attitude to the media in its War on Terror resonates strongly with that of successive US administrations. Under Obama's presidency, a 1 June 2012 Defense Department strategy for the Insider Threat Program, obtained by McClatchy, instructed officials to 'hammer this fact home[:] leaking is tantamount to aiding the enemies of the United States.'[17] President Trump's compromised attitude to the idea of a free media has been well covered elsewhere,[18] though at the time of writing coherent policy to reflect it has yet to emerge.

Back on Prinzengracht, evening approaches and I must leave to catch my plane. My phone pings and it's Abdalle, telling me that he just received a call from the US resettlement centre. His family are to go in person to receive their decision on Tuesday. It seems fitting finally to learn of an almost-conclusion to the Mumins' ordeal now, in this street. Once again I think of the Franks, made stateless under Nazi laws, their application for resettlement in the United States turned down because of a US government policy that amounted to a blanket ban on German Jews, refusing resettlement of anyone with close family remaining in Germany on the basis of a perceived risk that they could be blackmailed into spying for the Nazis. At this moment in time, it seems to me that, at least in one respect, US refugee policy has evolved. Several months later, with the Mumins' resettlement application apparently permanently stalled, words fail.

Anne Frank was a talented writer, and in a way she was already the journalist she confided to her diary that she wanted to become. She reported her experience, for us, from another time. One of her many enduring legacies has involved the renovation of the former Frank family residence on Merwedeplein, Amsterdam, where they lived from December 1933 until they went into hiding in July 1942. Since 2005, the apartment has been rented to the Stichting Amsterdam Vluchstad (part of the Network of Refugee Cities for Writers in Exile), and each year the Anne Frank House organisation invites a foreign writer to live and work in the residence, free from political constraints. The first resident writer was the young Algerian novelist and poet El-Mahdi Acherdour.[19]

For Abdalle, both basic safety and security for himself and his family, as well as that freedom to write without political pressure from governments and violent non-state actors, currently remain beyond his reach.

15

ENDINGS

I wrote in the Introduction that this book's nature as a fractured series of descriptions and the gaps in its explanatory narrative are, unavoidably, a product of the complex system of official secrecy surrounding national security matters, particularly in the United States and the United Kingdom. These restrictions and controls on who is permitted access to facts—and the implications for the quality, and reliability, of those facts that may never be exposed to the disinfectant of sunlight—goes to the heart of whether there can ever be a full public understanding of torture and other potential human rights violations occurring in the national security context.

The peculiarities and challenges for those seeking to use legal systems to access justice in this way cannot be fully explored here. In states such as the US and the UK, well-functioning legal systems, combined with the obvious hurdles for those seeking to gather evidence in order to initiate some form of claim, engender a sophisticated system of secrecy and information controls that skews the power balance from the outset, making it extremely difficult for claimants alleging state abuses in the national security context to succeed in court. In the US, the 'state secrets doctrine' has successfully blocked all civil claims against the state for alleged wrongs committed in US extraterritorial detention.

Eventually, Suleiman Abdallah became the lead claimant in a landmark US federal court case against James Mitchell and Bruce Jessen, the contract psychologists believed to have designed the CIA interrogation programme.[1] This case, which was settled in favour of the claimants in 2018, was the only legal avenue available to Suleiman in the US. All other cases brought by former CIA prisoners against the CIA directly, or other members of the US administration, have been summarily dismissed, on the basis that even a preliminary examination of the merits would risk the disclosure of state secrets.

In the absence of legal avenues in the US, Mohammed Saad Iqbal Madni attempted to bring a legal case in the UK, compelling disclosure of evidence relating to his alleged stop-over on the British territory of Diego Garcia. The case was struck out after the government took a position that for reasons of national security, despite a legal duty to monitor flights in and out of the territory, it could 'neither confirm nor deny' that Madni's plane had stopped for refuelling on British territory.[2]

In states with no secrecy regime for civil proceedings but with weak rule of law, such as Kenya and Uganda, other factors conspire to ensure that in practice, accessing truth, justice and accountability is often out of reach for victims of state violence. Some of the Kenyan victims of the 2007 'border operation' renditions brought a civil claim in Kenya against the Kenyan state, alleging constitutional violations related to their detention and rendition to Ethiopia. In 2011, they were awarded damages by a Kenyan court. The government appealed, and the case now appears to have stalled indefinitely.[3] There have, to date, been no fully human rights-compliant, adequate investigations into the growing epidemic of extrajudicial killings of Muslims on the

Kenyan coast, nor has there been any real Kenyan government follow-up into the plight of Somali refugees returned to Somalia since 2012.

Mohammed al-Asad brought a case against Djibouti at the African Commission on Human and People's Rights,[4] a regional human rights court that is supposed to provide a supranational forum to hold African governments to account. The case took many years and was ruled inadmissible in 2014.[5] This decision was subsequently reversed and the parties were ordered to brief on the merits. There was a hearing on this case in Mauritania in May 2018 and the case remains, at the time of writing, pending. Unfortunately the content of the 2018 hearing is not public. Before seeing any justice, Al-Asad sadly passed away in 2016.[6]

In cases of extrajudicial killing by drones, such as those of British citizens Bilal Berjawi and Mohammed Sakr, the extent, if any, of British involvement in their deaths remains unknown. The legal justifications and procedures in the US and the UK for planning, initiating, authorising and carrying out drone strikes against those believed to represent national security threats remain murky, and are not a matter of public record or debate.

Similarly, in the realm of digital surveillance, with its growing implications for East African citizens, the absence of real public debate is perpetuated by the national security justifications made by states. Understanding the mechanisms by which people may have been surveilled, let alone gathering reliable evidence, is a task for experts, well beyond the abilities of average citizens. The issue is also complicated by the proportional nature of the right to privacy: most people agree that states ought to have some surveillance powers, but these must be used properly, and against the right people. How this should happen is the million-dollar question. Systems for monitoring this and keeping the public informed without creating operational risks are hard to imagine in apparently well-functioning democracies, let alone in regimes that are highly corrupt or have overly centralised power structures, like many in East Africa. Where the surveillance is being carried out by a foreign government beyond its own borders, as with the US and its global surveillance capacities, or with technology and support provided by foreign, private companies, many further questions arise.

All this goes to say that the War on Terror in its various iterations raises many more questions than it answers, and that our systems of domestic and global justice and governance, including the level of public debate surrounding them, may not yet be functioning quite as they could be. As a result, important matters of public policy, such as the circumstances in which targeted killings and surveillance are carried out, are not accessible or understood by very many people. It is well accepted that human rights abuses such as systemic torture, unlawful detention and killings, and disappearances must first be publicly known and understood before affected societies can move on. The 'national security' card often serves to mute this imperative.

APPENDIX 1

APPENDICES OF DOCUMENTS

Rendition flight logs for mass renditions from Kenya to Somalia, obtained by the Nairobi-based Muslim Human Rights Forum through litigation in Kenya (reproduced with permission from Al-Amin Kimathi)

African Express Airways

PASSENGER MANIFEST
(I.C.A.O ANNEX 9, APPENDIX 2.)

Aircraft _____5Y–AND_____ Flight No. _XU527_ Date _20/1/07_
(Registration Marks and nationality)

Point of Lading _____HAIROBI_____ Port of Unlading _____MUGADISHU_____
(Place and Country) (Place and Country)

SURNAME AND INITIALS	SEX				FOR USE BY OWNER OR OPERATOR ONLY	PCS.	WT	FOR OFFICIAL USE ONLY
	M	F	C	I				
1. HUSSEIN MH	✓							
2. SAKATA SAKHAT	✓							
3. SAID CHIFA	✓							
4. NUR GIRARE	✓							
5. SHARIFF JAMA	✓							
6. SIIMA SOLIMAN	✓							
7. ABDI ABDULLAHI	✓							
8. ESFALET CHAN		✓						
7. OSMAN MOHA	✓							
10. SALAH IDRIS	✓							
11. SASANG NGANA	✓							
12. JAMAL ABDAL	✓							
13. AHMED HASSAN	✓							
13. MOH MAULIANI	✓							
14. AHID MOHD	✓							
15. TAFA DAISA	✓							
16. LAMA JAKAL	✓							
17. BABAH LAMI	✓							
18. LLICETA TASIN	✓							
19. CLEMPIM CUTUN	✓							
20. IBRAHIM OSMAN	✓							
21. NUR MOHD M	✓							
22. ALI ABDI	✓							
23. ABUKAR HUSEN	✓							
24. ABUKAR AHMED	✓							
25. OSMAN ABDI	✓							
26. MOHD HASSAN	✓							
27. SAGAWA ABDUU	✓							
28. ABDULLAHI MOH	✓							
29. OSMAN SULIMEN	✓							
30. MOHD FARLE	✓							
31. ABU SUFIM	✓							
32. NOHAMAR ADAN	✓							
33. ABDI ADEN AMAD	✓							

APPENDIX 1

African Express Airways

PASSENGER MANIFEST
(I.C.A.O. ANNEX 9. APPENDIX 2.)

Aircraft: 5Y-AXF
(Registration Marks and nationality)

Flight No. AXK527   Date: 27/01/07

Point of Lading: NAIROBI-KENYA   Port of Unlading: MOGADISHU
(Place and Country)   (Place and Country)

S.II NAME AND INITIALS	SEX M	F	C	I	FOR USE BY OWNER OR OPERATOR ONLY	PCS.	WT	FOR OFFICIAL USE ONLY
1 TOWFIK KAMILIA M?	✓							
2 MOHAMED ABSHIR S.	✓							
3 IBRAHIM MOHAMED	✓							
4 USAMA M. AL FAYUM	✓							
5 ISMAEL MUSLEH S	✓							
6 JAMIL ABDULLAHI	✓							
7 KHALID EL AHMED	✓							
8 MUNIER AWADH	✓							
9 AL-NASIE ABDUL A-U	✓							
10 SAFIJA BENAENDI		✓						
11 HELIMA SIMEREH H		✓						
12 JEWHERA KEMALA		✓						
13 SAIDIA HUSSEIN N	✓							
14 MARIAM ALI OMMA		✓						
15 SAINA M. ALI			✓					
16 FATUMA M. ALI			✓					
17 HASIRA MOHAMED			✓					
18 ABDI KADIR M. MAALU	✓							
19 HALIMA BADRONDINE		✓						
20 LUKMAN FAZUL H			✓					
21 ASIYA FAZUL			✓					
22 SUMAIYA FAZUL			✓					
23 OSMAN YASIN	✓							
24 SOPHIA ABDINASIR		✓						
25 MOHAMMED OSMAN			✓					
26 FATUMA OSMAN			✓					
27 SALIM ANOH S	✓							
28 FATUMA CHANDE	✓							
29 KASSIM MUSA	✓							
30 ALI MUSA MBARUS	✓							
31 ABDULLA KITATU T	✓							
32 SAIDI HAMISI	✓							
33 SISALEH ALI TUZA	✓							
34 ABDUL RASHID M	✓							

203

African Express Airways

PASSENGER MANIFEST
(I.C.A.O. ANNEX 9. APPENDIX 2.)

Aircraft STAXF
(Registration Marks and nationality)

Flight No _____ Date 27/01/07

Point of Lading NAIROBI - KENYA
(Place and Country)

Port of Unlading MOGADISHU - SOMALI
(Place and Country)

SURNAME AND INITIALS	SEX				FOR USE BY OWNER OR OPERATOR ONLY	PCS.	WT	FOR OFFICIAL USE ONLY
	M	F	C	I				
HASSAN SHABAN M	✓							
YUSUF ALI HAITAL I	✓							
MUKKI ABDINASURO		✓						
SAFIRA AHMED		W	✓					
IBRAHIM MOHAMED			✓					
ABDALLA AHMED			✓					
MR. S K TUM	✓							
MR. JOHN KOKI	✓							
MR. JOSEPHAT KIRINI	✓							
MR. RICHARD KERUS	✓							
MR. PAUL CHERUYOT	✓							
MR. MICHAEL YEGO	✓							
MR. PETER MULI	✓							
MR. IBRAHIM WANJE	✓							
MR. ZACHARY TALAM	✓							
MR. NIXON KEROS	✓							
MR. NICHLAS KHUVI	✓							
MR. DAVID KMINI	✓							
MR. PAUL KAIKAI	✓							
MR. DANIEL KIMAI	✓							
MR. WILLY MUTAI	✓							

"ZTL"

Bluebird Aviation Limited

GENERAL DECLARATION · INWARD · OUTWARD

Operator: Bluebird Aviation Ltd.
P.O. Box 52382, Nairobi, Kenya,

Aircraft Registration _5Y-VVP_ Date _15/02/07_

Point of Clearance _NAIROBI_ For Entry At _BAIDOA_
(Place & Country) (Place & Country)

ITINERARY OF AIRCRAFT & DECLARATION OF HEALTH

Airport	Departure Date	Airport	Departure Date

Illness (other than air sickness) that has occurred

Aboard during flight _____

For Official Use Only

Details of last disinfectization or sanitary treatment   Time of Departure _____

Date and Time _15/02/07_   Time of Arrival _____

CREW MANIFEST

Surname & Initials	Duties on Board	Nationality	Serial No. & Country of Issuance of Licence or Certificate of Passport
CAPT M. ADAN	CAPTAIN	KENYAN	~1K-31 4C-AC
CAPT. A. NGANGA	Co-PILOT	"	~1K-19 1C-AC

PASSENGER MANIFEST

Surname & Initials	Form	To	For use by Owner or Operator	Official Use Only
SHAH JEHAN TANJUA				
HAMZA CHENIOUF				
MOHAMED EZZOUER				
REZA AFSHER ZADELAN				
I NEJ CHINE				
ASSAD BASSAM SAWWAR				
MOHAMED ODEH MUSTAI				
AJUB ABDIRIZAK				
ADNAN NAJAH NAJJIH				
AMIR MOHAMED MESHAR				
KASSIM MUSA MWARUSI				
ALI MUSA MWARUSI				
ABDALLA KHALFAN IDDIE				
PC RICHARD KORES				
CPL JULIUS LOKALE				
PC MICHAL SEGO				
PC FRODLIN MWENDA				
PC RICHARD MURITA				
PC WESLEY MUTA				
PC STEPHEN MUGETI				

CARGO MANIFEST

Mark No. Of Packages	No. & Type of Packages	Nature of Goods	Form	To	Gross Weight	For use by Operator	Official Use

"ZTL"

Bluebird Aviation Limited
GENERAL DECLARATION · INWARD · OUTWARD
NAIROBI · KENYA

Operator: Bluebird Aviation Ltd.
P.O. Box 52382, Nairobi, Kenya,

Aircraft Registration _5Y-VVP_   Date _15/02/07_

Point of Clearance _NAIROBI_ (Place & Country)   For Entry At _BAIDOA_ (Place & Country)

ITINERARY OF AIRCRAFT & DECLARATION OF HEALTH

Airport	Departure Date	Airport	Departure Date

Illness (other than air sickness) that has occurred

Aboard during flight _____

Details of last disinfectization or sanitary treatment

Date and Time _15/02/07_

For Official Use Only

Time of Departure _____

Time of Arrival _____

CREW MANIFEST

Surname & Initials	Duties on Board	Nationality	Serial No. & Country of Issuance of Licence or Certificate of Passport
CAPT. M. ADAN	CAPTAIN	KENYAN	-K-3196-AE
CAP. A. NGANG	Co-PILOT	"	-K-196-AE

PASSENGER MANIFEST

Surname & Initials	Form	To	For use by Owner or Operator	Official Use Only
SHAH JEHAN TANJUA				
HAMZA CHENIOUI				
MOHAMED EZZOUEK				
REZA AFSHER ZANFLAN				
IFNEJ CHINE				
ASSAD BASSAN SALMAK				
MOHAMED ODIN MUSTAI				
AJUB ABDIRIZAK				
ADNAN NAJAH NAJAH				
AMIR MOHAMED MESFHAR				
KASSIM MUSA MWAKUSI				
ALI MUSA MWAKUSI				
ABDALLA KHALFAN TONDWE				
PC RICHARD KORGI				
CPL JULIUS LOKALE				
PC MICHAEL DEGO				
PC BRODLIN MWENDA				
PC RICHARD NJORIJKA				
PC WESLEY MUTA				
PC STEPHEN MUGETO				

CARGO MANIFEST

Mark No. Of Packages	No. & Type of Packages	Nature of Goods	Form	To	Gross Weight	For use by Operator	Official Use

APPENDIX 2

Photographs of Kenyan police post-mortem documents for Idris Mohamed, taken by HAKI Africa, reproduced with permission from HAKI Africa.

THE KENYA POLICE

POLICE 23x

(Section 386 C.P.C.)

POST-MORTEM FORM

Reference No. CR 341|619|2013　　　POLICE STATION CENTRAL M.SA

TO: THE PATHOLOGIST/MEDICAL OFFICER

CDAST GENERAL HOSPITAL

I have to request that you ascertain the cause of the death of ISMAEL MOHAMED ALIAS (IDRIS MOHAMED) whose body is sent herewith under escort of No. 46619 Pc JAMES JITUO

The undermentioned witnesses are able to identify the body to you:—

(1) FARID KLWI　　　(2) Fathmi Abdumani

The body was found at (Place) BONDENI on (Date) 14|9|14 at (Time) 4.00Am

Date and Time of Death (if known) 14|9|2014 AS 4.00Am

The circumstances of the death are as follows:—

(If natural causes is probable, give also a brief medical history, including the name and address of any medical officer consulted)

POLICE OFFICERS ON TIP OFF THAT
THERE WERE GANGSTERS WITHIN BONDENI
AREA VISITED THE SCENE AND ONE
OF THE SUSPECTS WAS GUNNED DOWN
WHO WAS LATER CONFIRMED CRIMINAL
HAVE BEEN A WANTED O/7 2383|2013
VIDE CR 341|619|2013 BY ARREST IN FORCE
AND A WARRANT

Note.—If death from poisoning is suspected, the officer requesting the examination should also give the following details (see also page 4).

(a) Date and time of onset and duration of symptoms ....

(b) Main symptoms. Please put a tick against any of the following symptoms that apply:—

			Delirium
Diarrhoea	Constipation	Shivering	Sweating
Vomiting	Cyanosis	Convulsions	Unconsciousness
Thirst	Jaundice	Eye pupil dilated	Internal pains/cramp
Blindness	Loss of weight	Eye pupil contracted	
Any Odour of Breath	Fever		

(c) Details of food, drink or drugs taken before and after onset of symptoms including times and quantities of any medicine given whilst under treatment ....

Date 14|7|2014

(d) Were other persons affected ....
CENTRAL POLICE
(e) Suspected O.C.G. STATION

Signature ....

Note.—Complete form in quadruplicate. One copy to be retained by the station and three copies to be supplied to Medical Officer. One is for his retention, one to be returned to Station with completed report, one to be forwarded with any exhibits submitted for toxicological or histological examination.

APPENDIX 2

THE KENYA POLICE

(Section 386 C.P.C.)

POST-MORTEM FORM

Reference No. CR 341|G19|2013   POLICE STATION CENTRAL MSA

TO: THE PATHOLOGIST/MEDICAL OFFICER

CDAST GENERAL HOSPITAL

I have to request that you ascertain the cause of the death of SWALEH MOHAMED whose body is sent herewith under escort of No. 46619 Pr. JAMES JITHO

The undermentioned witnesses are able to identify the body to you:—

(1) FARID AL-WI   (2) FATMA ADHUMAN

The body was found at (Place) BONDENI on (Date) 14|9|14 at (Time) 4:00AM

Date and Time of Death (if known) 14|9|2014 AS 4:00AM

The circumstances of the death are as follows:—

(If natural causes is probable, give also a brief medical history, including the name and address of any medical officer consulted.)

POLICE OFFICERS ON TIP OFF THAT THERE WERE GANGSTERS WITHIN BONDENI AREA VISITED THE SCENE AND ONE OF THE SUSPECTS WAS GUNNED DOWN WHO WAS LATTER CONFIRMED TO HAVE BEEN A WANTED CRIMINAL VIDE CR 341|G19|2013 C/F 2383|2013 AND A WARRANT OF ARREST IN FORCE.

Note.—If death from poisoning is suspected, the officer requesting the examination should also give the following details (see also page 4).

(a) Date and time of onset and duration of symptoms ....

(b) Main symptoms. Please put a tick against any of the following symptoms that apply:—

Diarrhoea	Constipation	Shivering	Delirium
Vomiting	Cyanosis	Convulsions	Sweating
Thirst	Jaundice	Eye pupil dilated	Unconciousness
Blindness	Loss of weight	Eye pupil contracted	Internal pains/cramp
Any Odour of Breath	Fever		

(c) Details of food, drink or drugs taken before and after onset of symptoms including times and quantities of any medicine given whilst under treatment ....

(d) Were other persons affected ....

(e) Suspect poison ....

Signature ....   Date 14|9|2014

Note—Complete form in quadruplicate. One copy to be retained by the station and three copies to be supplied to Medical Officer. One is for his retention, one to be returned to Station with completed report, one to be forwarded with any exhibits submitted for toxicological or histological examination.

209

NOTES

LIST OF ABBREVIATIONS

1. Foreword by Senate Select Committee on Intelligence Chairman Dianne Feinstein, Findings and Conclusions, Executive Summary, 3 December 2014.

1. A ZANZIBAR GHOST

1. The US Senate Select Committee on Intelligence carried out an extensive study of the CIA detention programme ('the SSCI Study'), sections of which were unclassified and published in December 2014. The Committee chose names for some of the CIA prisons referred to in its report, including COBALT. These names are not the same as the CIA's original codenames for the prisons. The SSCI report confirmed that Suleiman Abdallah was detained at COBALT. This is explored in detail later in this chapter. See US Senate Select Committee on Intelligence, 'Committee Study of the Central Intelligence Agency's Detention and Interrogation Program, Foreword by Senate Select Committee on Intelligence Chairman Dianne Feinstein, Findings and Conclusions, Executive Summary', 3 December 2014, https://www.amnestyusa.org/pdfs/sscistudy1.pdf [last checked 29 July 2016].

2. The description of Suleiman Abdallah's experience as described throughout this chapter has been largely adapted from the ACLU's Complaint and other related legal and advocacy documents in Suleiman Abdallah's civil claim against James Mitchell and Bruce Jessen, two CIA psychologists who it is alleged designed the CIA's torture programme. The case

is called Salim v Mitchell, United States District Court for the Eastern District of Washington, Civil Action 2: 15-CV-286-JLQ (13 October 2015). The pleadings and all public documents in this case can be found at the ACLU's website here: https://www.aclu.org/cases/salim-v-mitch-ell-lawsuit-against-psychologists-behind-cia-torture-program   [last checked 29 July 2016]. Further public source information about this case can be found here: *Out of the Darkness, How two psychologists teamed up with the CIA to devise a torture program and experiment on human beings*, ACLU, https://www.aclu.org/feature/out-darkness [last checked 29 July 2016]. Some minor details not included in the Complaint or other advocacy documents were related to me by Suleiman Abdallah in the course of legal interviews conducted over the past several years.

3. Figures 1.1–1.16 are extracts of a 2005 memo from the CIA to the DOJ, giving a 'generic description of the [rendition] process', published as a result of Freedom of Information litigation by the American Civil Liberties Union. HVD is short for 'high-value detainee', see ACLU Torture FOIA, CIA OLC Memo to Dan Levin, DOJ, *A Generic Description of the Process*, 30 December 2004, https://www.aclu.org/sites/default/files/torturefoia/released/082409/olcremand/2004olc97.pdf [last checked 18 June 2018].

4. US Senate Select Committee on Intelligence, 'Committee Study of the Central Intelligence Agency's Detention and Interrogation Program, Foreword by Dianne Feinstein', pp. 49 and 50.

5. Ibid.

6. 'Out of the Darkness: How two psychologists teamed up with the CIA to devise a torture program and experiment on human beings', ACLU, n.d., https://www.aclu.org/feature/out-darkness [last checked 29 July 2016].

7. Ibid.; Katherine Eban, 'Rorschach and Awe', *Vanity Fair*, July 2007, http://www.vanityfair.com/news/2007/07/torture200707 [last checked 26 July 2016].

8. Katherine Eban, 'Rorschach and Awe', *Vanity Fair*, July 2007, http://www.vanityfair.com/news/2007/07/torture200707 [last checked 26 July 2016].

9. US Senate Select Committee on Intelligence, 'Committee Study of the

Central Intelligence Agency's Detention and Interrogation Program, Foreword by Dianne Feinstein', p. 2.

10. US Senate Select Committee on Intelligence, 'Committee Study of the Central Intelligence Agency's Detention and Interrogation Program, Foreword by Dianne Feinstein', p. 50.

2. THE SPIDER'S WEB

1. 'The Spider's Web' is an updated and expanded version of 'How the US Rendered, Tortured and Discarded One Innocent Man' published in *The Nation 27* June 2012.

2. The global network of CIA prisons was confirmed and partially documented by the SSCI in its study: US Senate Select Committee on Intelligence, 'Committee Study of the Central Intelligence Agency's Detention and Interrogation Program, Foreword by Senate Select Committee on Intelligence Chairman Dianne Feinstein, Findings and Conclusions, Executive Summary', 3 December 2014, https://www.amnestyusa.org/pdfs/sscistudy1.pdf [last checked 29 July 2016].

3. Hilary Andersson, 'Red Cross Confirms "Second Jail" at Bagram, Afghanistan', BBC News, 11 May 2010, http://news.bbc.co.uk/1/hi/world/south_asia/8674179.stm [last checked 29 July 2016]; Scott Horton, 'Inside a Secret DOD Prison in Afghanistan', *Harper's Magazine*, 19 October 2010, http://harpers.org/blog/2010/10/inside-a-secret-dod-prison-in-afghanistan/ [last checked 29 July 2016].

4. US Senate Select Committee on Intelligence, 'Committee Study of the Central Intelligence Agency's Detention and Interrogation Program, Foreword by Dianne Feinstein'.

5. Ibid.

6. Ibid.

7. Dana Priest, 'Wrongful Imprisonment: Anatomy of a CIA Mistake', *The Washington Post*, 4 December 2005, http://www.washingtonpost.com/wp-dyn/content/article/2005/12/03/AR2005120301476.html [last checked 29 July 2016].

8. 'Statement: Khaled el-Masri', American Civil Liberties Union, https://www.aclu.org/statement-khaled-el-masri?redirect=human-rights_national-security/statement-khaled-el-masri [last checked 29 July 2016].

9. For more information on the state secrets doctrine and how it has been used to block cases in the years since 2001, see for example: Laura K Donohue, 'The Shadow of State Secrets', Georgetown Public Law and Legal Theory Research Paper, no. 10–10 (2010), http://scholarship. law.georgetown.edu/cgi/viewcontent.cgi?article=1291&context=facpub [last checked 29 July 2016].

10. In 2012, El-Masri won a landmark case at the European Court of Human Rights against Macedonia, *El-Masri v Macedonia*, Application no. 39630/09, (13 December 2012), for its failure to investigate the allegations about his mistreatment, or to honour his 'right to an effective remedy'. Further information on this case and the full judgement can be found here: 'El-Masri v. Macedonia', Open Society Foundations, 23 January 2013, https://www.opensocietyfoundations.org/litigation/el-masri-v-macedonia [last checked 29 July 2016].

11. Catherine Bond, 'Embassy Bomb Suspect Sent to U.S.', CNN, 27 March 2003, http://edition.cnn.com/2003/WORLD/africa/03/26/kenya.abdalla/index.html [last checked 29 July 2016].

12. 'How the US Backs its Old Enemies', *The Spectator* Archive, 15 November 2003, p. 28, http://archive.spectator.co.uk/article/15th-november-2003/28/ow-the-us-backs-its-old-enemies [last checked 29 July 2016].

13. Bond, 'Embassy Bomb Suspect Sent to US'.

14. Subsequently confirmed, for example, in US Senate Select Committee on Intelligence, 'Committee Study of the Central Intelligence Agency's Detention and Interrogation Program, Foreword by Dianne Feinstein'.

15. This hypothesis is supported by an early report in *The Spectator* citing security sources who described Suleiman's case as one of two 'dry run[s]...to see how easy it was to conduct more snatches in Mogadishu. [...] The challenge is to capture the more important and better protected terrorists in Somalia, such as Saleh Ali Nabhan.' Found at 'How the US Backs its Old Enemies', *The Spectator* Archive.

16. Harmony Project, Combating Terrorism Center at Westpoint, 'Appendix C-III: The (Disallowed) Confession of Omar Said Omar', in *Al-Qaida's (Mis)Adventures in the Horn of Africa*, https://www.ctc. usma.edu/wp-content/uploads/2010/06/Al-Qaidas-MisAdventures-in-the-Horn-of-Africa.pdf [last checked 29 July 2016], p. 147.

17. CJTF-HOA Public Affairs, 'CJTFHOA Coalition Pioneer Revisits Camp Lemonnier After Seven Years', 7 July 2010, http://www.africom.mil/Newsroom/Article/7529/cjtf-hoa-coalition-pioneer-revisits-camp-lemonnier [last checked 15 April 2016]; emphasis added. With thanks to Crofton Black for this research.

18. Matt Bryden, 'No Quick Fixes: Coming to Terms with Terrorism, Islam and Statelessness in Somalia', *The Journal of Conflict Studies*, vol. 23, no. 2 (Fall 2003), https://journals.lib.unb.ca/index.php/jcs/article/view/215/373 [last checked 29 July 2016].

19. 'How the US Backs its Old Enemies', *The Spectator* Archive.

20. An exit document shows his arrival at this time.

21. Sean D. Naylor, 'The Secret War: Africa ops may be just starting', *Military Times*, 5 December 2011, http://www.militarytimes.com/story/military/archives/2013/03/29/the-secret-war-africa-ops-may-be-just-starting/78535624/ [last checked 6 May 2016].

22. US Department of Defense, 'JTF-GTMO Detainee Assessment' for Gouled Hassan Dourad, 19 September 2008, available to view at 'The Guantánamo Docket', *The New York Times*, https://www.nytimes.com/interactive/projects/guantanamo/detainees/10023-gouled-hassan-dourad [last checked 23 May 2017].

23. Ibid.

24. 'Transcript: President Bush's Speech on Terrorism', *The New York Times*, 6 September 2006, http://www.nytimes.com/2006/09/06/washington/06bush_transcript.html [last checked 29 July 2016].

25. International Committee of the Red Cross, 'Report on the Treatment of Fourteen "High Value Detainees" in CIA Custody', February 2007, http://www.nybooks.com/media/doc/2010/04/22/icrc-report.pdf [last checked 29 July 2016].

26. Adam Goldman, 'Secret jails: Terror suspect's odyssey through CIA's "Black Sites"', Associated Press, 2010, http://hosted.ap.org/specials/interactives/wdc/binalshibh/content.swf [last checked 6 May 2016].

27. The Rendition Project, 'Gouled Dourad', https://www.therendition-project.org.uk/prisoners/dourad.html [last checked 29 July 2016].

28. See, for example, US Senate Select Committee on Intelligence, 'Committee Study of the Central Intelligence Agency's Detention and Interrogation Program, Foreword by Dianne Feinstein'; and the ACLU

Torture Database: https://www.thetorturedatabase.org/search/apache-solr_search [last checked 29 July 2016].

29. US Senate Select Committee on Intelligence, 'Committee Study of the Central Intelligence Agency's Detention and Interrogation Program, Foreword by Dianne Feinstein'.

30. See, for example, United Nations General Assembly, Human Rights Council, 'UN Joint Study on Secret Detention in the Context of Countering Terrorism', 19 February 2010, http://www2.ohchr.org/english/bodies/hrcouncil/docs/13session/A-HRC-13–42.pdf [last checked 29 July 2016].

31. 'Shadow Report to ACHPR on Djibouti Renditions', Justice Forum, April 2015, http://justiceforum.org/djiboutis-role-in-us-renditions/ [last checked 29 July 2016].

32. 'USA: Below the Radar: Secret flights to torture and "disappearance"', Amnesty International, 4 April 2006, https://www.amnesty.org/en/documents/AMR51/051/2006/en/ [last checked 6 May 2016], p. 11.

33. *Mohammed Abdullah Saleh Al-Asad v Djibouti, (African Commission on Human and Peoples' Rights), Communication No. 383/2010*, Declaration of Mohammed Abdullah Saleh Al-Asad, para 32. https://chrgj.org/wp-content/uploads/2016/11/Al-Asad-Signed-Declaration.pdf (last checked 22 May 2018).

34. *Mohammed Abdullah Saleh Al-Asad v Djibouti, (African Commission on Human and Peoples' Rights), Communication No. 383/2010*, Declaration of Mohammed Abdullah Saleh Al-Asad, para 32. https://chrgj.org/wp-content/uploads/2016/11/Al-Asad-Signed-Declaration.pdf (last checked 22 May 2018).

35. International Committee of the Red Cross, 'Report on the Treatment of Fourteen "High Value Detainees" in CIA Custody'.

36. ACLU Torture FOIA, CIA OLC Memo to Dan Levin, DOJ, *A Generic Description of the Process*, 30 December 2004, https://www.aclu.org/sites/default/files/torturefoia/released/082409/olcremand/2004olc97.pdf [last checked 29 July 2016].

37. Adam Goldman, 'The Hidden History of the CIA's Prison in Poland', *The Washington Post*, 23 January 2014, https://www.washingtonpost.com/world/national-security/the-hidden-history-of-the-cias-prison-

in-poland/2014/01/23/b77f6ea2–7c6f-11e3–95c6–0a7aa80874bc_story. html [last checked 29 July 2016].

38. By the SSIC, in US Senate Select Committee on Intelligence, 'Committee Study of the Central Intelligence Agency's Detention and Interrogation Program, Foreword by Dianne Feinstein'.

39. Ibid., p. 61.

40. Only one captive, Marwan Jabour, reports being allowed in 2006 to sit with another, Yassir al-Jazeeri. 'Ghost Prisoner: Two Years in Secret CIA Detention', *Human Rights Watch*, vol. 19, no. 1(G) (February 2007), pp. 22–3, http://www.hrw.org/reports/2007/us0207/us0207 webwcover.pdf [last checked 29 July 2016].

41. Center for Human Rights & Global Justice, *Surviving the Darkness: Testimony from the U.S. 'Black Sites'*, New York: NYU School of Law, 2007, p. 52. https://www.therenditionproject.org.uk/pdf/PDF%20 40%20[CHRGJ-2007–12-REP%20Surviving%20the%20Darkness]. pdf [last checked 23 May 2017].

42. Center for Human Rights & Global Justice, 'Surviving the Darkness', p. 36; 'Ghost Prisoner', p. 15; Amnesty International, 'USA: A case to answer: From Abu Ghraib to secret CIA custody: The case of Khaled al-Maqtari', 2008, p. 29, https://www.amnesty.org/en/documents/ AMR51/013/2008/en/ [last checked 23 May 2017]; Amnesty International, 'USA/Yemen/Jordan: Secret detention and torture: Case sheet 2: Salah Nasser Salim 'Ali', 31 July 2005, p. 2, https://www.amnesty. org/en/documents/amr51/126/2005/en/ [last checked 23 May 2017]; and Amnesty International, 'USA/Yemen: Case Sheet—"Disappearance", Secret Detention and Arbitrary Detention: Muhammed Abdullah Salah al-Assad', 8 November 2005, p. 2, https://www.amnesty.org/en/doc-uments/amr51/176/2005/en/ [last checked 23 May 2017].

43. 'Ghost Prisoner', p. 14.

44. US Senate Select Committee on Intelligence, 'Committee Study of the Central Intelligence Agency's Detention and Interrogation Program, Foreword by Dianne Feinstein', p. 62.

45. Ibid.

46. 'Transcript, President Bush's Speech on Terrorism'.

47. See, for example, *Haji Wajir v. Robert Gates*, Civil Action No. 1:06-cv-01697 (RBW), United States District Court for the District of

Columbia, 'Respondents' Motion to Dismiss for Lack of Subject Matter Jurisdiction and Memorandum in Support' (filed 10/03/2008); found at http://s3.amazonaws.com/propublica/assets/docs/wazir_gates_motion_dismiss_081003.pdf (last checked 16 July 2017).

48. Sondra S. Crosby, MD, 'A Doctor's Response to Torture', *Annals of Internal Medicine*, vol. 156, issue 6 (20 March 2012), http://annals.org/article.aspx?articleid=1090730 [last checked 29 July 2016].

49. Ibid.

50. US Senate Select Committee on Intelligence, 'Committee Study of the Central Intelligence Agency's Detention and Interrogation Program, Foreword by Dianne Feinstein', p. 459.

3. A GIANT FOOTPRINT AND A STRING OF PEARLS

1. See *Chagos Islanders v. the Attorney General & HMG British Indian Ocean Commissioner* [2003], EWHC 2222 (GB) (9 October 2003), para 74.

2. Peter H. Sand, 'The Chagos Archipelago Cases: Nature Conservation Between Human Rights and Power Politics', *The Global Community Yearbook of International Law and Jurisprudence* (2013, vol. 1), pp. 125–50.

3. 'Diego Garcia "Camp Justice"', GlobalSecurity.org, http://www.globalsecurity.org/military/facility/diego-garcia.htm, [last checked 1 August 2016].

4. Ibid.

5. Michael J. Green and Andrew Shearer, 'Defining U.S. Indian Ocean Strategy', *The Washington Quarterly* (The Center for Strategic Studies), vol. 34, no. 2 (Spring 2012), p. 175.

6. Ibid., p. 177.

7. Andrew Erickson, Walter Ladwig, Justin Mikolay, 'Diego Garcia: Anchoring America's Future in the Indo-Pacific', *Harvard Asia Quarterly*, vol. 15, no. 2 (2013), p. 21.

8. Ibid., p. 24.

9. A further current factor in the history of Diego Garcia is its connection to the UK/US deal over the controversial Trident nuclear weapons programme. As of 2017, in return for the island's lease to the US for operation of its naval base, the UK reportedly 'receives a significant discount on the research and development costs' of the US-led programme,

housed at the Faslane Naval Base on the west coast of Scotland. See Jamie Doward, 'Diego Garcia Guards its Secrets Even As The Truth on CIA Torture Emerges', *The Guardian*, 13 December 2014, http://www.theguardian.com/world/2014/dec/13/diego-garcia-cia-us-torture-rendition [last checked 24 May 2017].

10. UN, 'General Assembly Resolution 1514', 16 December 1965, UN Doc. A/RES/20/2066, http://wpik.org/Src/unga1514.html [last checked 1 August 2016].

11. *Chagos Islanders v. Attorney General* [2003] EWHC (QB) 2222, Annex A. Summary extracted from Peter Prows, 'Mauritius Brings UNCLOS Arbitration Against the United Kingdom over the Chagos Archipelago', *American Society of International Law Insights*, vol. 15, no. 8 (5 April 2011).

12. See *Bancoult v. McNamara*, 445 F.3d 427 (D.C. Cir. 2006), *cert. denied*, 549 U.S. 1166 (2007) (dismissing the Chagossians' challenge under the Alien Tort Claims Act on the decision to establish Diego Garcia and remove the Chagossians, as a non-reviewable political question because it directly involved national security and foreign policy); *R (Bancoult) v. Foreign Secretary* [2008] UKHL 61, pp. 52–58 (rejecting challenge to BIOT immigration order excluding Chagossians from the Archipelago and deferring to the Crown's reasonable preference in favoring the military and foreign policy interests supporting the order over the interests of the Chagossians 'to return to live Crusoe-like in poor and barren conditions of life'). References found in Peter Prows, 'Mauritius Brings UNCLOS Arbitration'.

13. 'European Court of Human Rights Decision on Chagos Islanders Case', Chagos Conservation Trust, http://chagos-trust.org/news/european-court-of-human-rights-decision-on-chagos-islanders-case [last checked 24 May 2017].

14. 'In the Matter of the Chagos Marine Protected Area Arbitration, before an Arbitral Tribunal Constituted Under Annex VII of the United Nations Convention on the Law of the Sea, between The Republic of Mauritius and The United Kingdom: Award', Permanent Court of Arbitration, 18 March 2015, http://www.pcacases.com/pcadocs/MU-UK%2020150318%20Award.pdf [last checked 1 August 2016].

15. Henry Mance, 'Extended US Lease Blocks Chagossians' Return Home',

Financial Times, 16 November 2016, https://www.ft.com/content/abbc879a-ac1d-11e6-ba7d-76378e4fef24 [last checked 1 April 2017].

16. 'US embassy cables: Foreign Office does not regret evicting Chagos islanders', *The Guardian*, 2 December 2010, http://www.theguardian.com/world/us-embassy-cables-documents/207149 [last checked 1 August 2016].

17. Mauritius's Notification and Statement of Claim. See 'In the Matter of the Chagos Marine Protected Area Arbitration'.

18. Ibid.

19. See, for example, Geoffrey Robertson QC, 'Who Owns Diego Garcia? Decolonisation and Indigenous Rights in the Indian Ocean', June 2012, available at http://www.austlii.edu.au/au/journals/UWALawRw/2012/1.pdf [last checked 25 May 2017].

20. 'Letter to Prime Minister Tony Blair: British Territory Must Not Be Used for Torture', Human Rights Watch, 28 December 2002, http://www.hrw.org/press/2002/12/uk1230ltr.htm [last checked 1 August 2016].

21. See these collected in the Bar Human Rights Committee of England and Wales, 'Diego Garcia. Footprint of Freedom? Briefing paper on reports of unlawful detentions', 17 November 2003, pp. 16–17, https://www.barhumanrights.org.uk/diego-garcia-footprint-of-freedom-briefing-paper-on-reports-of-unlawful-detentions/ [last checked 24 May 2017].

22. Simon Elegant, 'The Terrorist Talks', *Time Magazine*, 5 October 2003, http://content.time.com/time/magazine/article/0,9171,493256,00.html [last checked 24 May 2017].

23. Bar Human Rights Committee of England and Wales to Foreign Secretary Jack Straw, letter, 19 November 2003, p. 2, http://www.barhumanrights.org.uk/wp-content/uploads/2016/10/Jack_Straw_DG.pdf [last checked 24 May 2017].

24. Andrew Selsky, 'Guantánamo transcripts paint portraits of detainees, but much remains cloudy', Associated Press, 3 April 2006, http://www.globalsecurity.org/org/news/2006/060403-gtmo-transcripts.htm, [last checked 1 August 2016]; 'Transcript of: Background Briefing By A Senior Administration Official And A Senior Intelligence Official On The Transfer Of Cia Detainees To The Department Of Defense's

Guantánamo Bay Detention Facility', Washington DC: The White House Conference Center, 6 September 2006. In February 2008, Gen. Michael Hayden, director of the CIA, admitted that two of these prisoners had been subjected in CIA custody to waterboarding, an ancient torture technique that involves controlled drowning. (See Director's Statement to the Senate Select Committee on Intelligence, 5 February 2008, found at https://www.cia.gov/news-information/speeches-testimony/speeches-testimony-archive-2008/february08-statement-to-ssci.html, last checked 16 July 2017). Abu Zubaydah, Ramzi bin al-Shibh and Khaled Sheikh Mohammed are also confirmed in the SSCI report to have been in CIA detention and subjected to 'enhanced interrogation techniques'—see US Senate Select Committee on Intelligence, 'Committee Study of the Central Intelligence Agency's Detention and Interrogation Program, Foreword by Senate Select Committee on Intelligence Chairman Dianne Feinstein, Findings and Conclusions, Executive Summary', 3 December 2014, https://www.amnestyusa.org/pdfs/sscistudy1.pdf [last checked 29 July 2016]; 'Out of the Darkness: How two psychologists teamed up with the CIA to devise a torture program and experiment on human beings', ACLU, n.d., https://www.aclu.org/feature/out-darkness [last checked 29 July 2016].

25. Jamie Doward and Mark Townsend, 'Al-Qaida Suspect "Held on British Island"', *The Observer*, 2 August 2009, https://www.theguardian.com/uk/2009/aug/02/diego-garcia-rendition-mustafa-naser [last checked 1 August 2016]. For my research and field-trip to Syria on his detention there, see William Maclean, 'Al Qaeda ideologue in Syrian detention—lawyers', Reuters, 10 June 2009, http://www.reuters.com/article/idUSLA456186 [last checked 21 July 2017].

26. UK Parliament Select Committee on Foreign Affairs, Written Evidence, 'Submission from Reprieve: Enforced Disappearance, Illegal Interstate Transfer and Other Human Rights Abuses Involving the UK Overseas Territories', 18 October 2007, http://www.publications.parliament.uk/pa/cm200708/cmselect/cmfaff/147/147we47.htm [last checked 1 August 2007].

27. '"Deborah Norville Tonight" for May 6', MSNBC on NBC News, 6 May 2007, transcript at http://www.msnbc.msn.com/id/4924989 [last checked 24 May 2017].

28. 'Two Generals' View of Gates, Troop Levels', NPR, 5 December 2006, audio at http://www.npr.org/templates/story/story.php?storyId=6582 945 [last accessed 1 August 2016].

29. Parliamentary Assembly of the Council of Europe, 'Illegal Interstate Transfers involving Council of Europe Member States', Parliamentary Assembly Report, June 2008, p. 17, pt 70.

30. 'US Faces Prison Ship Allegations', BBC News, 28 June 2005, http://news.bbc.co.uk/2/hi/americas/4632087.stm [last checked 1 August 2016].

31. Original interview by Rupert Stone. See Ian Cobain, 'CIA Interrogated Suspects on Diego Garcia, Says Colin Powell Aide', *The Guardian*, 30 January 2015, https://www.theguardian.com/world/2015/jan/30/cia-interrogation-diego-garcia-lawrence-wilkerson [last checked 2 August 2016].

32. International Committee of the Red Cross, 'Report on the Treatment of Fourteen 'High Value Detainees' in CIA Custody', February 2007, p. 5, http://www.nybooks.com/media/doc/2010/04/22/icrc-report.pdf [last checked 29 July 2016].

33. Ibid., p. 14.

34. Ibid., p. 19.

35. US Senate Select Committee on Intelligence, 'Committee Study of the Central Intelligence Agency's Detention and Interrogation Program, Foreword by Dianne Feinstein'. Summary found at Alan Yuhas, 'Controversial "rectal feeding" technique used to control detainees' behaviour', *The Guardian*, 9 December 2014, https://www.theguardian.com/us-news/2014/dec/09/cia-report-rectal-feeding-detainees [last checked 1 August 2016].

36. Elegant, 'The Terrorist Talks'.

37. International Committee of the Red Cross, 'Report on the Treatment of Fourteen "High Value Detainees"', p. 17.

38. Ibid., p. 20.

39. Ibid.

40. *Hansard* HC Deb., vol. 422, col. 1221W (21 June 2004), http://hansard.millbanksystems.com/written_answers/2004/jun/21/diego-garcia-chagos-islands [last checked 25 May 2017]. [last checked 2 August 2016].

41. *Hansard* HC Deb., vol. 483, col. 191W (17 November 2008), http://www.publications.parliament.uk/pa/cm200708/cmhansrd/cm081117/text/81117w0045.htm [last checked 25 May 2017].

42. *Hansard* HC Deb, vol. 422, col. 1222W (21 June 2004).

43. UK Intelligence and Security Committee of Parliament, 'Rendition', special report (July 2007), para 197, http://isc.independent.gov.uk/committee-reports/special-reports [last checked 1 August 2016].

44. 'Exchange of notes constituting an agreement…concerning a United States naval support facility on Diego Garcia, British Indian Ocean Territory and replacing the supplementary agreement of 24 October 1972 (with annexed plan)', Foreign and Commonwealth Office, (25 February 1976), para 3, https://treaties.un.org/doc/Publication/UNTS/Volume%201018/volume-1018-I-8737-English.pdf [last checked 16 July 2017].

45. 'Answer by Baroness Amos to a question by Lord Wallace of Saltaire, Diego Garcia', *Hansard*, HL Deb, *HL Deb.*, vol 642, cols cc1019–21, 1019, (8 January 2003), http://hansard.millbanksystems.com/lords/2003/jan/08/diego-garcia [last checked 16 July 2017].

46. Bar Human Rights Committee, 'Diego Garcia. Footprint of Freedom?', p. 5.

47. D. Proctor and V. Fleming (eds), *Biodiversity: The UK Overseas Territories*, London: Joint Nature Conservation Committee, 1999, p. 42; Peter Sand, 'Diego Garcia: British-American legal Black Hole in the Indian Ocean?', *Journal of Environmental Law*, vol. 21, no. 1 (January 2009), pp. 113–37.

48. US Navy 'Welcome to Diego Garcia' (document for new military personnel), Naval Computer and Telecommunications Station, Far East Detachment Diego Garcia British Indian Ocean Territory, January 2011, p. 14, found at http://www.public.navy.mil/fcc-c10f/nctsfedetdg/Documents/WELCOME_ABOARD_JAN%202011_.pdf [last checked 16 July 2017].

49. Ibid., p. 3.

50. *Husayn (Abu Zubaydah) v. Poland* (Application no. 7511/13), European Court of Human Rights, 24 July 2014; and *Al Nashiri v. Poland* (Application no. 28761/11), European Court of Human Rights, 24 July 2014.

51. United Nations Human Rights Committee, 'Concluding observations of the Human Rights Committee: United Kingdom of Great Britain and Northern Ireland', 30 July 2008 (UN Doc. CCPR/C/GBR/CO/6, para 22, Annex 8); see also UN Committee on the Elimination of Racial Discrimination, 'Concluding Observations of the Committee on the Elimination of Racial Discrimination: United Kingdom of Great Britain and Northern Ireland', 10 December 2003 (UN Doc. CERD/C/63/CO/11, para 26, Annex 9).

52. United Nations Committee Against Torture, 'Concluding Observations of the Committee Against Torture: United Kingdom of Great Britain and Northern Ireland', 2013, para 9.

53. *Hansard* HC Deb., vol. 584, col. 172W (8 July 2014), http://www.publications.parliament.uk/pa/cm201415/cmhansrd/cm140708/text/140708w0001.htm#140708125000874 [last checked 1 August 2016].

54. Jamie Doward and Ian Cobain, 'Emails Shed New Light on UK Link to CIA "Torture Flights"', *The Observer*, Saturday 12 July 2014, http://www.theguardian.com/world/2014/jul/12/uk-cia-torture-flights-rendition-programme [last checked 1 August 2016].

55. *Hansard* HC Deb., vol. 584, col. 643W (15 July 2014), http://www.publications.parliament.uk/pa/cm201415/cmhansrd/cm140715/text/140715w0002.htm#14071576001196 [last checked 25 May 2017]; *Hansard* HC Deb., vol. 584, col. 873W (21 July 2014), http://www.publications.parliament.uk/pa/cm201415/cmhansrd/cm140721/text/140721w0002.htm#14072134004340 [last checked 25 May 2017].

56. *Hansard* HC Deb., vol. 584, col. 643W (15 July 2014).

57. Ibid.

58. Weather Underground, 'Diego Garcia, British Indian Ocean: Weather History for FJDG—June, 2014', http://www.wunderground.com/history/airport/FJDG/2014/6/30/DailyHistory.html?req_city=NA&req_state=NA&req_statename=NA [last checked 25 May 2017].

59. *Hansard* HC Deb., vol. 584, col. 1047W (22 July 2014), http://www.publications.parliament.uk/pa/cm201415/cmhansrd/cm140722/text/140722w0002.htm#14072281003081 [last checked 25 May 2017].

60. Ibid.; and *Hansard* HC Deb., vol. 584, col. 691W, 16 July 2014, http://

www.publications.parliament.uk/pa/cm201415/cmhansrd/cm140716/
text/140716w0001.htm [last checked 25 May 2017].

4. 'WE FORGIVE YOU: JUST ACCEPT YOU MET OSAMA BIN LADEN'

1. The Secretary of State for Foreign and Commonwealth Affairs (David Miliband), statement on 'Terrorist Suspects (Renditions)', *Hansard* HC Deb., vol. 472, col. 547 (21 February 2008), https://www.publications. parliament.uk/pa/cm200708/cmhansrd/cm080221/debext/80221–0008. htm [last checked 25 May 2017].

2. BBC News, 'In Full: CIA Statement on Renditions', 21 February 2008, http://news.bbc.co.uk/1/hi/uk_politics/7257524.stm ([ast checked 16 July 2017).

3. Ibid.

4. *Hansard* HC Deb., vol. XXX, col. 2002W (11 February 2009), https:// publications.parliament.uk/pa/cm200809/cmhansrd/cm090211/ text/90211w0007.htm [last checked 21 July 2017].

5. Rajiv Chandrasekaran and Peter Finn, 'US Behind Secret Transfer of Terror Suspects,' *The Washington Post*, 11 March 2001.

6. *Mohammed Saad Iqbal Madni v. The Commissioner of the British Indian Ocean Territory*, (Supreme Court of the British Indian Ocean Territory), 'Witness Statement of the Claimant', 1 July 2009, para 3, found at https://www.therenditionproject.org.uk/pdf/PDF%20200%20 [Madni%20Witness%20Statement,%20v%20BIOT,%2018%20 Aug%202009].pdf [last checked 1 April 2017].

7. *Mohammed Saad Iqbal Madni v. The Commissioner of the British Indian Ocean Territory*, 'Witness Statement'.

8. Duncan Campbell, 'US sends suspects to face torture', *The Guardian*, 12 March 2002, https://www.theguardian.com/world/2002/mar/12/ september11.usa [last checked 21 June 2017].

9. *Mohammed Saad Iqbal Madni v. The Commissioner of the British Indian Ocean Territory*, 'Witness Statement of the Claimant', paras 8–10.

10. Jane Perlez, Raymond Bonner, Salman Masood, 'An Ex-Detainee of the U.S. describes a 6-Year Ordeal', *The New York Times*, 27 May 2009, http://www.nytimes.com/2009/01/06/world/asia/06iqbal.html?_ r=2&hp=&pagewanted=all [last checked 26 May 2017].

11. Mohammed Saad Iqbal Madni, 'Combatant Status Review Tribunal Transcript (unclassified)', Guantanamo (9 November 2004); found at *The New York Times* Guantánamo Docket, 'Muhammad Saad Iqbal', https://www.nytimes.com/interactive/projects/guantanamo/detainees/743-muhammad-saad-iqbal/documents/4 [last checked 21 July 2017].

12. Chandrasekaran and Finn, 'US Behind Secret Transfer of Terror Suspects'.

13. Raymond Bonner, 'Terror Suspect's Ordeal in U.S. Custody', *The New York Times*, 18 December 2005, http://www.nytimes.com/2005/12/18/world/asia/terror-suspects-ordeal-in-us-custody.html?_r=0 [last checked 26 May 2017].

14. Stephen Grey, 'US Accused of Torture Flights', *The Sunday Times*, 14 November 2004.

15. Perlez, Bonner, Masood, 'An Ex-Detainee of the U.S. describes a 6-Year Ordeal'.

16. *Mohammed Saad Iqbal Madni v. The Commissioner of the British Indian Ocean Territory*, 'Witness Statement of the Claimant', para 4.

17. Khaled El-Masri and Mohamed Al-Zeri reported being photographed during their renditions. 'Khaled El-Masri said: "They took off my blindfold. ... As soon as it was removed, a very bright flashlight went off and I was temporarily blinded. I believed from the sounds that they had taken photographs of me from throughout." See: *Declaration of Khaled El-Masri in support of Plaintiff's Opposition to the United States' Motion to Dismiss*, in El-Masri v. Tenet et al, Eastern District Court of Virginia in Alexandria, 6 April 2006, at p. 9. See also: Office of the Parliamentary Ombudsman (Sweden), "Interview Conducted with State Official X of the Security Police (Sapo)", Case No. 2169–2004, 30 September 2004, comment made at p.13: "He wasn't naked, he had his underpants on; the upper body was undressed and then his picture was taken." See also Amnesty International, *Human Cargo*, p. 42, which describes Al-Maqtari being stripped naked and photographed. See also Center for Human Rights & Global Justice, *Surviving in the Darkness: Testimony from the U.S. "Black Sites"*, New York: NYU School of Law, 2007, p. 15, where Bashmilah describes being stripped and photographed. See also: Human Rights Watch, "The Case of Marwan

Jabour", online report, in which Jabour describes being stripped naked and videoed: http://www.hrw.org/reports/2007/us0207/2.htm [last checked 26 May 2017].' This citation is taken from a report I authored: Reprieve, '"Human Cargo": Binyam Mohamed and the Rendition Frequent Flier Programme', 10 June 2008, available at https://www.therenditionproject.org.uk/pdf/PDF%20100%20[Reprieve,%20Jun%202008.%20Human%20Cargo,%20report%20on%20Binyam].pdf [last checked 21 July 2017].

18. Reprieve file, Sultana Noon email to Clara Gutteridge, 27 April 2009.

19. Amnesty International, 'USA: A case to answer: From Abu Ghraib to secret CIA custody: The case of Khaled al-Maqtari', 2008, p. 16, https://www.amnesty.org/en/documents/AMR51/013/2008/en/ [last checked 23 May 2017] AI Index: AMR 51/03/2008.

20. 1 international knot = 1.852 km/hr (1 nautical mile per hour).

21. Anita Bhatt, *The Strategic Role of the Indian Ocean in World Politics: The Case of Diego Garcia*, New Delhi: Ajanta, 1992, p. 7.

22. Guantánamo tribunal hearing transcript (unclassified). When the plane landed, he was told he was in Cairo.

23. Perlez, Bonner, Masood, 'An Ex-Detainee of the U.S. describes a 6-Year Ordeal'.

24. Ibid.

25. Ibid.

26. Raymond Bonner, 'Detainee Says He Was Tortured While in U.S. Custody', *The New York Times*, 13 February 2005, http://www.nytimes.com/2005/02/13/world/middleeast/detainee-says-he-was-tortured-while-in-us-custody.html [last checked 16 July 2017]; Dana Priest, Dan Eggen, 'Terror Suspect Alleges Torture: Detainee Says U.S. Sent Him to Egypt Before Guantánamo', *The Washington Post*, 6 January 2005, http://www.washingtonpost.com/wp-dyn/articles/A51726–2005Jan5.html [last checked 25 May 2017].

27. Dana Priest, 'Detainee Sent Home to Australia', *The Washington Post*, 29 January 2005, http://www.washingtonpost.com/wp-dyn/articles/A45643–2005Jan28.html [last checked 26 May 2017].

28. Andy Worthington, 'Rendered to Egypt for Torture, Mohammed Saad Iqbal Madni is Released from Guantánamo', andyworthington.co.uk,

4 September 2008, http://www.andyworthington.co.uk/2008/09/04/rendered-to-egypt-for-torture-mohammed-saad-iqbal-madni-is-released-from-guantanamo/ [last checked 26 May 2017]. Worthington's meticulously researched book, *The Guantánamo Files* (London: Pluto Press, 2007), was more or less used as a reference by Guantánamo lawyers. See also Amnesty International, 'USA: Guantánamo. Lives Torn Apart: The Impact of Indefinite Detention on Detainees and Their Families', 6 February 2006, https://www.amnesty.org/en/documents/amr51/007/2006/en/ [last checked 21 July 2017].

29. Perlez, Bonner, Masood, 'An Ex-Detainee of the U.S. describes a 6-Year Ordeal'.
30. Bonner, 'Terror Suspect's Ordeal in U.S. Custody'.
31. Perlez, Bonner, Masood, 'An Ex-Detainee of the U.S. describes a 6-Year Ordeal'.
32. Reprieve interviews; see Reprieve's report to the UK Parliament Foreign Affairs Committee (20 May 2009).
33. Amnesty International, 'USA: Guantánamo. Lives Torn Apart'.
34. Ibid.
35. *Mohammed Saad Iqbal Madni v. The Commissioner of the British Indian Ocean Territory*, 'Witness Statement of the Claimant', para 16.
36. Perlez, Bonner, Masood, 'An Ex-Detainee of the U.S. describes a 6-Year Ordeal'.
37. Ibid.
38. *Mohammed Saad Iqbal Madni v The Commissioner of the British Indian Ocean Territory*.
39. Jason Leopold, 'Revealed: Senate Report Contains New Details on Black Sites', Al Jazeera America, 9 April 2014, http://america.aljazeera.com/articles/2014/4/9/senate-cia-torture.html [last checked 26 May 2017].
40. US Senate Select Committee on Intelligence, 'Committee Study of the Central Intelligence Agency's Detention and Interrogation Program, Foreword by Dianne Feinstein', cover page.
41. Jamie Doward, "UK Ambassador 'Lobbied Senators to Hide Diego Garcia Role in Rendition'", *The Observer*, 16 August 2014, https://www.theguardian.com/world/2014/aug/16/uk-ambassador-senators-hide-diego-garcia-rendition-cia [last checked 1 August 2016].

5. GOODBYE AFRICA

1. On 13 June 1997, Jimmy Carter's national security advisor Zbigniew Brzezinski admitted in a television interview that the US had 'actively and directly' supported the mujahideen to fight the Soviets following the latter's invasion of Afghanistan, including 'providing weapons'. See The National Security Archive [a non-profit private collective of scholars and journalists], 'Interview with Dr Zbigniew Brzezinksi',transcript for the CNN documentary series *The Cold War*, Episode 17, 'Good Guys, Bad Guys', first aired 1998: http://nsarchive.gwu.edu/coldwar/interviews/episode-17/brzezinski2.html). Among the mujahideen's ranks were Osama bin Laden and other founding members of al-Qaeda. The former director of the CIA, Robert Gates, also stated in his memoirs, *From the Shadows* (New York: Simon & Schuster, 1996), that US intelligence services began to aid the Mujahideen in Afghanistan, six months before the Soviet invasion.

2. Jane Mayer, 'Outsourcing Torture: The secret history of America's "extraordinary rendition" program', *The New Yorker*, 14 February 2005, http://www.newyorker.com/magazine/2005/02/14/outsourcing-torture [last checked 30 May 2017].

3. Johnnie Carson, 'Kenya: The Struggle Against Terrorism', in Robert L. Rotberg (ed.), *Battling Terrorism in the Horn of Africa*, Cambridge, MA/Washington DC: World Peace Foundation/Brookings Institution Press, 2005, p. 181.

4. Presidential Decision Directive 39, 21 June 1995, available via the Federation of American Scientists, Intelligence Resource Program: http://www.fas.org/irp/offdocs/pdd39.htm [last checked 30 May 2017].

5. 9/11 Commission, Staff Statement no. 5, in Thomas H. Kean and Lee Hamilton, 'The 9/11 Commission report: final report of the National Commission on Terrorist Attacks upon the United States', Washington DC, 2004, p. 68. The list of all ten policy programmes can be found in Roger Cressey, Director, Transnational Threats, 'U.S. Counter-Terrorism Policy and Organization', Washington DC: National Security Council, 27 September 2000. The full text of PDD 62 (22 May 1998), is available via the Federation of American Scientists, Intelligence Resource Program: http://www.fas.org/irp/offdocs/pdd-62.htm [last checked 30 May 2017].

6. Cofer Black, former chief of the CIA Counterterrorism Center, stated: 'All I want to say is that there was "before" 9/11 and "after" 9/11. After 9/11 the gloves come off.' See Black's unclassified testimony to the Joint House/Senate Intelligence Committee Hearing, 'Joint Investigation into September 11th: Fifth Public Hearing' (26 September 2002), available at https://fas.org/irp/congress/2002_hr/092602black.html [last checked 1 August 2016].

7. White House Office of the Press Secretary, 'News Release: President Discusses Creation of Military Commissions to Try Suspected Terrorists', 6 September 2006,https://georgewbush-whitehouse.archives.gov/news/releases/2006/09/20060906–3.html [last checked 30 May 2017]; Office of the Director of National Intelligence, 'Summary of the High Value Terrorist Detainee Program', 6 September 2006, available at http://cryptome.info/cia-hvdp.htm [last checked 30 May 2017].

8. Douglas Jehl and David Johnston, 'Rule Change Lets C.I.A. Freely Send Suspects Abroad to Jails', *The New York Times*, 6 March 2005, http://www.nytimes.com/2005/03/06/politics/06intel.html [last checked 30 May 2017].

9. US Department of State, 'The Antiterrorism Assistance Program, Report to Congress for Fiscal Year 2004', February 2005, p. 7, http://www.au.af.mil/au/awc/awcgate/state/44890.pdf [last checked 30 May 2017]. Interestingly, the ATA report notes that 'missing in these efforts has been a central command with the authority to investigate, plan, coordinate, and implement CT operations. The JTTF will provide this linchpin, bringing together representatives from all the major stakeholder organizations under one central command' (p. 7). In fact, Kenya's Joint Terrorism Task Force never got off the ground and no longer exists.

10. Amnesty International 'Kenya: The impact of "anti-terrorism" operations on human rights', AI Index: AFR 32/002/2005, 23 March 2005, pp. 35–6, https://www.amnesty.org/en/documents/afr32/002/2005/en/ [last checked 30 May 2017].

11. Combating Terrorism Center, 'Al-Qaeda's (Mis)Adventures in the Horn of Africa', West Point: US Military Academy (2 July 2007), https://www.ctc.usma.edu/wp-content/uploads/2010/06/Al-Qaidas-MisAdventures-in-the-Horn-of-Africa.pdf [last checked 1 August 2016].

12. UN Human Rights Council, 'Joint Study on Global Practices in Relation to Secret Detention in the Context of Countering Terrorism', 19 February 2010, Annex II, Case 2 (Suleiman Abdallah), http://www2.ohchr.org/english/bodies/hrcouncil/docs/13session/A-HRC-13–42.pdf [last checked 30 May 2017], p. 154. Abdallah's detention in Afghanistan is now also confirmed by the SSIS Report: US Senate Select Committee on Intelligence, 'Committee Study of the Central Intelligence Agency's Detention and Interrogation Program, Foreword by Senate Select Committee on Intelligence Chairman Dianne Feinstein, Findings and Conclusions, Executive Summary', 3 December 2014, https://www.amnestyusa.org/pdfs/sscistudy1.pdf (last checked 29 July 2016).

13. See, for example: Muslim Human Rights Forum, 'Horn of Terror: Report of US-Led Mass Extraordinary Renditions from Kenya to Somalia, Ethiopia and Guantánamo Bay, January–June 2007', revised edition, September 2008; Amnesty International, 'Horn of Africa: Unlawful Transfers in the War on Terror', AI Index: AFR 25/006/2007, June 2007; Cageprisoners, 'Inside Africa's War on Terror: War on Terror Detentions in the Horn of Africa', May 2006; Cageprisoners and Reprieve, 'Mass Rendition, Incommunicado Detention, and Possible Torture of Foreign Nationals in Kenya, Somalia and Ethiopia', 22 March 2007; Human Rights Watch, 'Why Am I Still Here? The 2007 Horn of Africa Renditions and the Fate of those Still Missing', October 2008.

14. Karen de Young, 'U.S. Strike in Somalia Targets Al-Qaeda Figure', *The Washington Post*, 9 January 2007, http://www.washingtonpost.com/wp-dyn/content/article/2007/01/08/AR2007010801635.html [last checked 20 July 2007].

15. Prisoners were of British, Canadian, Comorian, Eritrean, Ethiopia, Jordanian, Kenyan, Moroccan, Omani, Rwandese, Saudi, Somali, South African, Swedish, Sudanese, Syrian, Tanzanian, Tunisian, United Arab Emirates, United States, and Yemeni nationality. Muslim Human Rights Forum, 'Horn of Terror', 6 July 2007 (first edition).

16. Combating Terrorism Center, 'Al-Qaeda's (Mis)Adventures in the Horn of Africa', p. 99; Xan Rice, 'Africa's Secret: the men, women and chil-

231

dren "vanished" in the war on terror', *The Guardian*, 23 April 2007, https://www.theguardian.com/world/2007/apr/23/international.mainsection2 [last checked 17 July 2017].

17. Reprieve and Cageprisoners, interview with detainees, 14–15 February 2007.

18. These manifests are annexed to Muslim Human Rights Forum, 'Horn of Terror' (first edition).

19. 'Report of the Presidential Special Action Committee to Address Specific Concerns of the Muslim Community in Regard to Alleged Harassment and/or Discrimination in the Application/Enforcement of the Law', Chapter 3.4, 31 March 2008 (unpublished).

20. Muslim Human Rights Forum, 'Horn of Terror', p. 6.

21. Ibid. (see flight logs and other official Kenyan documents annexed to the report), pp. 15, 132–51. Samia Josephs was six months old when first detained (see Redress and Reprieve, 'Kenya and Counter-terrorism: A Time for Change', 2009, p. 13).

22. *Mohammed Abdulmalik v. Barack Obama*, United States District Court for the District of Columbia, Civil Action No. CV-01440-CKK, declaration of Mohammed Abdulmalik (unclassified).

23. *Ayan Jayama Warsame (on behalf of Ahmed Abdullahi and another) v. the Police Commissioner and the Commandant of the ATPU* (Misc. Criminal Application No. 329 of 2009), replying affidavit of Boniface Mwaniki, para 9.

24. Hassan's account, cited in author interview with his former fellow prisoner.

25. Jeremy Scahill, 'The CIA's Secret Sites in Somalia', *The Nation*, 1 August 2011, https://www.thenation.com/article/cias-secret-sites-somalia/ [last checked 23 July 2016].

26. Ibid.

27. Author interview with former detainee (2011).

28. Ibid.

6. RULE BY LAW: THE KAMPALA BOMBINGS CASE

1. Paul D. Williams, 'Four questions—and answers—about U.S. support of peacekeeping in Africa', *The Washington Post*, 15 May 2015, https://www.

washingtonpost.com/news/monkey-cage/wp/2015/05/15/four-questions-and-answers-about-u-s-support-of-peacekeeping-in-africa/?utm_term=.6a9089fe0075 [last checked 21 July 2017]; *Stars and Stripes*, 'US sending MRAPS to Somalia for African Union mission', 20 January 2015, https://www.stripes.com/news/us-sending-mraps-to-somalia-for-african-union-mission-1.324797#.WXCU-9Pyuu4 [last checked 21 July 2017]; see also the search function on the US government website http://foreignassistance.gov/categories/Peace-and-Security.

2. Dan Damon, 'Why is Uganda fighting in "hellish" Somalia?', BBC World Service, 15 March 2012, http://www.bbc.co.uk/news/world-africa-16853499 [last checked 2 June 2017].

3. Lindsay McLain and Allan Ngari, 'Pay Us so We Can Forget: Reparations for Victims and Affected Communities in Northern Uganda', Justice and Reconciliation Project-Institute for Justice and Reconciliation Policy Brief No. 2, August 2011, p.6, http://justiceandreconciliation.com/wp-content/uploads/2011/09/JRP-IJR_Policy-Brief_Reparations.pdf [last checked 2 June 2017].

4. 'Kampala Bomb Blast Victims' Compensation Unaccounted for', *Red Pepper*, 20 January 2014, http://www.redpepper.co.ug/kampala-bomb-blast-victims-compensation-unaccounted-for/ [last checked 2 June 2017].

5. Human Rights Watch, 'Violence Instead of Vigilance: Torture and Illegal Detention by Uganda's Rapid Response Unit', March 2011, https://www.hrw.org/news/2011/03/23/uganda-torture-extortion-killings-police-unit [last checked 19 July 2017].

6. In two cases, those of the Claimant Habib Suleiman Njoroge and of Omar Awadh Omar, the renditions are denied by the Kenyan and Ugandan authorities. In the other cases the fact of the rendition is accepted, although it is contended that it was 'lawful'.

7. See: *Omar Awadh Omar and others v Attorney General of Uganda* (Constitutional Court of Uganda), consolidated constitutional petition nos 55 and 56 (2011), affidavits of Omar Awadh, Idris Magondu, Hussein Hassan Agade, Mohammed Hamid Suleiman, Mohamed Adan Abdow, Yahya Suleiman Mbuthia, Habib Suleiman Njoroge.

8. Nzau Musau, 'UK Envoy Censures Illegal Rendition of Terror Suspects', *The Star*, 14 October 2010; Richard Lough and Wangui Kanina, 'Kenya

justice minister criticizes Uganda Renditions', Reuters, 30 September 2010, http://af.reuters.com/article/topNews/idAFJOE68T0M320100 930 [last checked 2 June 2017].

9. Judicial review proceedings seeking disclosure of British security service notes of interrogations were initiated by two defendants who alleged that they had been abusively interrogated by Americans in the company of people they believed were British agents. *The Queen on the Application of Omar Awadh Omar & Ors v. Secretary of State for Foreign & Commonwealth Affairs*, High Court of Justice, [2012] EWCH 1737 (Admin), judgment found at https://www.judiciary.gov.uk/wp-content/uploads/JCO/Documents/Judgments/omar-and-others-judgment-260612.pdf) [last checked 2 June 2017].

10. *Zuhura Suleiman (on behalf of Mohammed Hamid Suleiman) v. The Commissioner of Police, the Commandant of the Anti-Terror Police Unit, and the Attorney-General*, High Court of Kenya at Nairobi, Misc. Crim. App. No. 441 of 2010.

11. See ibid.; *Asha Suleiman (on behalf of Habib Suleiman Njoroge) v. The Commissioner of Police, the Commandant of the Anti-Terror Police Unit, and the Attorney-General*, High Court of Kenya, Misc. Crim. Application No 469 of 2010; *Asha Suleiman (on behalf of Yahya Mbuthia Suleiman) v. The Commissioner of Police, the Commandant of the Anti-Terror Police Unit, and the Attorney-General*, High Court of Kenya, Misc. Crim. Application No. 470 of 2010; and a constitutional case in the Kenyan High Court initiated by Mohammed Aktar Kana.

12. *Asha Suleiman (on behalf of Yahya Mbuthia Suleiman) v The Commissioner of Police, the Commandant of the Anti-Terror Police Unit, and the Attorney-General*; *Raabia Mohammed (on behalf of Omar Awadh Omar) v. The Commissioner of Police, the Commandant of the Anti-Terror Police Unit, and the Attorney-General*, High Court of Kenya.

13. *Omar Awadh & 10 ors v Attorney General* (Constitution Application No.02 of 2015)(2015) UGCC 2 (26 March 2015), judgment found at http://www.ulii.org/ug/judgment/court-appeal/2015/29 [last checked 1 August 2016].

14. There is no evidence to suggest that the assassination had anything to do with this case.

15. Nicholas Bariyo, 'Life Sentences for Seven Men Convicted of 2010 Kampala Bombings', *The Wall Street Journal*, 27 May 2016, http://www.wsj.com/articles/life-sentences-for-seven-men-convicted-of-2010-kampala-bombings-1464363980 [last accessed 1 August 2016].

16. *Nyambura v. The Attorney General of the Republic of Uganda and The Attorney General of the Republic of Kenya*, petition to the East African Court of Justice (EACJ), Reference no. 11 (2011).

17. Human Rights Watch, 'Uganda: Kenyan Rights Defender to Be Tried for Kampala Bombings', 30 November 2010, https://www.hrw.org/news/2010/11/30/uganda-kenyan-rights-defender-be-tried-kampala-bombings [last checked 2 June 2017].

18. Human Rights House, 'Kenya/Uganda Update: Human Rights Investigator Deported, Human Rights House', 14 May 2011, http://humanrightshouse.org/noop/page.php?p=Articles/16396.html&d=1 [last checked 1 August 2016].

19. *Samuel Mukira Mohochi v. The Attorney General of the Republic of Uganda*, EACJ, Case no. 5 of 11, http://eacj.org/?cases=samuel-mukira-mohochi-vs-the-attorney-general-of-the-republic-of-uganda [last checked 1 August 2016].

7. EAST AFRICA'S 'PHOENIX PROGRAMME'

1. AFRICOM's 'official' headquarters are located on a US military base in Stuttgart, Germany; however, the operational headquarters are at Camp Lemonnier, Djibouti.

2. US Navy, 'CNIC, Camp Lemonnier, Djibouti: History', http://www.cnic.navy.mil/regions/cnreurafswa/installations/camp_lemonnier_djibouti/about/history.html [last checked 2 August 2016].

3. CJTF-HOA's mission is billed as primarily to provide military cooperation and training to allied African states. In practice, these currently comprise Ethiopia, Kenya, Tanzania and Uganda, as well as the Indian Ocean states of Mauritius, the Comoros and the Seychelles. The US base provides selective support for the African Union force in Somalia, AMISOM, as well as complementing French training of Djibouti's small armed forces. US military ties with Ethiopia have also steadily increased, and the Americans have established small outposts in southwest Ethiopia and northern Uganda

as well. See David Styan, 'Djibouti: Changing Influence in the Horn's Strategic Hub', Chatham House Briefing Paper, April 2013, https://www. chathamhouse.org/sites/files/chathamhouse/public/Research/ Africa/0413bp_djibouti.pdf [last checked 2 August 2016].

4. Nick Turse, 'The Stealth Expansion of a Secret U.S. Drone Base in Africa', *The Intercept*, 21 October 2015, https://theintercept.com/ 2015/10/21/stealth-expansion-of-secret-us-drone-base-in-africa/ [last checked 2 August 2016].

5. 'Transcript, President Bush's Speech on Terrorism', 6 September 2006, *The New York Times*, http://www.nytimes.com/2006/09/06/washington/ 06bush_transcript.html [last checked 29 July 2016].

6. US Department of Defense, 'JTF-GTMO Detainee Assessment: Abdul Malik', 22 May 2007, *The New York Times* Guantánamo Docket, https://www.nytimes.com/interactive/projects/guantanamo/ detainees/10026-abdul-malik [last checked 5 June 2017].

7. *Unclassified declaration of Mohammed Abdulmalik—Supplement to motion to obtain additional discovery in the form of depositions of interrogators*, 13 Oct. 2010; this was part of his US *habeas* case. These cases show that the change in practice whereby the US has increasingly positioned itself as one step removed from the operational reality of detention operations began under President Bush, thus predating Obama's presidency and any publicly proclaimed change of US detention policy under him.

8. *Unclassified declaration of Mohammed Abdulmalik—Supplement to motion to obtain additional discovery in the form of depositions of interrogators*, 13 October 2010.

9. US Department of Defense, 'JTF-GTMO Detainee Assessment: Abdullahi Sudi Arale', 22 May 2007, *The New York Times* Guantánamo Docket, https://www.nytimes.com/interactive/projects/guantanamo/ detainees/10027-abdullahi-sudi-arale [last checked 5 June 2017].

10. 'Al-Qaeda Arrest in East Africa', BBC News, 7 June 2007, http://news. bbc.co.uk/1/hi/6729015.stm [last checked 2 August 2016]; Andy Worthington, 'The Stories of the Two Somalis Freed from Guantánamo', 21 December 2009, http://www.andyworthington.co.uk/2009/12/21/ the-stories-of-the-two-somalis-freed-from-guantanamo/ [last checked 2 August 2016].

11. 'US Kills al-Qaeda Suspects in Yemen', *USA Today*, 5 November 2002, http://usatoday30.usatoday.com/news/world/2002-11-04-yemen-explosion_x.htm [last checked 2 August 2016].

12. James Bamford, '"He's in the Backseat!"', *The Atlantic*, April 2006, http://www.theatlantic.com/magazine/archive/2006/04/-hes-in-the-backseat/304712/ [last checked 2 August 2016].

13. Dana Priest, 'US Citizen Among Those Killed in Yemen Predator Missile Strike', *The Washington Post*, 8 November 2002, found in MIT newspaper *The Tech*, vol. 122, no. 54, 8 November 2002, http://tech.mit.edu/V122/N54/long4–54.54w.html [last checked 2 August 2016].

14. Seymour M. Hersh, 'Moving Targets: Will the Counter-insurgency plan in Iraq Repeat the Mistakes of Vietnam', *The New Yorker*, 15 December 2003, http://www.newyorker.com/magazine/2003/12/15/moving-targets [last checked 2 August 2016].

15. Later incorporated into Executive Order 12332 (1981), signed by President Reagan and remaining in force.

16. Gabriella Blum and Philip P. Heymann, 'Law and Policy of Targeted Killing', *Harvard National Security Journal*, vol. 1 (2010), pp. 145–70.

17. Eric Schmitt and Jeffrey Gettleman, 'Qaeda Leader Reported Killed in Somalia', *The New York Times*, 2 May 2008, http://www.nytimes.com/2008/05/02/world/africa/02somalia.html [last checked 18 July 2017].

18. Mohamed Oled Hassan, 'Saleh Ali Nabhan Killed; Somali Insurgents Vow to Avenge U.S. Raid', *The Huffington Post*, 15 September 2009.

19. Associated Press, 'Al Qaeda Death a Blow to Terror Group', CBS News, 16 October 2009, http://www.cbsnews.com/news/al-qaeda-death-a-blow-to-terror-group/ [last checked 2 August 2016].

20. Jeffrey Gettleman and Eric Schmitt, 'US Kills Top Qaeda Militant in Southern Somalia', *The New York Times*, 14 September 2009, http://www.nytimes.com/2009/09/15/world/africa/15raid.html?_r=0 [last checked 2 August 2016].

21. *Ayan Jayama Warsame (on behalf of Ahmed Abdullahi and another) v. the Police Commissioner and the Commandant of the ATPU* (Misc. Criminal Application No. 329 of 2009), replying affidavit of Boniface Mwaniki, para 9.

22. Jeremy Scahill, 'The CIA's Secret Sites in Somalia', *The Nation*, 10 December 2014, https://www.thenation.com/article/cias-secret-sites-somalia/ [last checked 23 July 2016].

23. Craig Whitlock, 'Remote U.S. base at core of secret operations', *The Washington Post*, 25 October 2012, http://www.washingtonpost.com/world/national-security/remote-us-base-at-core-of-secret-operations/2012/10/25/a26a9392–197a-11e2-bd10–5ff056538b7c_story.html [last checked 2 August 2016].

24. Intelligence, Surveillance and Reconnaissance Task Force, 'ISR Support to Small Footprint CT Operations—Somalia/Yemen', February 2013, available at *The Intercept*: https://theintercept.com/document/2015/10/15/small-footprint-operations-2–13/ [last checked 2 August 2016].

25. Jack Serle and Abigail Fielding-Smith, 'Monthly Updates on the Covert War October 2014 Update: US Covert Actions in Pakistan, Yemen and Somalia', The Bureau of Investigative Journalism, 3 November 2014, http://www.thebureauinvestigates.com/2014/11/03/october-2014-update-us-covert-actions-in-pakistan-yemen-and-somalia/ [last checked 5 June 2017]. The number of reported strikes in Somalia is clearly extremely low and must be treated with care in the context of a national population desensitised to warfare, and a state extremely dangerous for journalists, with effectively no centralised government or state structures.

26. The Bureau of Investigative Journalism, 'Drone Wars—Somalia: Reported US Covert Actions 2001–2016', 22 February 2012, https://www.thebureauinvestigates.com/2012/02/22/get-the-data-somalias-hidden-war/ [last checked 2 August 2016].

27. Whitlock, 'Remote U.S. base at core of secret operations'.

28. Jacey Fortin, 'Djibouti Government Forces US Drones To Leave Airport After Tense Summer For American Troops at Camp Lemonnier', *International Business Times*, 26 September 2013, http://www.ibtimes.com/djibouti-government-forces-us-drones-leave-airport-after-tense-summer-american-troops-camp-lemonnier [last checked 2 August 2016].

29. Craig Whitlock, 'Chaos in Skies, Danger in Skies at Base in Africa', *The Washington Post*, 30 April 2015, https://www.washingtonpost.com/world/national-security/miscues-at-us-counterterrorism-base-

put-aircraft-in-danger-documents-show/2015/04/30/39038d5a-e9bb-11e4–9a6a-c1ab95a0600b_story.html [last checked 2 August 2016].

30. Whitlock, 'Chaos in Skies'.
31. Ibid.
32. Turse, 'The Stealth Expansion of a Secret US Drone Base in Africa'.
33. Nick Turse, 'Target Africa: The U.S. Military's Expanding Footprint in East Africa and the Arabian Peninsula', *The Intercept*, The Drone Papers no. 08, 15 October 2015, https://theintercept.com/drone-papers/target-africa/ [last checked 2 August 2016].
34. Ibid.
35. Whitlock, 'Remote U.S. base at core of secret operations'.
36. Cora Currier, 'The Kill Chain—the Lethal Bureaucracy Behind Obama's Drone War', *The Intercept*, Drone Papers No. 03, 15 October 2015, https://theintercept.com/drone-papers/the-kill-chain/ [last checked 2 August 2016].
37. Marcy Wheeler, 'The Disposition of Informants and Citizens', emptywheel, 4 January 2013, http://www.emptywheel.net/2013/01/04/the-disposition-of-informants-and-citizens/ [last checked 2 August 2016].
38. Ian Cobain, British 'al-Qaida Member' Killed in US Drone Attack in Somalia, *The Guardian*, 22 January 2012, http://www.guardian.co.uk/world/2012/jan/22/british-al-qaida-suspect-drone-somalia [last checked 2 August 2016],
39. Ryan Gallagher, 'The Life and Death of Objective Peckham', *The Intercept*, The Drone Papers No. 07, 15 October 2015, https://theintercept.com/drone-papers/the-life-and-death-of-objective-peckham/ [last checked 2 August 2016].
40. Abdi Guled, 'Al-Shabaab Executes 3 Members', *The Washington Times*, 22 July 2012, http://www.washingtontimes.com/news/2012/jul/22/al-shabab-executes-3-members/ [last checked 2 August 2016].
41. Ryan Gallagher, 'The Life and Death of Objective Peckham'.
42. Benjamin Weiser, 'Terrorist has Cooperated With U.S. Since Secret Guilty Plea in 2011, Papers Show', *The New York Times*, 25 March 2013, http://www.nytimes.com/2013/03/26/nyregion/since-2011-guilty-plea-somali-terrorist-has-cooperated-with-authorities.html [last checked 1 April 2017].

43. FBI, New York Field Office, 'Guilty Plea Unsealed in New York Involving Ahmed Warsame, a Senior Terrorist Leader and Liaison Between al Shabaab and al Qaeda in the Arabian Peninsula, for Providing Material Support to Both Terrorist Organizations', press release, U.S. Attorney's Office & Southern District of New York, 25 March 2013, available at http://www.fbi.gov/newyork/press-releases/ 2013/guilty-plea-unsealed-in-new-york-involving-ahmed-warsame-a-senior-terrorist-leader-and-liaison-between-al-shabaab-and-al-qaeda-in-the-arabian-peninsula-for-providing-material-support-to-both-terrorist-organizations [last checked 5 June 2017].

44. Charlie Savage, 'U.S. Tests New Approach to Terrorism Cases on Somali Suspect', 6 July 2011, *The New York Times*, http://www. nytimes.com/2011/07/07/world/africa/07detain.html [last checked 2 August 2016].

45. Channel 4 News, 'Somali terror suspect appears before US civilian court', 6 July 2011, http://www.channel4.com/news/somali-terror-suspect-appears-before-us-civilian-court [last checked 2 August 2016].

46. See America's Navy, 'USS Boxer MH-60S Flight Operatoins', 27 May 2011, http://www.public.navy.mil/surfor/lhd4/Pages/USSBoxerMH-60SFlightOperations.aspx#.Uv5uh0J_uR8 [last checked 5 June 2017]; 13th Marine Expeditionary Unit unofficial blog, 'Marines Graduate Inaugural Corporal's Course', 29 April 2011, http://13thmeu.blogspot. co.uk/2011_04_01_archive.html; 'BLT 1/1 train with GIGN', 31 May 2011, http://13thmeu.blogspot.co.uk/2011_05_01_archive.html; 13th MEU blog, 'GIGN complete BLT 1/1 training', 30 June 2011, http://13thmeu.blogspot.co.uk/2011_06_01_archive.html; 13th MEU blog, 'Charlie Company conduct demo traiing with GIGN troops', 18 July 2011, http://13thmeu.blogspot.co.uk/2011_07_01_archive.html [all last checked 5 June 2017].

47. According to the Bureau of Investigative Journalism, the first took place on 23 June 2011, killing at least two people, and injuring two to three others. Bureau of Investigative Journalism, 'Somalia: Reported US Covert Actions 2001–2016', 22 February 2012 (BIJ database item Som010), http://www.thebureauinvestigates.com/2012/02/22/get-the-data-somalias-hidden-war/ [last checked 2 August 2016].

48. Cora Currier and Peter Maass, 'Firing Blind: Flawed Intelligence and the Limits of Drone Technology', *The Intercept*, The Drone Papers No. 6, 15 October 2015, https://theintercept.com/drone-papers/firing-blind/ [last checked 2 August 2016].

49. Ibid.

50. Weiser, 'Terrorist has Cooperated with US Since Secret Guilty Plea in 2011, Papers Show'.

8. DEATH SQUADS

1. Gabriel Gatehouse, 'The Muslim Cleric Who Predicted He Would Be Killed', BBC News, 9 April 2014, http://www.bbc.co.uk/news/world-africa-26958455 [last checked 8 June 2017].

2. United Nations High Commissioner for Human Rights, 'UN Special Rapporteur on Extrajudicial, Arbitrary or Summary Executions, Addendum—Mission to Kenya', 16–25 February 2009, available at http://reliefweb.int/report/kenya/report-special-rapporteur-extrajudicial-summary-or-arbitrary-executions-mr-philip [last checked 1 April 2017].

3. Ibid.

4. Associated Press, 'Two Grenade Blasts Rattle Nairobi; 1 Dead', 24 October 2011.

5. Reuters, 'Nairobi bus station blast toll rises to five: Red Cross', 11 March 2012.

6. Bosire Boniface, 'Timeline: Grenade and Landmine Attacks in Kenya', SabahiOnline, 30 August 2012, http://sabahionline.com/en_GB/articles/hoa/articles/features/2012/08/30/feature-01 [last checked 2 August 2016].

7. Boniface, 'Timeline'.

8. Ibid.; Julius Mokaya, 'Police arrest 4 suspects in connection with Nairobi bus station blast', SabahiOnline, 12 March 2012, http://sabahionline.com/en_GB/articles/hoa/articles/features/2012/03/12/feature-01 [last checked 2 August 2016].

9. 'We're Tired of Taking You to the Court: Human Rights Abuses by Kenya's Anti-Terrorism', Open Society Justice Initiative, 2013, p. 42, https://www.opensocietyfoundations.org/sites/default/files/human-

rights-abuses-by-kenya-atpu-20140220.pdf [last checked 8 June 2017]; IRIN Africa News, 'Gunned down in Mombasa—the Clerics that have died', http://www.irinnews.org/report/100412/gunned-down-in-mombasa-the-clerics-that-have-died [last checked 2 August 2016].

10. According to HAKI Africa.

11. Human Rights Watch, 'Kenya: Killings, Disappearances by Anti-Terror Police', 18 August 2014, https://www.hrw.org/news/2014/08/18/kenya-killings-disappearances-anti-terror-police [last checked 2 August 2016].

12. In forming the category descriptions, we followed the very useful approach used in the Cambridge University Centre for Governance and Human Rights report 'Unlawful Killings in Africa' (p. 13, http://www.cghr.polis.cam.ac.uk/research-themes/right_to_life/unlawful_killings_in_africa/unlawful_killings_report/Unlawful_Killings_Africa.pdf [last checked 2 August 2016]).

13. Human Rights Watch, Kenya: Killings, Disappearances by Anti-Terror Police'.

14. Ibid.

15. BBC, 'Kenya Police Seize Weapons in Mombasa Mosque Raid', 17 November 2014, http://www.bbc.co.uk/news/world-africa-30078973 [last checked 2 August 2016].

16. Capital FM Kenya, 'Makaburi killers no different from Baby Satrine attackers—Lenku' https://www.youtube.com/watch?v=O-jtJ6ipIBQ [last checked 17 November 2014].

17. Cambridge University Centre for Governance and Human Rights, 'Unlawful Killings in Africa', p. vi.

9. WHERE THERE IS A SEA

1. Spencer Ackerman, 'US delays prison for Somali man as officials tell of "intelligence watershed"', *The Guardian*, 4 December 2013, https://www.theguardian.com/world/2013/dec/04/somali-terrorism-intelligence-us-officials [last checked 19 July 2017].

2. See, for example, Jerika Richardson, 'Somali Pirate Asks Forgiveness, Sentenced To Nearly 34 Years In Prison', ABC News, 16 February 2011, http://abcnews.go.com/Blotter/somali-pirate-muse-sentenced-34-years/story?id=12930166 [last checked 19 July 2017].

3. The CMF is comprised of three main task forces: CTF-150 (maritime security and counter-terrorism), CTF-151 (counterpiracy), and CTF-152 (Arabia Gulf Security and Cooperation). All three commands are located at US Naval Support Activity Bahrain. The CMF has 27 member nations: Australia, Bahrain, Belgium, Canada, Denmark, France, Germany, Greece, Italy, Japan, Jordan, Republic of Korea, Kuwait, Malaysia, the Netherlands, New Zealand, Pakistan, Portugal, Saudi Arabia, Singapore, Spain, Thailand, Turkey, UAE, UK and US (see: Combined Maritime Forces Blog, 'CMF hosts 21st SHADE Meeting', 27 September 2011, http://combinedmaritimeforces.com/2011/09/27/cmf-hosts-21st-shade-meeting/ [last checked 2 August 2016]).

4. Council of the European Union, 'Council Conclusions on the Horn of Africa, 3124th Foreign Affairs Council Meeting', 14 November 2011, http://www.consilium.europa.eu/uedocs/cms_data/docs/pressdata/EN/foraff/126052.pdf [last checked 2 August 2016]. EUNAVFOR operates within the framework of the European Commission Security and Defence Policy (CSDP). The Council of the EU has recently extended the operation until the end of 2018 (see Council of the European Union, 'EUNAVFOR Somalia Operation Atalanta: operation's mandate extended until 31 December 2018', press release, 28 November 2016, http://www.consilium.europa.eu/en/press/press-releases/2016/11/28-eu-navfor-somalia-operation-mandate-extended/ [last checked 21 July 2017]).

5. On 1 May 2007, American Navy News reported 'coalition ships from the British-led Combined Task Force (CTF) 150 continue to maintain a presence off the east coast of Africa in response to the recent events in Somalia. CTF 150 includes USS Ramage (DDG 61) and USS Bunker Hill (CG 52) and other coalition ships. These warships are conducting maritime security operations (MSO) to ensure continued security and stability of international waters surrounding the Horn of Africa. Coalition naval forces are performing boardings on a number of vessels to deter individuals with links to al-Qaida and other terrorist organizations the use of the sea as a potential escape route. The coalition ships of CTF 150 maintain a maritime presence in the international waters of the Gulf of Oman, North Arabian Sea, parts of the Indian Ocean, Gulf of Aden, and the Red Sea.'

6. Shashank Bengali, 'Somalis say Illegal Fishing by Foreign Trawlers Drove Them to Piracy', McClatchy, 29 April 2009, available at Information Clearing House: http://www.informationclearinghouse. info/article22522.htm [last checked 2 August 2016].

7. John Vidal, 'Will overfishing by foreigners drive Senegalese fishermen to piracy?', *The Guardian*, https://www.theguardian.com/global-development/poverty-matters/2012/apr/03/overfishing-foreigners-senegal-fishermen-piracy [last checked 8 June 2017].

8. Ghassan Schbley and William Rosenau, 'Piracy, Illegal Fishing and Maritime Insecurity in Somalia, Kenya and Tanzania', CNA Strategic Studies, September 2013, p. 31, http://oceansbeyondpiracy.org/sites/default/files/attachments/CNA_Sep%202013_Piracy-Illegal-Fishing-and%20Maritime-Insecurity.pdf [last checked 9 June 2017].

9. Task Force on IUU Fishing on the High Seas, 'Closing the net: Stopping illegal fishing on the high seas'. Governments of Australia, Canada, Chile, Namibia, New Zealand, and the United Kingdom, WWF, IUCN and the Earth Institute at Columbia University, High Seas Task Force, 2006, p. 14, http://www.imcsnet.org/imcs/docs/hstf_final_report.pdf [last checked 2 August 2016].

10. Ibid., p. 14.

11. Ibid., p. 22.

12. Ibid.

13. Ibid., p. 80.

14. The High Seas Task Force (HSTF) notes that 'IUU fishing therefore imposes significant economic costs on some of the poorest countries in the world where dependency on fisheries for food, livelihoods and revenues is high.' Ibid., p. 3.

15. Greenpeace, 'The Toxic Ships: The Italian Hub, the Mediterranean Area and Africa', June 2010, p. 17, http://www.greenpeace.it/Report-The-toxic-ship.pdf [last checked 2 August 2016].

16. Ibid., pp. 12–13.

17. Chris Milton, 'Somalia Used as Toxic Dumping Ground', *The Ecologist*, 1 March 2009, http://www.theecologist.org/News/news_analysis/268581/somalia_used_as_toxic_dumping_ground.html [last checked 2 August 2016].

18. Greenpeace, 'The Toxic Ships', p. 21.

19. Milton, 'Somalia Used as Toxic Dumping Ground'.

20. See, for example: the HSTF: 'One of the key difficulties throughout has been to gather the necessary political leadership needed to carry internationally agreed targets and declarations into effect. This has been reflected in a lack of willingness on the part of some states to participate in multilateral arrangements or, when they do, to do so without any deep sense of commitment—a phenomenon by no means confined to fishing. The 153 paragraphs that emerged as the Johannesburg Plan of Action from the 2002 World Summit on Sustainable Development make repeated reference to the need to fulfil previously agreed commitments. It was the uneven and sometimes ambivalent nature of political leadership that led the Round Table on Sustainable Development at the OECD3 to focus on just one of the many items contained in the Johannesburg Plan. A meeting of fisheries ministers at the Round Table in June 2003 was invited to review progress and discuss how best to bring leverage to bear on a global problem which lay beyond the enforcement capabilities of any one country or even any single regional or international agency.' Task Force on IUU Fishing on the High Seas, 'Closing the net', p. 17.

21. 'Somalia: Fishermen Driven From the Sea By Illegal Trawlers, IRIN News, 27 June 2011, http://www.irinnews.org/report/93079/somalia-fishermen-driven-from-the-sea-by-illegal-trawlers [last checked 2 August 2016].

22. 'The "Benefit" of Somalia's Pirates', Channel 4 News, 25 October 2009, http://www.channel4.com/news/articles/world/africa/the+aposbenefi tapos+of+somaliaaposs+pirates/3399027.html [last checked 2 August 2016].

23. Ken Silverstein, 'Pirates and the CIA: What would Thomas Jefferson have done?', *Harper's Magazine*, 9 April 2009, http://harpers.org/blog/2009/04/pirates-and-the-cia-what-would-thomas-jefferson-have-done/ [last checked 2 August 2016].

24. International Chamber of Commerce Commercial Crime Services, 'Attacks off the Somali coast drive piracy to record high, reports IMB', 14 April 2011, http://www.icc-ccs.org/news/304-attacks-off-the-

somali-coast-drive-piracy-to-record-high-reports-imb [last checked 2 August 2016].

25. Risk and strategic consulting firm Control Risks attributed this massive decline in pirate activity from 2012 to a range of factors, including the greater use of armed private security personnel, which after 2011 took an increasing role in the conduct of international counter-piracy efforts in the Indian Ocean.

26. 'The Human Cost of Maritime Piracy 2012', Working Paper, Oceans Beyond Piracy, p. 3, http://oceansbeyondpiracy.org/sites/default/files/attachments/View%20Full%20Report_0.pdf [last checked 9 June 2017].

27. Ibid., p. viii.

28. Noah Rayman, 'Did 2013 Mark the End of Somali Piracy?', *Time Magazine*, 6 January 2013, http://world.time.com/2014/01/06/did-2013-mark-the-end-of-somali-piracy/ [last checked 2 August 2016].

29. Martin Plaut, 'Private Patrol Boats to Tackle Somali Pirates', BBC World Service, 30 May 2012, http://www.bbc.co.uk/news/world-africa-18209357 [last checked 2 August 2016].

30. Ibid.; Jonathan Ibun, 'Typhon Fights Back Against Pirates', *The Daily Telegraph*, 15 January 2012, http://www.telegraph.co.uk/news/world-news/piracy/9016188/Typhon-fights-back-against-pirates.html [last checked 2 August 2016]. As founder Anthony Sharp described in a promotional video: 'The Typhon force will be the first of its kind for probably 200 years and will protect private ship owners' assets at sea. Somali piracy has grown from entrepreneurial Somalis taking advantage of the closeness of shipping to their shores and their complete lack of coast guards to a fully-fledged criminal activity.'

31. Michelle Wiese Bockmann and Alan Katz, 'Shooting to Kill Pirates Risks Blackwater Moment', *Bloomberg*, 8 May 2012, http://www.bloomberg.com/news/2012–05–08/shooting-to-kill-pirates-risks-blackwater-moment.html [last checked 2 August 2016].

32. ICC International Maritime Bureau, 'Piracy and Armed Robbery Against Ships: Report for the Period 1 January–31 December 2011', January 2012, http://psm.du.edu/media/documents/industry_initiatives/industry_reports/maritime_imb_annual-report-2011.pdf [last checked 2 August 2016].

33. Vellientertain, 'Private Security Guards Shoot Somali Pirates', 6 April 2012, http://www.youtube.com/watch?v=ESFFFW0B64I [last checked 2 August 2016]; 'The Human Cost of Maritime Piracy 2012', p. 32.

34. 'The Human Cost of Maritime Piracy 2012', p. 32.

35. US Embassy, 'Djibouti Approves Blackwater For Commercial Counter-piracy Operations', confidential cable, 12 February 2009, https://wikileaks.org/plusd/cables/09DJIBOUTI113_a.html [last checked 9 June 2017]. On the Counter Piracy Coordination Cell, see also US Embassy, 'Djibouti seeks to host Somali Counter-Piracy Coordination Center', confidential cable, 12 January 2009, http://cablegatesearch.net/cable.php?id=09DJIBOUTI27

36. Drazen Jorgic, 'Rise in Illegal Fishing Threatens to Revive Somali Piracy', Reuters, 31 March 2015, http://www.reuters.com/article/2015/03/31/us-somalia-piracy-crime-idUSKBN0MR17S20150331 [last checked 9 June 2017]; US Embassy, 'Djibouti Approves Blackwater For Commercial Counter-piracy Operations'.

37. Associated Press, 'Pirates Demand Ransom for Oil Tanker Captured Off Coast of Somalia', *The Guardian*, 14 March 2017, https://www.theguardian.com/world/2017/mar/14/pirates-demand-ransom-for-oil-tanker-captured-off-coast-of-somalia [last checked 9 June 2017].

38. UN Somalia and Eritrea Sanctions Committee Monitoring Group, 'Report of the Monitoring Group on Somalia and Eritrea pursuant to Security Council resolution 2060 (2012): Somalia', Annex 3.1: Spoiler networks in northern Somalia, 12 July 2013, Report S/2013/413, p. 101, https://www.un.org/sc/suborg/en/sanctions/751/work-and-mandate/reports [last checked 9 June 2017].

39. 'Somali Pirates Now Protecting Illegal Fishing Ships, Says UN Report', Associated Press, 26 July 2013, available at Hiraan Online, http://www.hiiraan.com/news4/2013/July/30468/somali_pirates_now_protecting_illegal_fishing_ships_says_un_report.aspx; [last checked 9 June 2017]; US Embassy, Djibouti Approves Blackwater For Commercial Counter-piracy Operations'.

40. Schbley and Rosenau, 'Piracy, Illegal Fishing and Maritime Insecurity in Somalia, Kenya and Tanzania', p. 31; US Embassy, 'Djibouti Approves Blackwater For Commercial Counter-piracy Operations'.

10. CIVIL SOCIETY STIFLED

1. National Authorities of Ethiopia, 'Proclamation No. 652/2009 of 2009, Anti-Terrorism Proclamation', 7 July 2009, preamble, available at http://www.refworld.org/docid/4ba799d32.html [last checked 2 August 2016].

2. See, for example, Human Rights Watch, 'Ethiopia: Amend Draft Terror Law', 30 June 2009, http://www.hrw.org/news/2009/06/30/ethiopia-amend-draft-terror-law [last checked 2 August 2016].

3. National Authorities of Ethiopia, 'Anti-Terrorism Proclamation'.

4. Ibid.

5. National Authorities of Ethiopia, 'Proclamation No. 621/2009 of 2009, Charities and Societies Proclamation', 13 February 2009, http://www.refworld.org/docid/4ba7a0cb2.html, [last checked 2 August 2016].

6. Amnesty International, 'Annual Report: Ethiopia 2010', http://www.amnestyusa.org/research/reports/annual-report-ethiopia-2010?page=2 [last checked 2 August 2016].

7. Ibid.

8. Ibid.

9. Amnesty International, 'Annual Report: Ethiopia 2011', http://www.amnestyusa.org/research/reports/annual-report-ethiopia-2011?page=2 [last checked 2 August 2016].

10. Ibid.

11. For further information, see Human Rights Watch, 'Ethiopia: 4 Journalists Win Free Speech Prize', 20 December 2012, http://www.hrw.org/news/2012/12/20/ethiopia-4-journalists-win-free-speech-prize [last checked 12 June 2017].

12. Human Rights Watch, 'Kenya: Rights Defenders Under Attack', 4 October 2013, http://www.hrw.org/news/2013/10/04/kenya-rights-defenders-under-attack [last checked 2 August 2016].

13. Lily Lui, 'Help Not Needed: Kenya is pressurising thousands of expat NGO workers and volunteers to go home', *Quartz Africa*, 19 July 2016, http://qz.com/716518/kenya-is-pressuring-thousands-of-expat-ngo-workers-and-volunteers-to-go-home/ [last checked 29 July 2016].

14. 'Kenya "Deregisters" NGOs in Anti-Terror Clampdown', BBC News,

16 December 2014, http://www.bbc.co.uk/news/world-africa-30494259 [last checked 29 July 2016].

15. 'NGOs in Kenya Protest Threatened Deregistration of 959 Organisations', IRIN News, 30 October 2015, http://www.irinnews.org/report/102174/ ngos-kenya-protest-threatened-deregistration-959-organisations, [last checked 29 July 2016].

16. 'Kimaiyo Warns NGOs to Keep Off Government's Crackdown on Terrorists and Radical Muslims—We Will Finish Them', *The Kenyan Daily Post*, 7 April 2014.

17. 'Mombasa NGOs to be Investigated for Inciting Youth', My News 24, 19 March 2014, http://www.news24.co.ke/MyNews24/Mombasa-NGOs-to-be-investigated-for-inciting-youth-20140319 [last checked 2 August 2016].

11. MOTIFS OF EXCLUSION: SECURITISATION AND COLLECTIVE PUNISHMENT IN KENYAN COUNTERTERRORISM OPERATIONS

1. Kenya Ministry of State and Planning, Hon. Wycliffe Ambesta Oparanya (Minister of State for Planning, National Development and Vision 2030), '2009 Population and Housing Census Results', 31 August 2010, https:// web.archive.org/web/20130115103229/http://www.knbs.or.ke/docs/ PresentationbyMinisterforPlanningrevised.pdf [last checked 2 August 2016].

2. UNHCR, 'Refugees in the Horn of Africa: Somalia Displacement Crisis', http://data.unhcr.org/horn-of-africa/regional.php [last checked 2 August 2016].

3. Human Rights Watch, 'Kenya: Counterterrorism Operations Undermine Human Rights, No Justice for Security Force Abuses', 29 January 2015, https://www.hrw.org/news/2015/01/29/kenya-counterterrorism-oper-ations-undermine-rights [last checked 2 August 2016].

4. Amnesty International, 'Kenya 2016/17', annual report, https://www. amnesty.org/en/countries/africa/kenya/report-kenya/ [last checked 13 June 2017].

5. Names have been changed for confidentiality.

6. Kenya Human Rights Commission, 'Briefing Paper on Kenya', 56th

Session of the African Commission on Human and People's Rights, 21 April–7 May 2015, http://www.khrc.or.ke/publications/20-country-brief-at-the-56th-ordinary-session-of-the-african-commission-on-human-and-people-s-rights/file.html [last checked 13 June 2017].

7. 'Tripartite Agreement Between the Government of the Republic of Kenya, the Government of the Federal Republic of Somalia and the United Nations High Commissioner for Refugees Governing the Voluntary Repatriation of Somali Refugees Living in Kenya, 2013', Preamble J, http://www.refworld.org/pdfid/5285e0294.pdf [last checked 13 June 2017]. Emphasis added.

8. Independent Policing Oversight Authority (IPOA), 'Monitoring Report on Operation Sanitization Eastleigh, Publically Known as "Usalama Watch"', 2014, available at http://www.regionalmms.org/images/sector/IPOA%20report%20on%20Usalama%20Watch%20operation%20in%20Eastleigh,%20Kenya.pdf [last checked 20 July 2017].

9. Ibid.

10. Hannah Whittaker, 'Legacies of Empire: State Violence and Collective Punishment in Kenya's North Eastern Province, c. 1963–Present', *The Journal of Imperial and Commonwealth History*, vol. 43, no. 4 (2015), pp. 641–57, DOI: 10.1080/03086534.2015.1083232, http://dx.doi.org/10.1080/03086534.2015.1083232 [last checked 31 March 2017].

11. Ibid.

12. *Salim Awadh Salim & 10 Others v Commissioner of Police & 3 Others*, Kenya High Court, Constitutional & Judicial Review Division, Case No. 822 of 2008, http://kenyalaw.org/caselaw/cases/view/89752/ [last checked 21 July 2017].

13. Amnesty International, 'Kenya: Somalis trapped in "catch-22" amid crackdown on refugees', 11 April 2014, https://www.amnesty.org/en/latest/news/2014/04/kenya-somalis-placed-catch-amid-crackdown-refugees/ [last checked 13 June 2017].

14. Refugees International, 'Kenya: Government Directive Leads to Severe Abuses and Forced Returns', field report, 27 February 2012, http://reliefweb.int/sites/reliefweb.int/files/resources/Government%20Directive%20Leads%20to%20Severe%20Abuses%20and%20Forced%20Returns.pdf [last checked 13 June 2017].

15. Lydia Matata, 'Kenya: Xenophobia Becoming a Reality in Kenya', *The Star*, 13 May 2014, http://allafrica.com/stories/201405130974.html? viewall=1 [last checked 13 June 2017].

12. CYBER WARS

1. Nick Hopkins, 'Militarisation of cyberspace: how the global power struggle moved online', *The Guardian*, 16 April 2012, https://www.theguardian.com/technology/2012/apr/16/militarisation-of-cyberspace-power-struggle [last checked 25 July 2016].

2. Glenn Greenwald, 'NSA collecting phone records of millions of Verizon customers daily', *The Guardian*, 6 June 2013, http://www.theguardian.com/world/2013/jun/06/nsa-phone-records-verizon-court-order [last checked 13 June 2017]; Ellen Nakashima, 'Verizon providing all call records to U.S. under court order', *The Washington Post*, 6 June 2013, https://www.washingtonpost.com/world/national-security/verizon-providing-all-call-records-to-us-under-court-order/2013/06/05/98656606-ce47-11e2-8845-d970ccb04497_story.html [last checked 2 August 2016].

3. Cameron Stewart and Paul Maley, 'Edward Snowden Stole Up to 20,000 Aussie Files', *The Australian*, 5 December 2013; David Miranda Row, 'Seized Files Endanger Agents', BBC News, 30 August 2013, http://www.bbc.co.uk/news/uk-23898580 [last checked 2 August 2016]

4. Laura Poitras, Marcel Rosenbach, Holger Stark, '"A" for Angela: GCHQ and NSA Targeted Private German Companies and Merkel', *Der Spiegel Online*, http://www.spiegel.de/international/germany/gchq-and-nsa-targeted-private-german-companies-a-961444.html [last checked 2 August 2016].

5. R Ryan Devereaux, Glenn Greenwald, Laura Poitras, 'Data Pirates of the Caribbean', *The Intercept*, 19 May 2014, https://theintercept.com/2014/05/19/data-pirates-caribbean-nsa-recording-every-cell-phone-call-bahamas/ [last checked 2 August 2016].

6. Wikileaks, 'Wikileaks statement on the mass recording of Afghan telephone calls by the NSA', 23 May 2014, https://wikileaks.org/WikiLeaks-statement-on-the-mass.html [last checked 21 July 2017].

7. Ibid.

8. Privacy International, 'State of Privacy: Kenya', https://www.privacy-international.org/node/980 [last checked 13 June 2017; last modified 14 March 2017].

9. Ibid.

10. Michael Rispoli, 'Kenyans face new privacy threats as state expands surveillance powers', Privacy International, 8 January 2015, https://www.privacyinternational.org/node/99 [last checked 2 August 2016].

11. 'High Court Suspends Eight Clauses in the Security Law', Kenyan Judiciary Portal, 2 January 2015, http://www.judiciary.go.ke/portal/blog/post/high-court-suspends-eight-clauses-in-the-security-law [last checked 2 August 2016].

12. Rispoli, 'Kenyans face new privacy threats'.

13. Arguably, systems of secrecy obstructing such oversight in states with a stronger rule of law such as the US and the UK could similarly end up preventing effective functionality of proportionality assessments. In any case, there is no means of public, non-classified reckoning.

14. Interviews with both the author and Al-Amin Kimathi.

15. President Uhuru Kenyatta's director of digital media and diaspora affairs, Dennis Itumbi, was originally accused of being responsible for the hacking, which he denied. See: *The Prosecutor v. Francis Kirimi Muthaura and Uhuru Muigai Kenyatta*, Situation in the Republic of Kenya (ICC-01/09–02/11), 28/09/2012, https://www.icc-cpi.int/iccdocs/doc/doc1477582.pdf [last checked 2 August 2016].

16. Peace Brigades International, 'An Assessment of the Feasibility and Effectiveness of Protective Accompaniment in Kenya', July 2012, http://www.peacebrigades.org.uk/fileadmin/user_files/international/files/special_report/PBI_Kenya_report.pdf [last checked 2 August 2016].

17. Wikileaks Hacking Team Archive, 'R: HT-Italy, Email ID 14276 from e.shehata@hackingteam.com to d.milan@hackingteam.com, rsales@hackingteam.com, 7 May 2015', https://wikileaks.org/hackingteam/emails/emailid/14276 [last checked 2 August 2016].

18. Bill Marczak, John Scott-Railton, Adam Senft, Irene Poetranto, Sarah McKune, 'Pay No Attention to the Server Behind the Proxy: Mapping Finfisher's Continuing Proliferation', Citizenlab, Munk School of Global Affairs, University of Toronto, 15 October 2015, https://citi-

zenlab.org/2015/10/mapping-finfishers-continuing-proliferation/ [last checked 2 August 2016].

19. David Leigh, 'Offshore Company Directors' Links to Military and Intelligence Revealed', *The Guardian*, 28 November 2012, http://www.theguardian.com/uk/2012/nov/28/offshore-company-directors-military-intelligence [last checked 2 August 2016].

13. BIG BROTHER INC.

1. See, for example, 'WikiLeaks Spy Files: GAMMA', YouTube, uploaded on 9 December 2011, https://www.youtube.com/watch?v=oNsXK PHBR3s [last checked 19 September 2016].

3. Amar Toor and Russel Brandon, 'A Spy in the Machine: How a Brutal Government Used Cutting-Edge Spyware to Hijack One Activist's Life', *The Verge*, 21 January 2015, http://www.theverge.com/2015/1/21/7861645/finfisher-spyware-let-bahrain-government-hack-political-activist [last checked 2 August 2016].

4. Bill Marczak, John Scott-Railton, Adam Senft, Irene Poetranto, Sarah McKune, 'Pay No Attention to the Server Behind the Proxy: Mapping Finfisher's Continuing Proliferation', The Citizen Lab, Munk School of Global Affairs, University of Toronto, 15 October 2015, https://citizenlab.org/2015/10/mapping-finfishers-continuing-proliferation/ [last checked 2 August 2016].

5. Liat Clark, 'Ethiopian Refugee "Illegally" Spied on Using British Software', *Wired*, 17 February 2014, http://www.wired.co.uk/news/archive/2014–02/17/illegal-spying-ethiopian-refugee; *Kidane v. Ethiopia*, Washington DC, see Electronic Frontier Foundation website, https://www.eff.org/cases/kidane-v-ethiopia [last checked 2 August 2016].

6. Ibid.

7. 'Global Surveillance: The Open Market', Justice Forum and Spirited Pictures, 2015, https://www.youtube-nocookie.com/embed/GWbFIh EVE9c?autoplay=1 [last checked 2 August 2016].

8. Human Rights Watch, '"They Know Everything We Do": Telecom and Internet Surveillance in Ethiopia', 25 March 2014, https://www.hrw.org/report/2014/03/25/they-know-everything-we-do/telecom-and-internet-surveillance-ethiopia [last checked 2 August 2016].

9. Human Rights Watch, 'Ethiopia: Digital Attacks Intensify', 9 March 2015, https://www.hrw.org/news/2015/03/09/ethiopia-digital-attacks-intensify [last checked 2 August 2016].

10. Privacy International, 'For God and My President: State Surveillance in Uganda', 15 October 2015, https://privacyinternational.org/node/656 [last checked 2 August 2016].

11. 'RE: I: Somtel', email from Ismail Dualeh to Marco Bettini, 30 October 2012, Email ID 435037, WikiLeaks, 8 July 2015, https://wikileaks.org/hackingteam/emails/emailid/435037 [last checked 29 July 2016].

12. 'RE: I: Somtel', email from Marco Bettini to Ismail Dualeh, 13 November 2012, Email ID 435037, Wikileaks, 8 July 2015, https://wikileaks.org/hackingteam/emails/emailid/435037 [last checked 29 July 2016].

13. 'RE: I: Somtel', email from Ismail Dualeh to Marco Bettini.

14. Human Rights Watch, '"They Know Everything We Do"'.

14. BETWEEN TWO FIRES

1. Michael Onyiego, 'The Day They Came to Kill Me: A Somali journalist remembers the day armed men attacked him', Al-Jazeera, 1 November 2015, http://www.aljazeera.com/indepth/features/2015/11/day-kill-151101161035093.html [last checked 23/07/16].

2. Abdalle Ahmed Mumin, 'Somalia: A Threat By Any Name', *Financial Mail*, 28 May 2015, http://www.financialmail.co.za/features/2015/05/28/somalia-a-threat-by-any-name [last checked 23 July 2016].

3. 'Al Jazeera Kabul Offices Hit in US Raid', BBC News, 13 November 2001, http://news.bbc.co.uk/1/hi/world/south_asia/1653887.stm [last checked 23 July 2016].

4. Clive Stafford-Smith, 'Embedded in Gitmo', *The Guardian*, 28 March 2006, https://www.theguardian.com/commentisfree/2006/mar/28/athomewithaljazeera [last checked 19 July 2017].

5. Sami al-Hajj, 'Sami al-Hajj: Remembering Guantánamo', Al-Jazeera, 11 January 2016, http://www.aljazeera.com/indepth/features/2016/01/sami-al-hajj-remembering-Guantánamo-160106182602246.html [last checked 23 July 2016].

6. Dahr Jamail, 'Iraq: The Deadliest War for Journalists', Al-Jazeera,

11 April 2013, http://www.aljazeera.com/humanrights/2013/04/2013
481202781452.html [last checked 23 July 2016].

7. Committee to Protect Journalists, 'Iraq, The Islamic State Group
Silences the Press', https://cpj.org/mideast/iraq/ [last checked 20 June
2017].

8. Nadia Massih, 'Infographic: Islamic State's Assault on the Press',
Committee to Protect Journalists, 8 June 2016, https://cpj.org/blog/
2016/06/infographic-islamic-states-assault-on-the-press.php [last
checked 23 July 2016].

9. Jack Shafer, 'Spare Me Your Hypocritical Journalism Lecture, Mr
President', *POLITICO Magazine*, 29 March 2016, http://www.polit-
ico.com/magazine/story/2016/03/obama-hypocritical-journalism-lec-
ture-213775 [last checked 23 July 2016].

10. Cora Currier, 'Charting Obama's Crackdown on National Security
Leaks', ProPublica, 30 July 2013, https://www.propublica.org/special/
sealing-loose-lips-charting-obamas-crackdown-on-national-security-
leaks [last checked 23 July 2016].

11. Leonard Downie Jr., 'The Obama Administration and the Press: Leak
Investigations and Surveillance in post-9/11 America', Committee to
Protect Journalists, 10 October 2013, https://www.cpj.org/reports/
2013/10/obama-and-the-press-us-leaks-surveillance-post-911.php
[last checked 23 July 2016].

12. Ed Pilkington, 'Journalist James Risen ordered to testify in CIA leaker
trial', *The Guardian*, 19 July 2013, https://www.theguardian.com/
media/2013/jul/19/us-press-publishing-us-constitution-and-civil-lib-
erties [last checked 19 July 2017].

13. Marisa Taylor and Jonathan S. Landay, 'Obama's Crackdown Views
Leaks as Aiding Enemies of US', McClatchy, 20 June 2013, http://
www.mcclatchydc.com/news/special-reports/insider-threats/arti-
cle24750244.html#.UkSv9dKsgyo [last checked 2 August 2016].

14. Downie Jr., 'Leak Investigations and Surveillance in post-9/11 America'.

15. Mumin, 'Somalia: A Threat By Any Name'.

16. Human Rights Watch, 'Somalia: Journalists Under Attack', 3 May
2016, https://www.hrw.org/news/2016/05/03/somalia-journalists-
under-attack [last checked 30 March 2017].

17. Taylor and Landay, 'Obama's Crackdown Views Leaks as Aiding Enemies of US'.

18. See, for instance, Callum Borchers, 'The Remarkable Inconsistency of Trump's Attacks on the Media', *The Washington Post*, 25 February 2017, https://www.washingtonpost.com/news/the-fix/wp/2017/02/25/the-remarkable-inconsistency-of-trumps-attacks-on-the-media/?utm_term=.9d7e190ad67c [last checked 30 March 2017].

19. Anne Frank House, 'Annual Report 2005', https://web.archive.org/web/20080216031433/http://annefrankhuis.nl/upload/downloads/AFreport2005.pdf [last checked 20 June 2017].

15. ENDINGS

1. *Salim v. Mitchell*, Case 2:15-cv-00286-JLQ (ED. WA., 20015); see American Civil Liberties Union, 'Salim v. Mitchell—Lawsuit Against Psychologists Behind CIA Torture Program', 1 July 2017, https://www.aclu.org/cases/salim-v-mitchell-lawsuit-against-psychologists-behind-cia-torture-program [last checked 21 July 2017].

2. *The Queen on the Application of Mohammed Saad Iqbal Madni v. the Secretary of State for Commonwealth Affairs*, High Court of Justice, Queen's Bench Division, Claim No. CO/9212/2009.

3. *Salim Awadh Salim & 10 Others v. Commissioner of Police & 3 Others*, High Court of Kenya, Constitutional & Judicial Review Division, Petition No. 822 of 2008.

4. *Mohammed Abdullah Saleh Al-Asad v. the Republic of Djibouti*, 383/10. See http://www.achpr.org/communications/decision/383.10/ [last checked 21 July 2017].

5. Mohammed Abdullah Saleh al-Asad v The Republic of Djibouti (African Commission on Human and People's Rights), Communication 383/10 http://www.achpr.org/files/sessions/55th/comunications/383.10/achpr55_383_10_eng.pdf (last checked 22 May 2018).

6. Matt Apuzzo, Sheri Fink, James Risen, 'How US Torture Left a Legacy of Damaged Minds', New York Times, October 2016, https://www.nytimes.com/2016/10/09/world/cia-torture-guantanamo-bay.html (last checked 22 May 2018).

INDEX

INDEX

INDEX

259

INDEX

INDEX

INDEX

INDEX

INDEX

INDEX

INDEX

INDEX

INDEX

INDEX

INDEX

INDEX

INDEX

INDEX